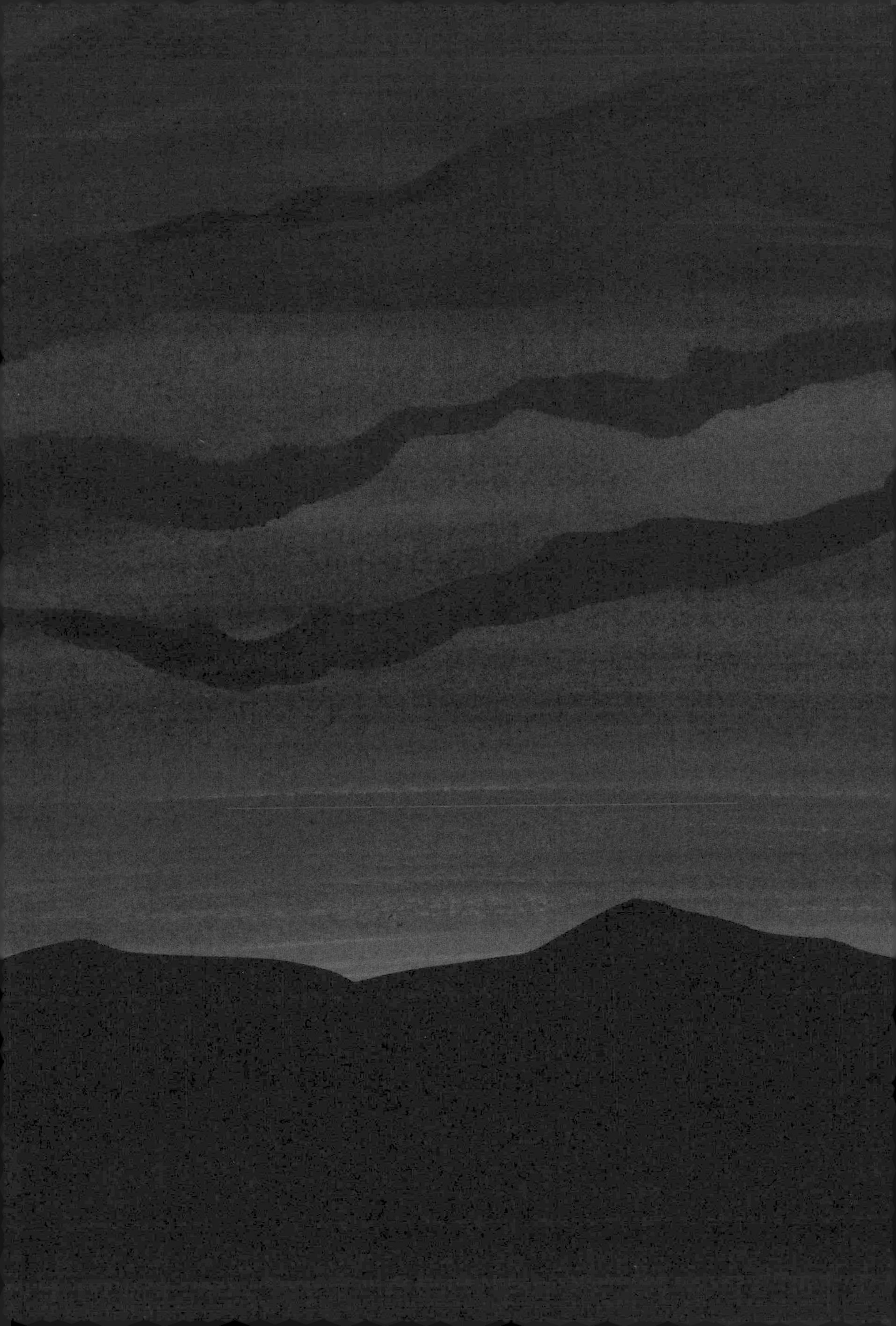

BUÑUEL

in the labyrinth of the turtles

First published in English in 2021
by SelfMadeHero
139–141 Pancras Road
London NW1 1UN
www.selfmadehero.com

Written and illustrated by Fermín Solís
Translated by Lawrence Schimel

Publishing Director: Emma Hayley
Editorial & Production Director: Guillaume Rater
Publishing Assistant: Stefano Mancin
Designer: Txabi Jones
UK Publicist: Paul Smith
US Publicist: Maya Bradford
With thanks to: Nick de Somogyi

A CIP record for this book is available from the British Library

ISBN: 978-1-910593-84-4

10 9 8 7 6 5 4 3 2 1

Printed and bound in Slovenia

BUÑUEL

in the labyrinth of the turtles

FERMÍN SOLÍS

TRANSLATED BY
LAWRENCE SCHIMEL

SELF
MADE
HERO

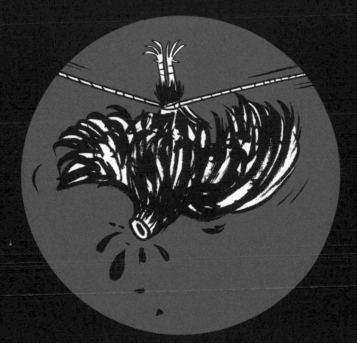

DO NOT DISTURB! ARTIST DREAMING

"THERE IS NO GOD, AND WE ARE HIS PROPHETS."
- CORMAC MCCARTHY, *THE ROAD*

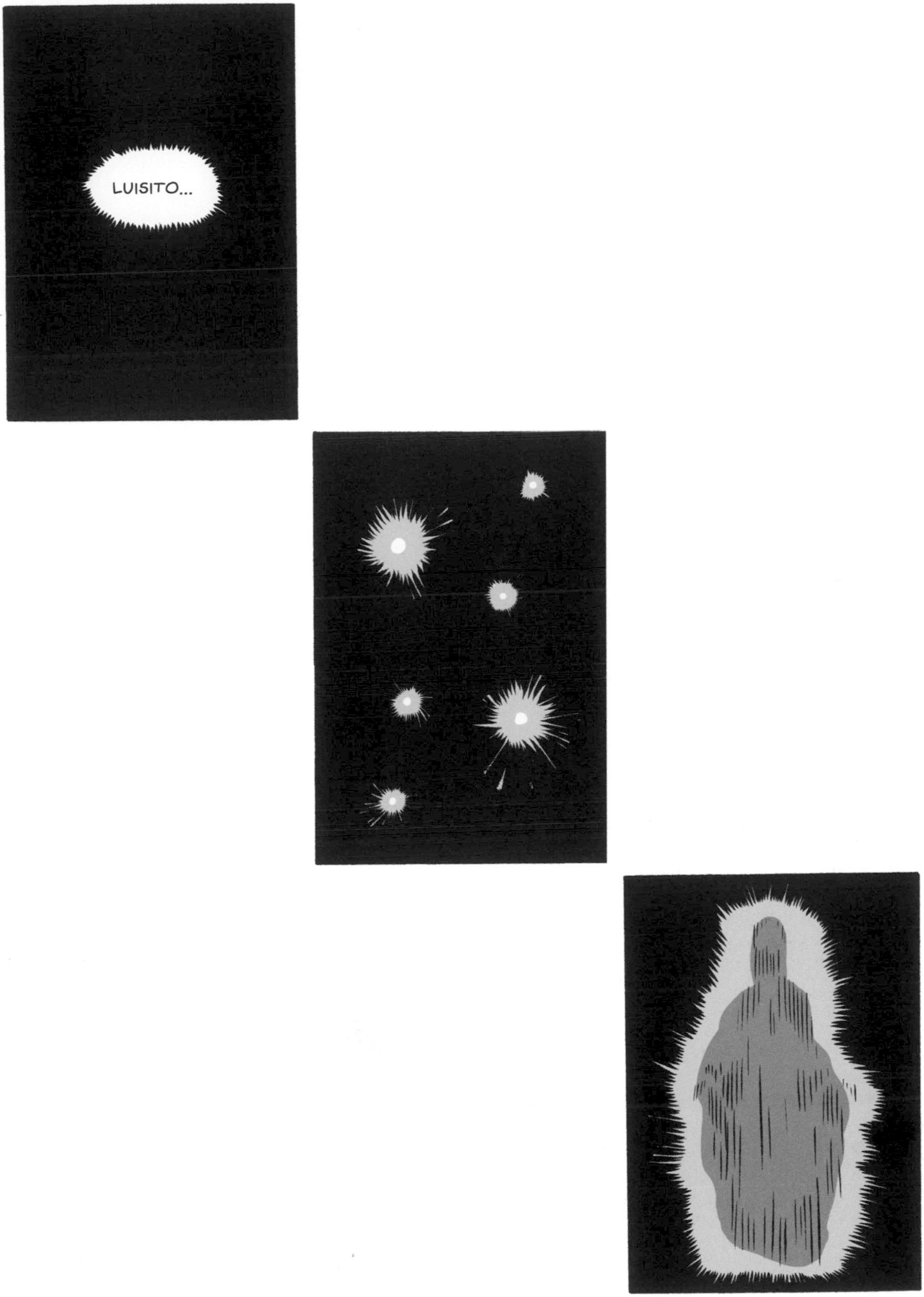
LUISITO...

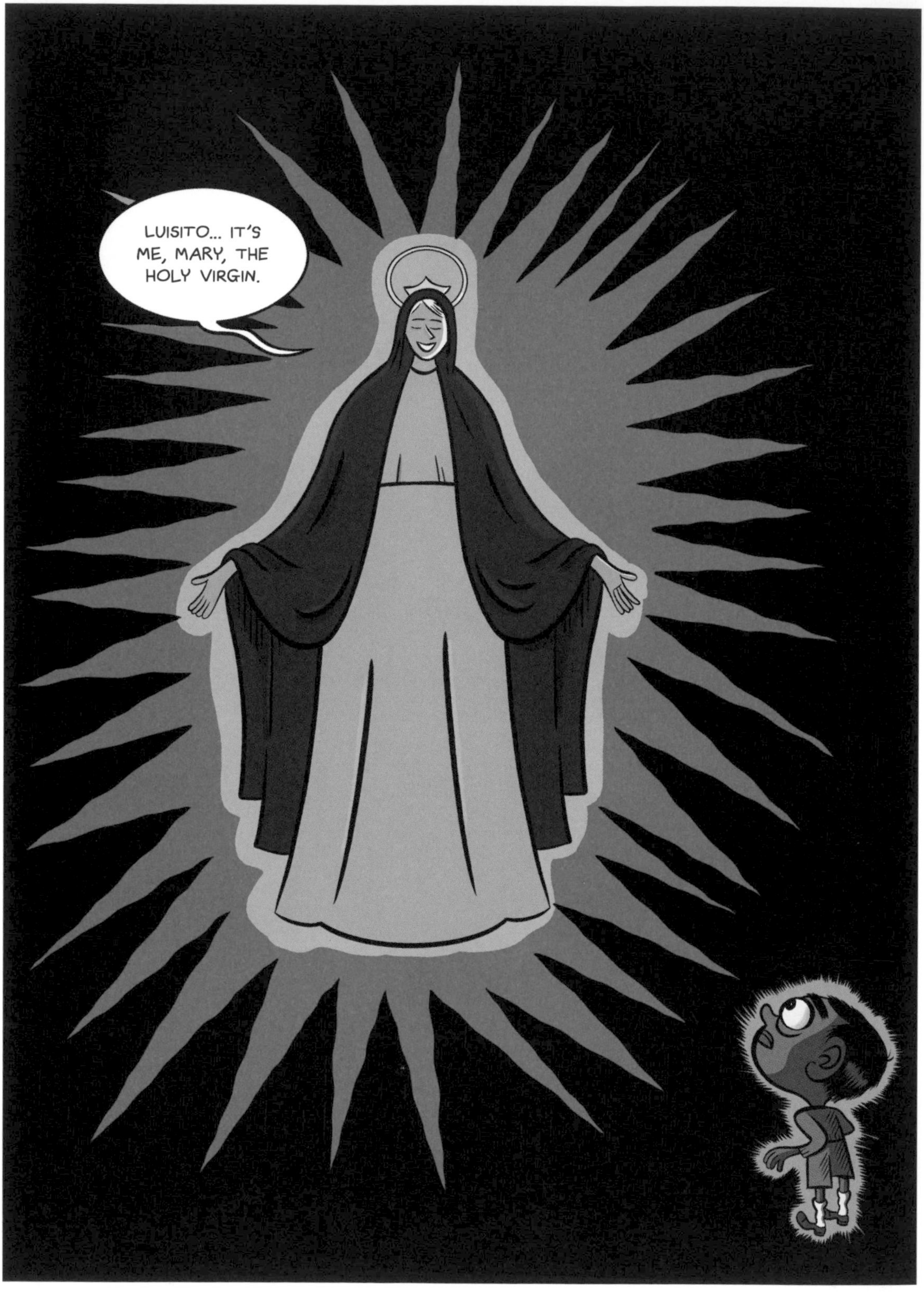
LUISITO... IT'S ME, MARY, THE HOLY VIRGIN.

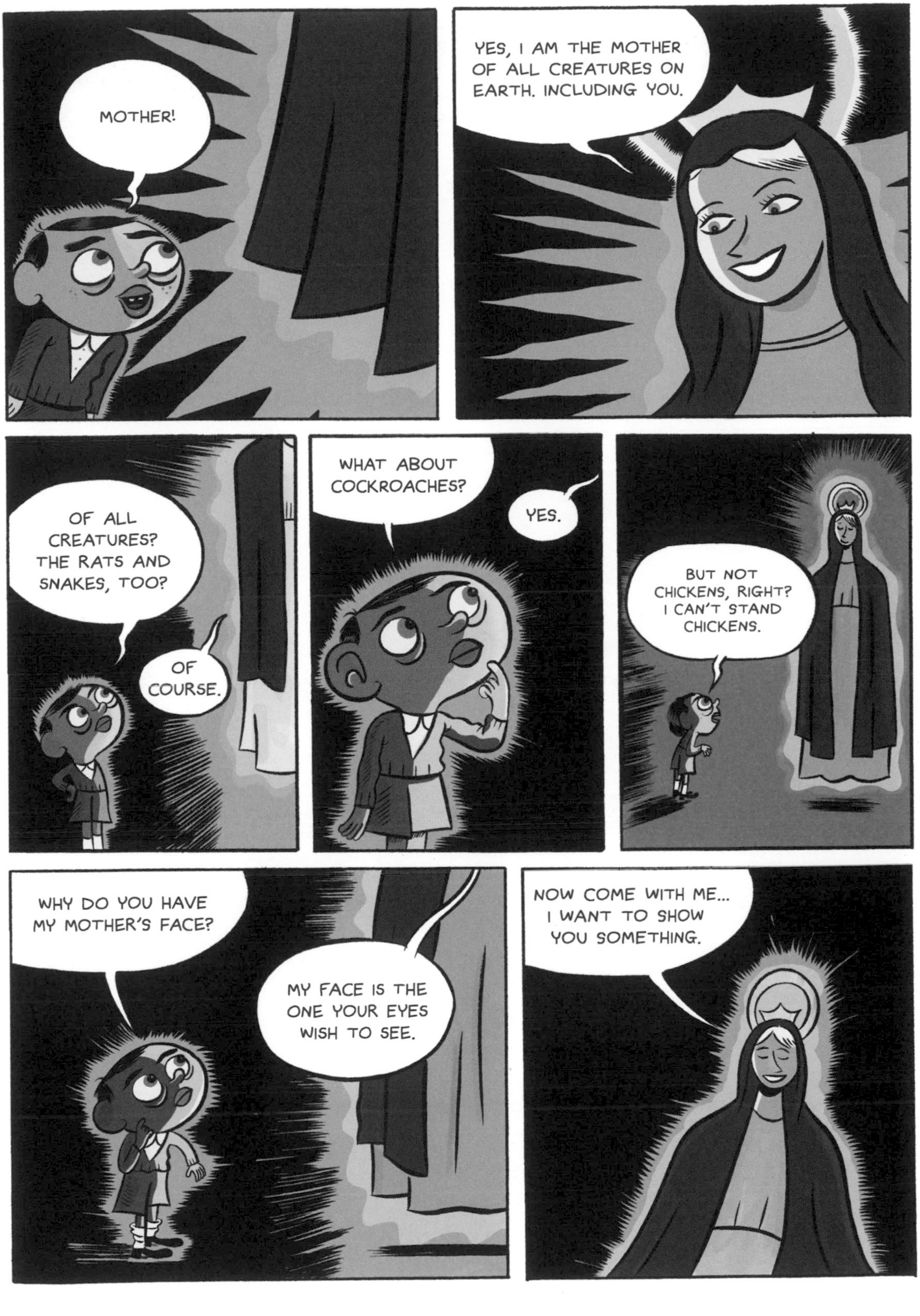
MOTHER!
YES, I AM THE MOTHER OF ALL CREATURES ON EARTH. INCLUDING YOU.
OF ALL CREATURES? THE RATS AND SNAKES, TOO?
OF COURSE.
WHAT ABOUT COCKROACHES?
YES.
BUT NOT CHICKENS, RIGHT? I CAN'T STAND CHICKENS.
WHY DO YOU HAVE MY MOTHER'S FACE?
MY FACE IS THE ONE YOUR EYES WISH TO SEE.
NOW COME WITH ME... I WANT TO SHOW YOU SOMETHING.

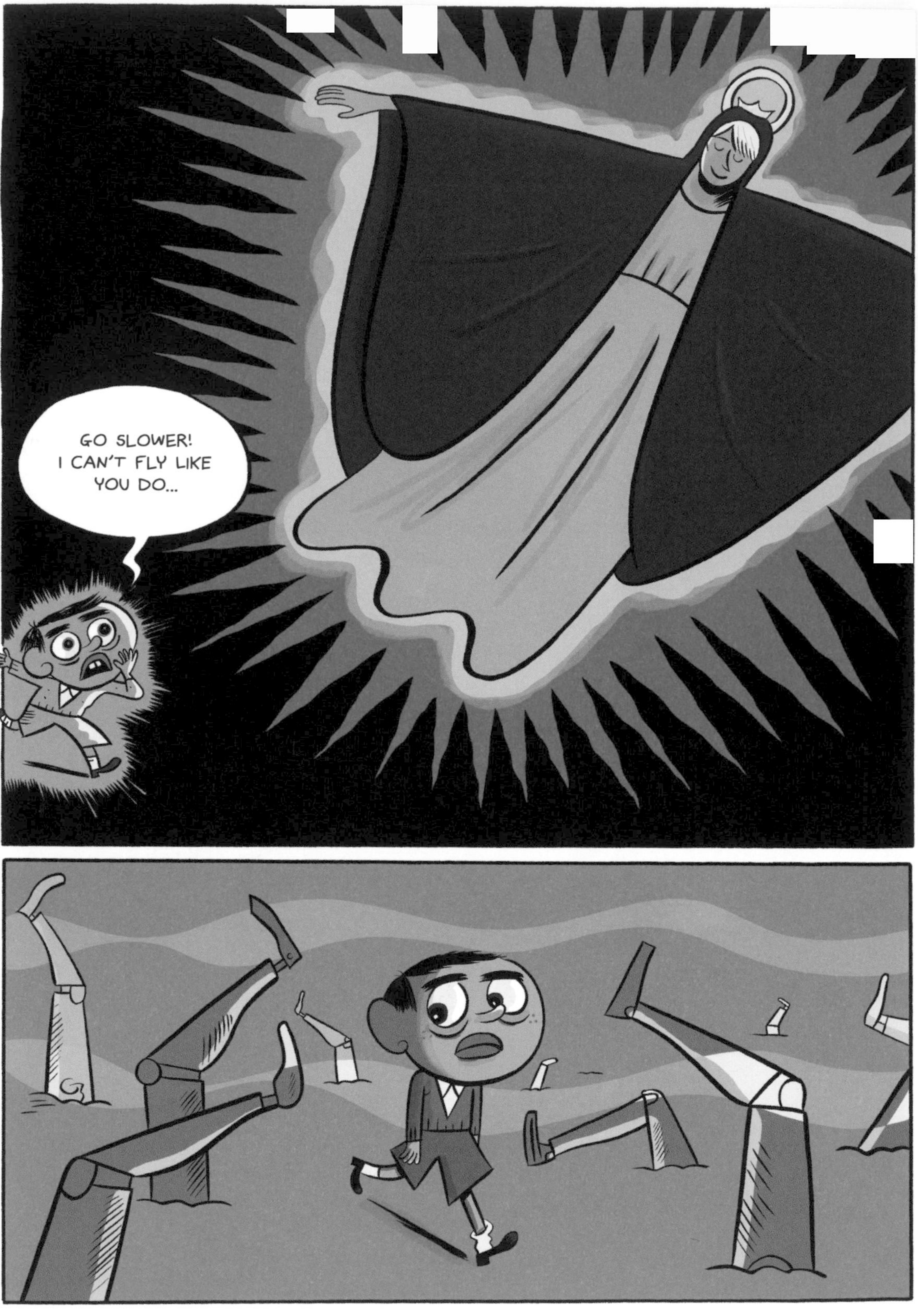
GO SLOWER! I CAN'T FLY LIKE YOU DO...

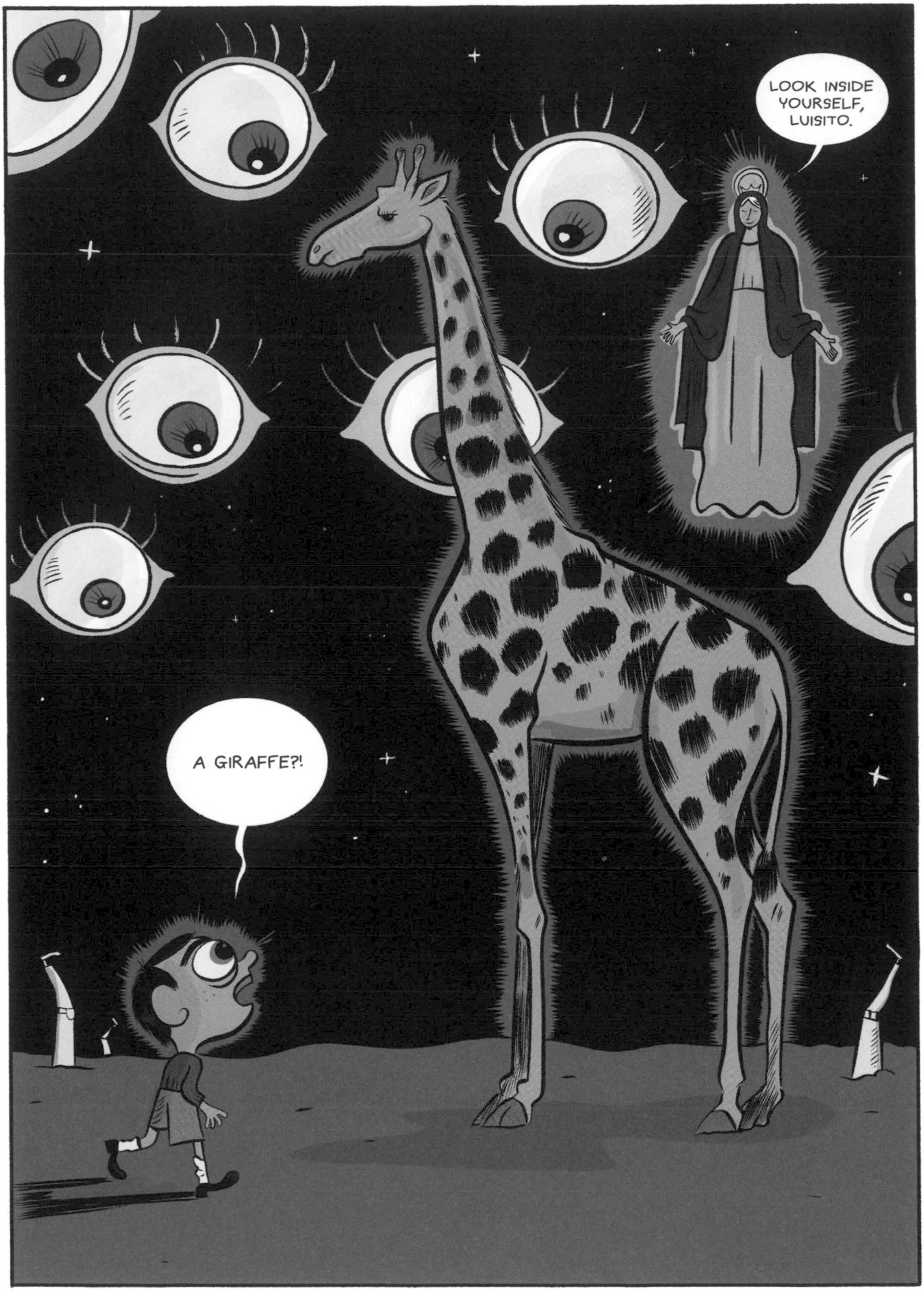
LOOK INSIDE YOURSELF, LUISITO.
A GIRAFFE?!

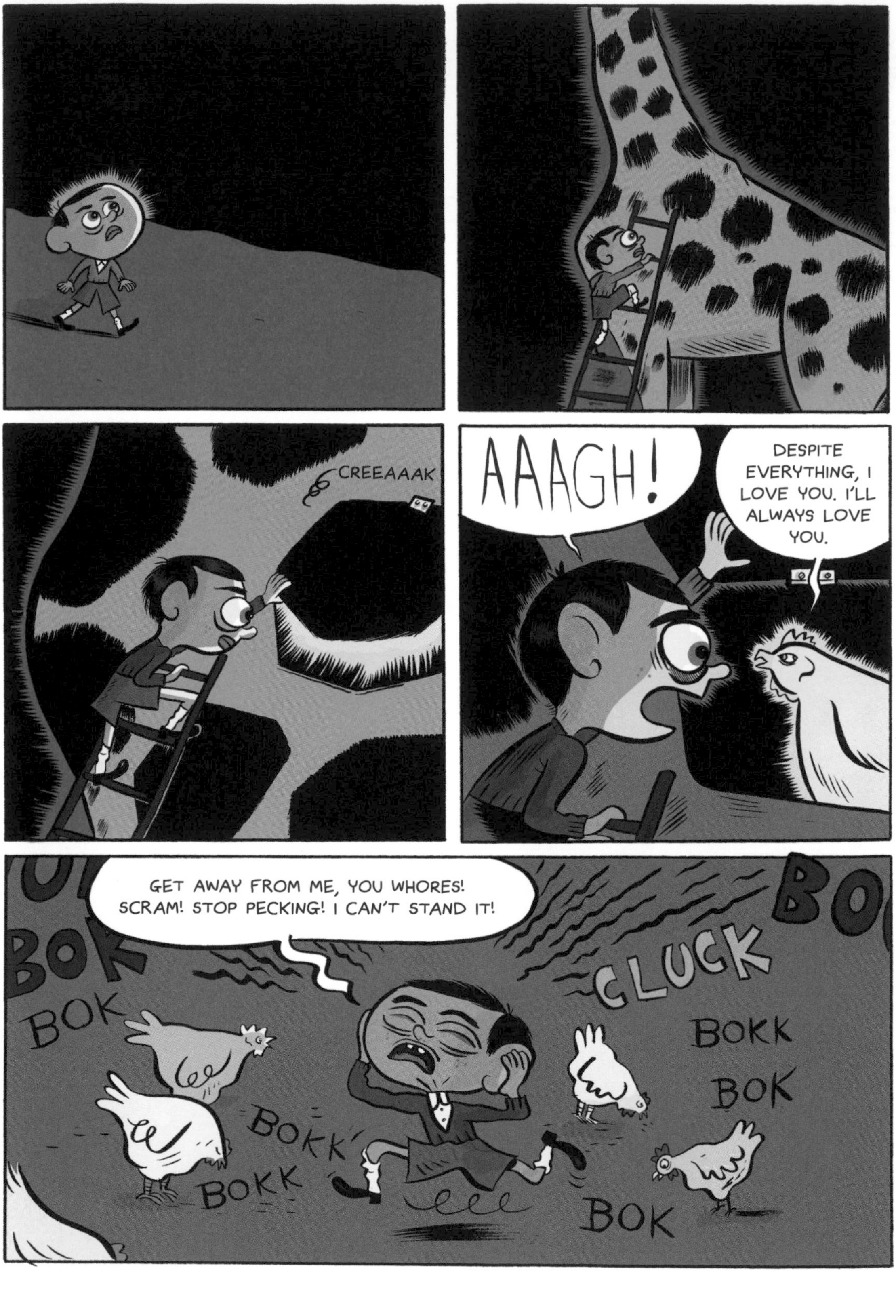
CREEAAAK
AAAGH!
DESPITE EVERYTHING, I LOVE YOU. I'LL ALWAYS LOVE YOU.
GET AWAY FROM ME, YOU WHORES! SCRAM! STOP PECKING! I CAN'T STAND IT!
BOK
CLUCK
BOK
BOKK
BOKK
BOKK
BOK
BOK

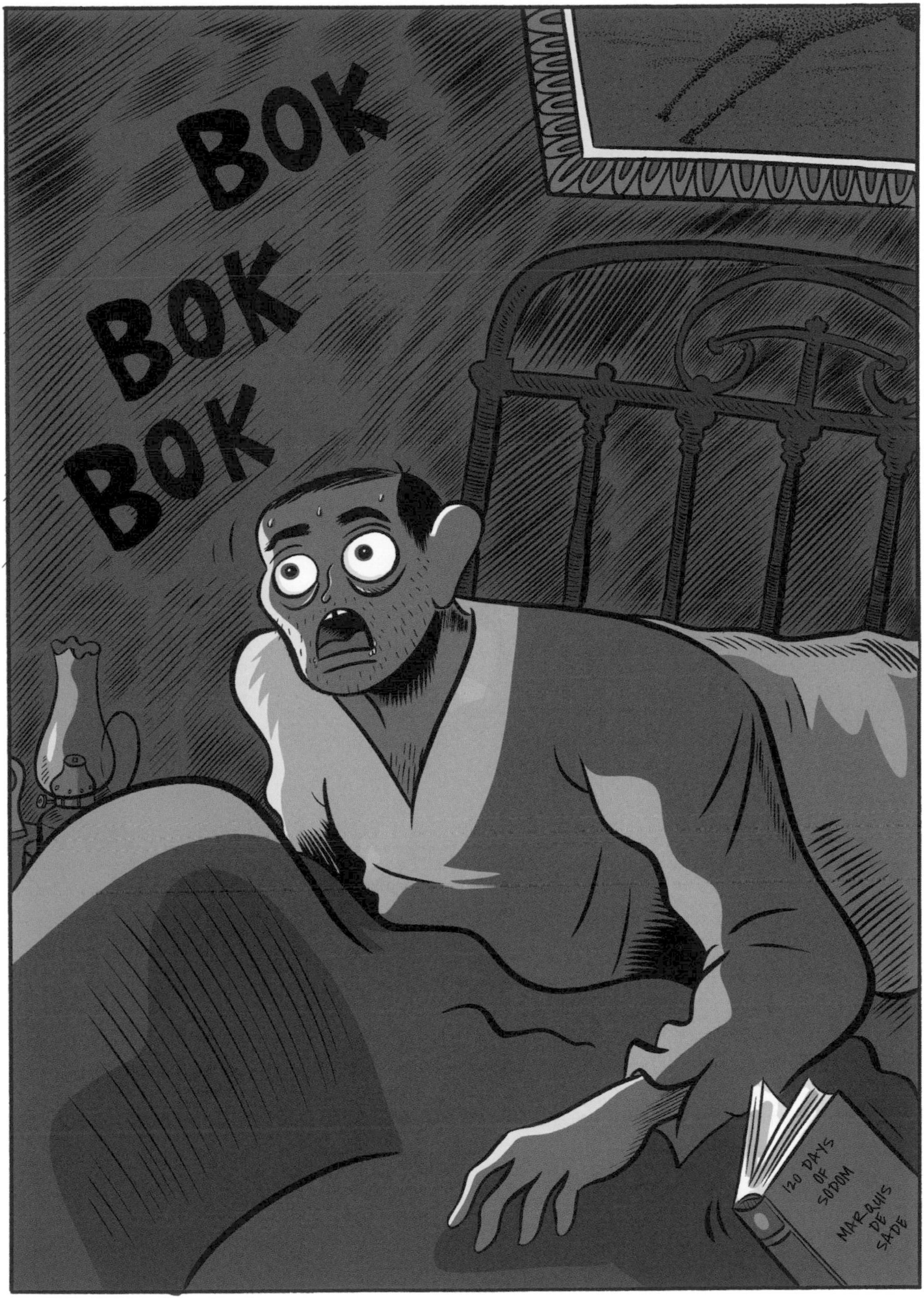
BOK
BOK
BOK
120 DAYS OF SODOM
MARQUIS DE SADE

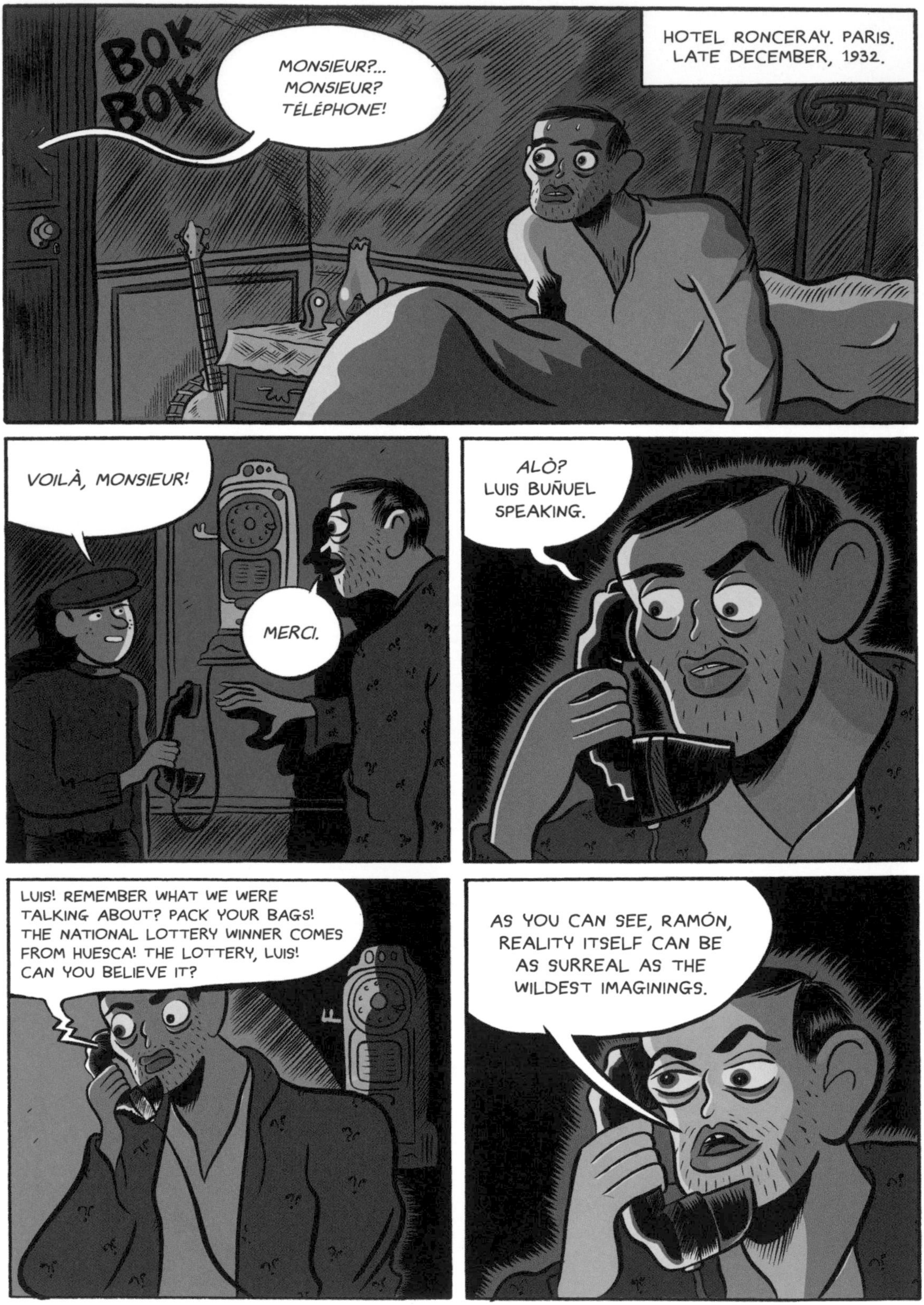
HOTEL RONCERAY. PARIS. LATE DECEMBER, 1932.
BOK BOK
MONSIEUR?... MONSIEUR? TÉLÉPHONE!
VOILÀ, MONSIEUR!
MERCI.
ALÒ? LUIS BUÑUEL SPEAKING.
LUIS! REMEMBER WHAT WE WERE TALKING ABOUT? PACK YOUR BAGS! THE NATIONAL LOTTERY WINNER COMES FROM HUESCA! THE LOTTERY, LUIS! CAN YOU BELIEVE IT?
AS YOU CAN SEE, RAMÓN, REALITY ITSELF CAN BE AS SURREAL AS THE WILDEST IMAGININGS.

2

PARIS NO LONGER LOVES US

"THE MORE STITCHES, THE LESS RICHES."
– ALDOUS HUXLEY, *BRAVE NEW WORLD*

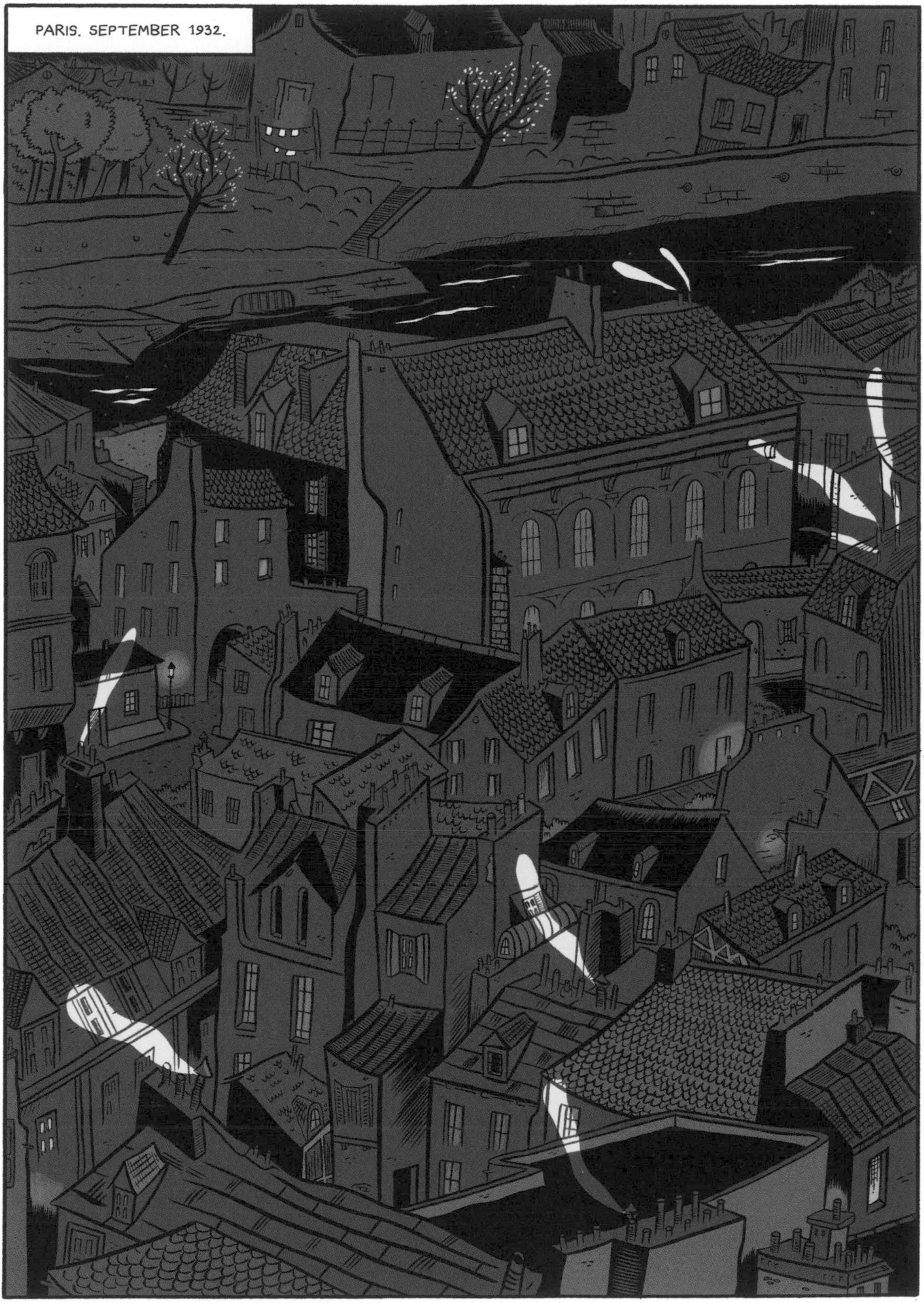
PARIS. SEPTEMBER 1932.

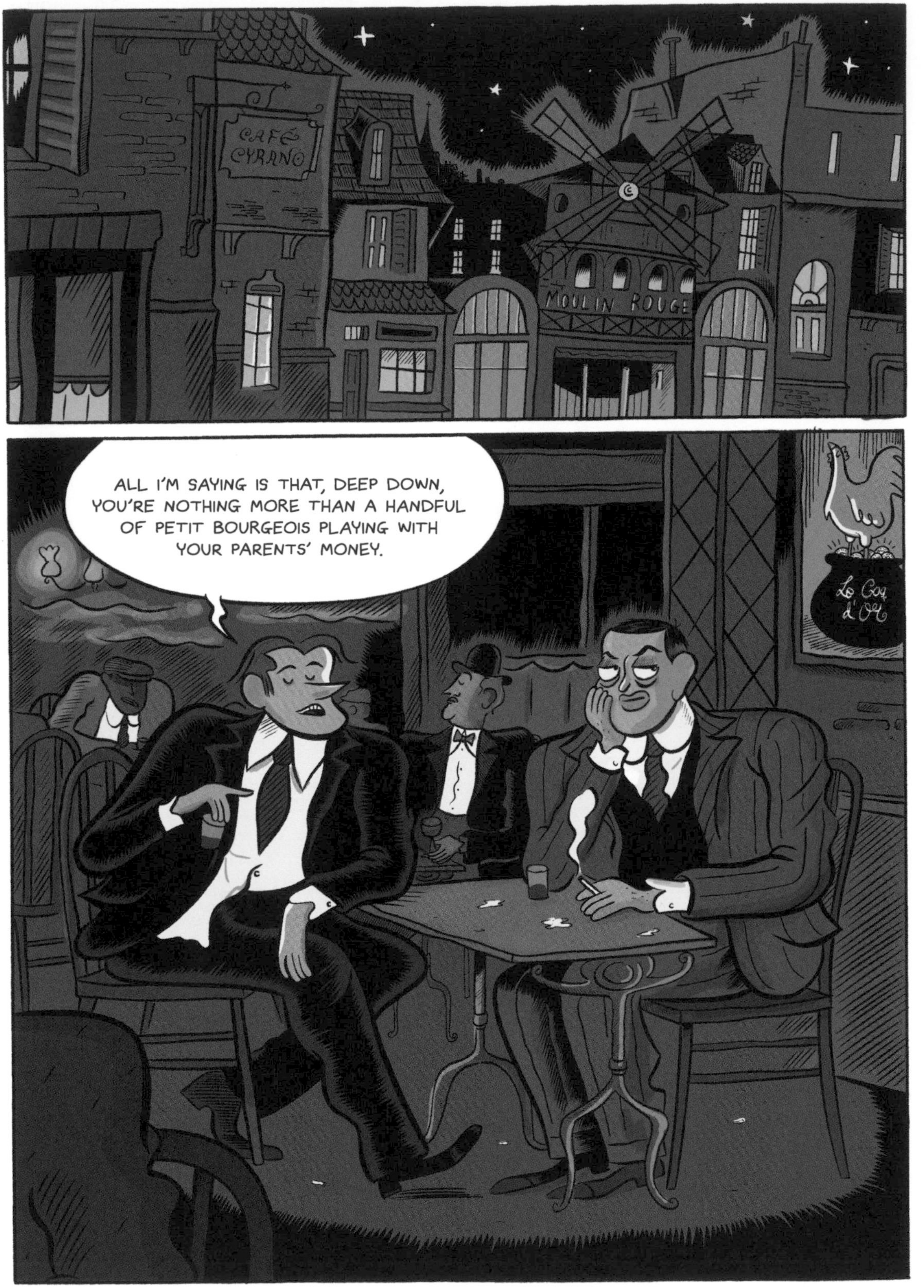
CAFÉ CYRANO
MOULIN ROUGE
ALL I'M SAYING IS THAT, DEEP DOWN, YOU'RE NOTHING MORE THAN A HANDFUL OF PETIT BOURGEOIS PLAYING WITH YOUR PARENTS' MONEY.
Le Coq d'Or

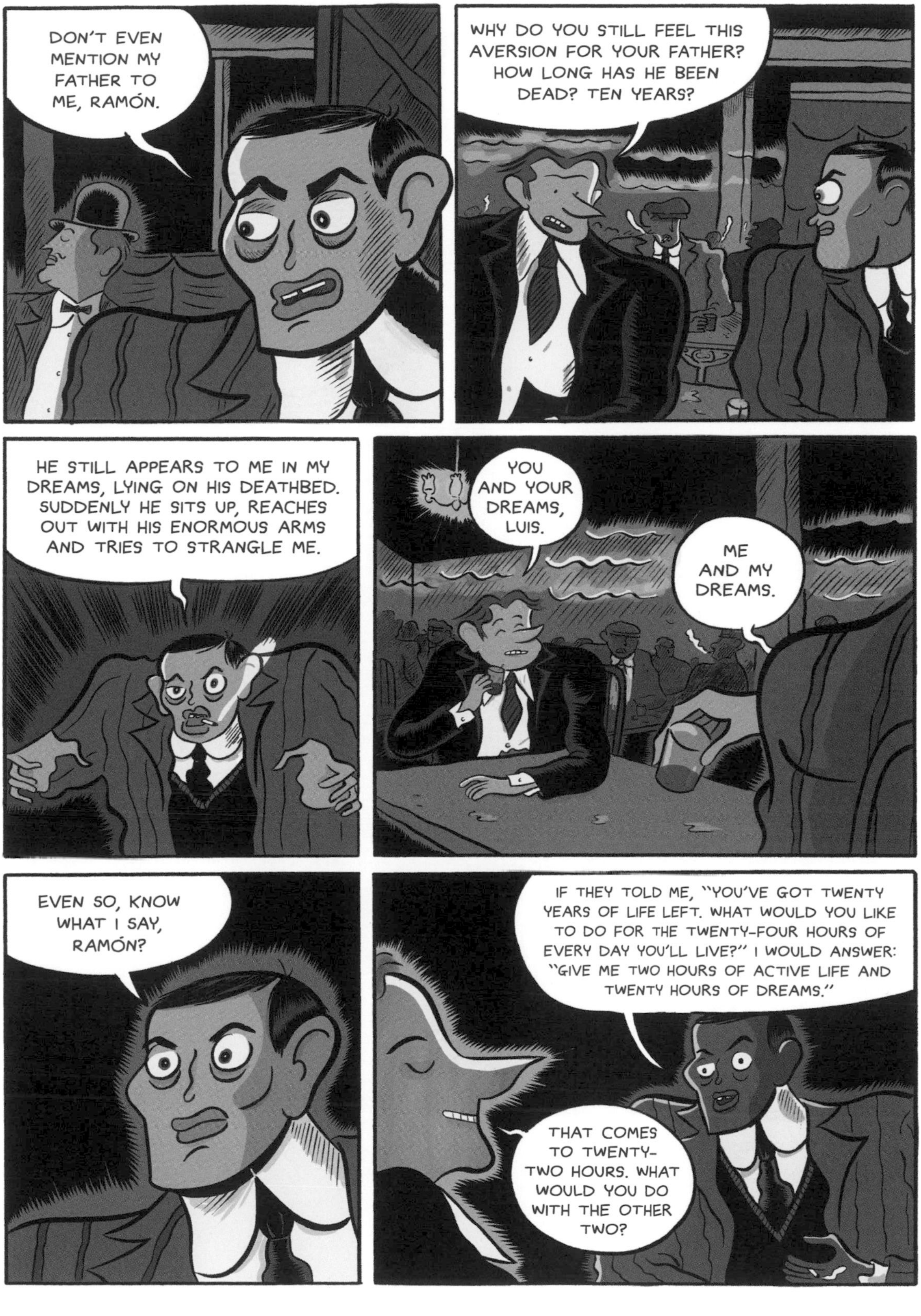

DON'T EVEN MENTION MY FATHER TO ME, RAMÓN.
WHY DO YOU STILL FEEL THIS AVERSION FOR YOUR FATHER? HOW LONG HAS HE BEEN DEAD? TEN YEARS?
HE STILL APPEARS TO ME IN MY DREAMS, LYING ON HIS DEATHBED. SUDDENLY HE SITS UP, REACHES OUT WITH HIS ENORMOUS ARMS AND TRIES TO STRANGLE ME.
YOU AND YOUR DREAMS, LUIS.
ME AND MY DREAMS.
EVEN SO, KNOW WHAT I SAY, RAMÓN?
IF THEY TOLD ME, "YOU'VE GOT TWENTY YEARS OF LIFE LEFT. WHAT WOULD YOU LIKE TO DO FOR THE TWENTY-FOUR HOURS OF EVERY DAY YOU'LL LIVE?" I WOULD ANSWER: "GIVE ME TWO HOURS OF ACTIVE LIFE AND TWENTY HOURS OF DREAMS."
THAT COMES TO TWENTY-TWO HOURS. WHAT WOULD YOU DO WITH THE OTHER TWO?

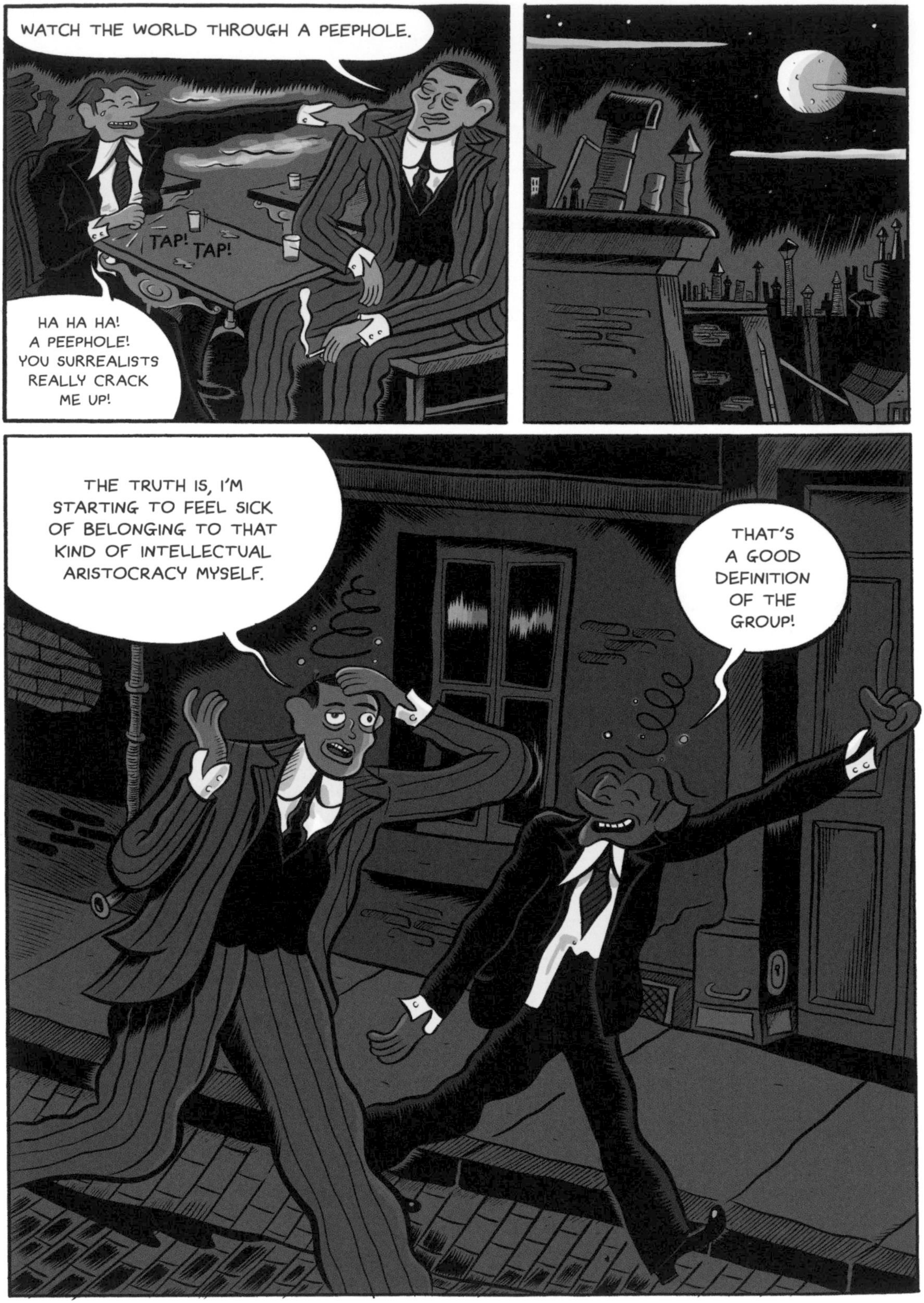
WATCH THE WORLD THROUGH A PEEPHOLE.
TAP! TAP!
HA HA HA! A PEEPHOLE! YOU SURREALISTS REALLY CRACK ME UP!
THE TRUTH IS, I'M STARTING TO FEEL SICK OF BELONGING TO THAT KIND OF INTELLECTUAL ARISTOCRACY MYSELF.
THAT'S A GOOD DEFINITION OF THE GROUP!

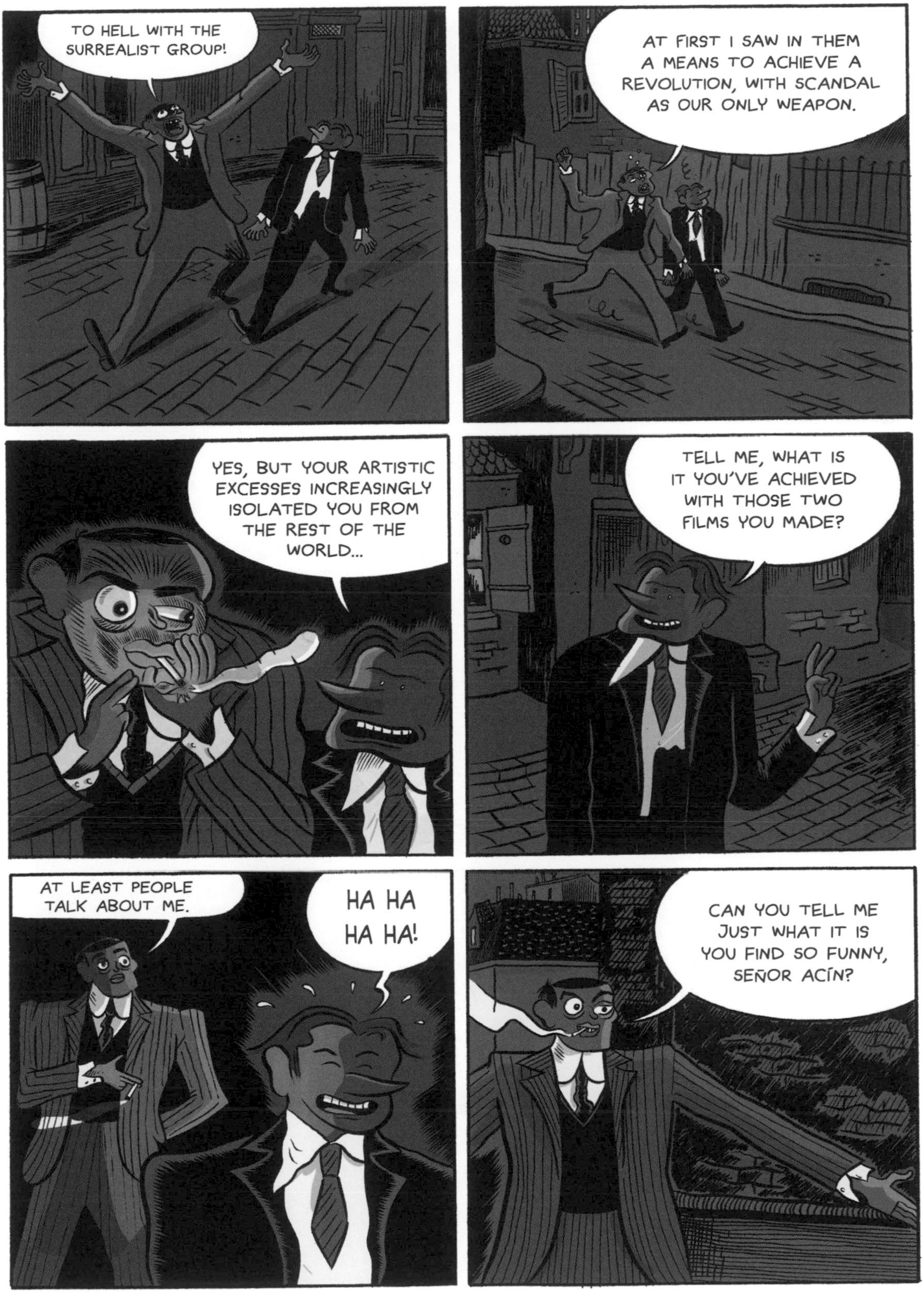
TO HELL WITH THE SURREALIST GROUP!
AT FIRST I SAW IN THEM A MEANS TO ACHIEVE A REVOLUTION, WITH SCANDAL AS OUR ONLY WEAPON.
YES, BUT YOUR ARTISTIC EXCESSES INCREASINGLY ISOLATED YOU FROM THE REST OF THE WORLD...
TELL ME, WHAT IS IT YOU'VE ACHIEVED WITH THOSE TWO FILMS YOU MADE?
AT LEAST PEOPLE TALK ABOUT ME.
HA HA HA HA!
CAN YOU TELL ME JUST WHAT IT IS YOU FIND SO FUNNY, SEÑOR ACÍN?

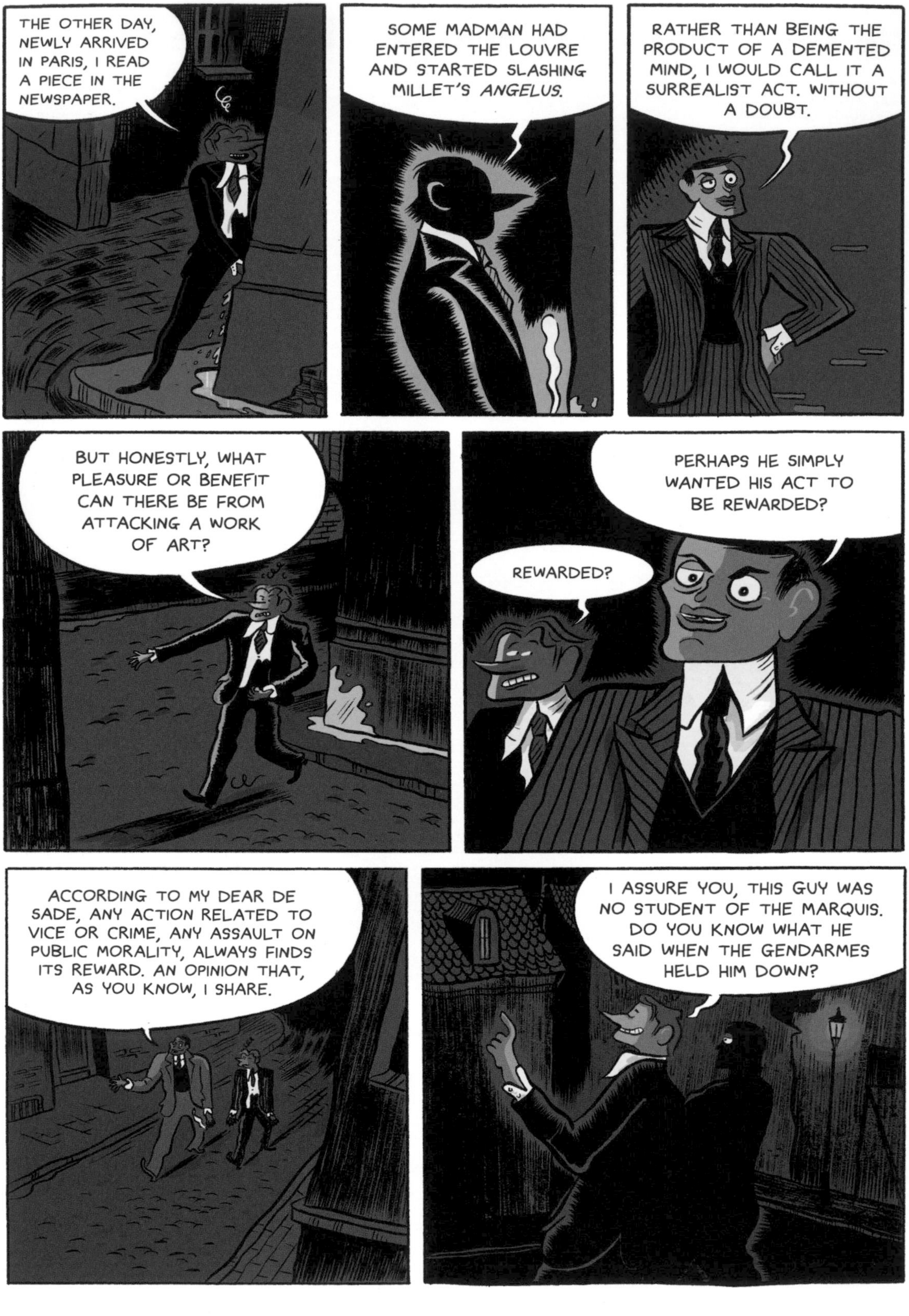
THE OTHER DAY, NEWLY ARRIVED IN PARIS, I READ A PIECE IN THE NEWSPAPER.
SOME MADMAN HAD ENTERED THE LOUVRE AND STARTED SLASHING MILLET'S *ANGELUS*.
RATHER THAN BEING THE PRODUCT OF A DEMENTED MIND, I WOULD CALL IT A SURREALIST ACT. WITHOUT A DOUBT.
BUT HONESTLY, WHAT PLEASURE OR BENEFIT CAN THERE BE FROM ATTACKING A WORK OF ART?
PERHAPS HE SIMPLY WANTED HIS ACT TO BE REWARDED?
REWARDED?
ACCORDING TO MY DEAR DE SADE, ANY ACTION RELATED TO VICE OR CRIME, ANY ASSAULT ON PUBLIC MORALITY, ALWAYS FINDS ITS REWARD. AN OPINION THAT, AS YOU KNOW, I SHARE.
I ASSURE YOU, THIS GUY WAS NO STUDENT OF THE MARQUIS. DO YOU KNOW WHAT HE SAID WHEN THE GENDARMES HELD HIM DOWN?

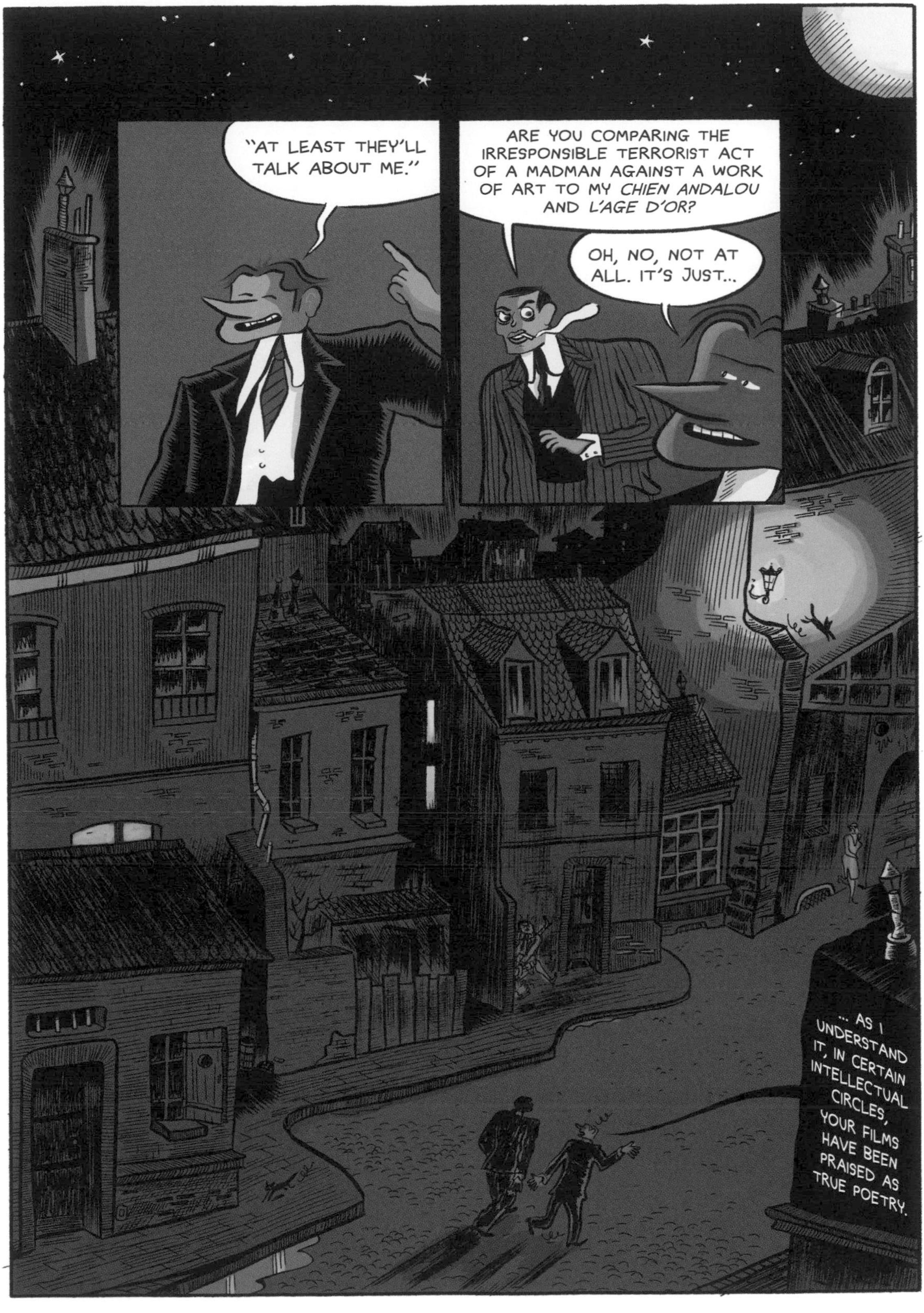
"AT LEAST THEY'LL TALK ABOUT ME."
ARE YOU COMPARING THE IRRESPONSIBLE TERRORIST ACT OF A MADMAN AGAINST A WORK OF ART TO MY *CHIEN ANDALOU* AND *L'AGE D'OR?*
OH, NO, NOT AT ALL. IT'S JUST...
... AS I UNDERSTAND IT, IN CERTAIN INTELLECTUAL CIRCLES, YOUR FILMS HAVE BEEN PRAISED AS TRUE POETRY.

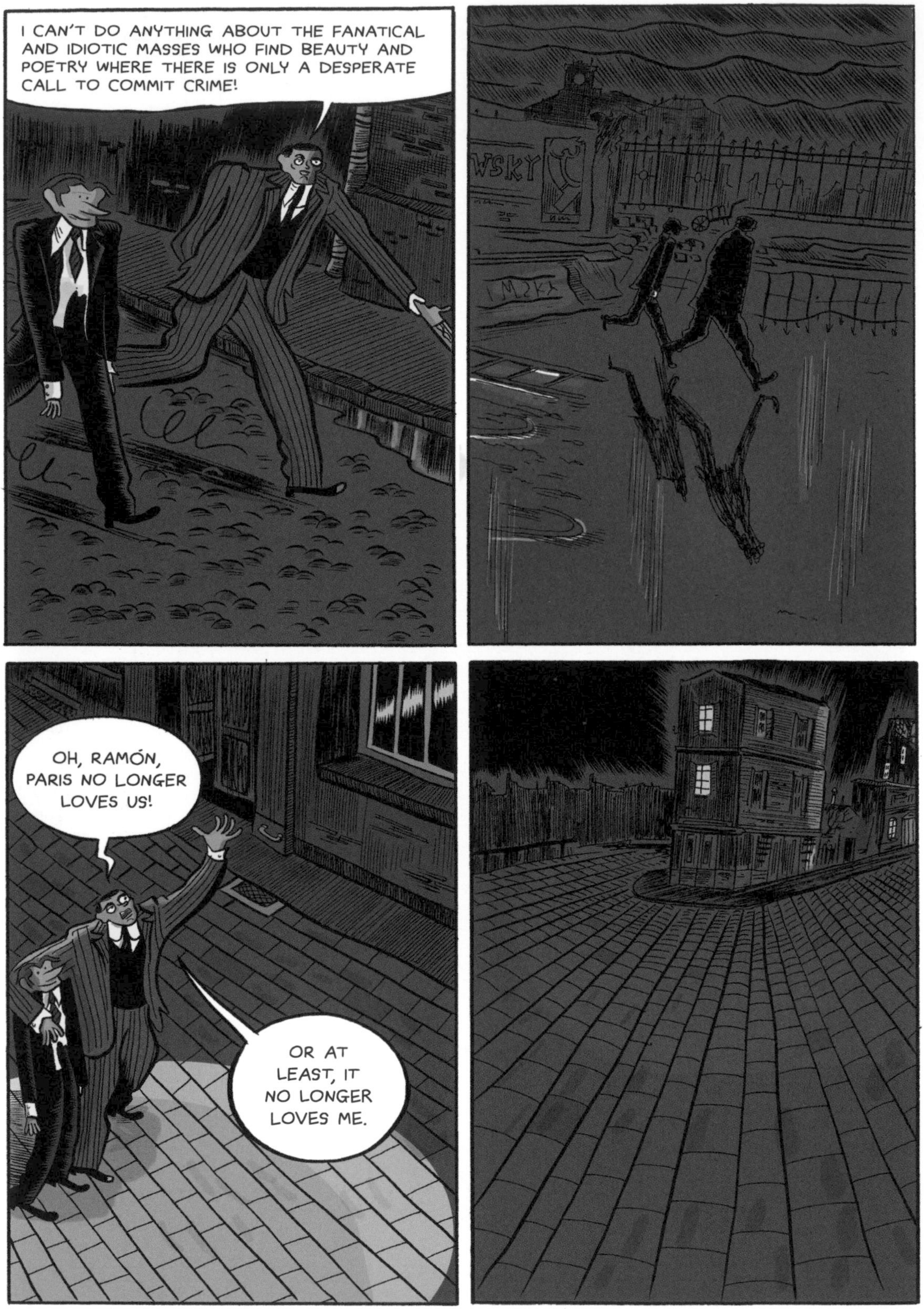
I CAN'T DO ANYTHING ABOUT THE FANATICAL AND IDIOTIC MASSES WHO FIND BEAUTY AND POETRY WHERE THERE IS ONLY A DESPERATE CALL TO COMMIT CRIME!
OH, RAMÓN, PARIS NO LONGER LOVES US!
OR AT LEAST, IT NO LONGER LOVES ME.

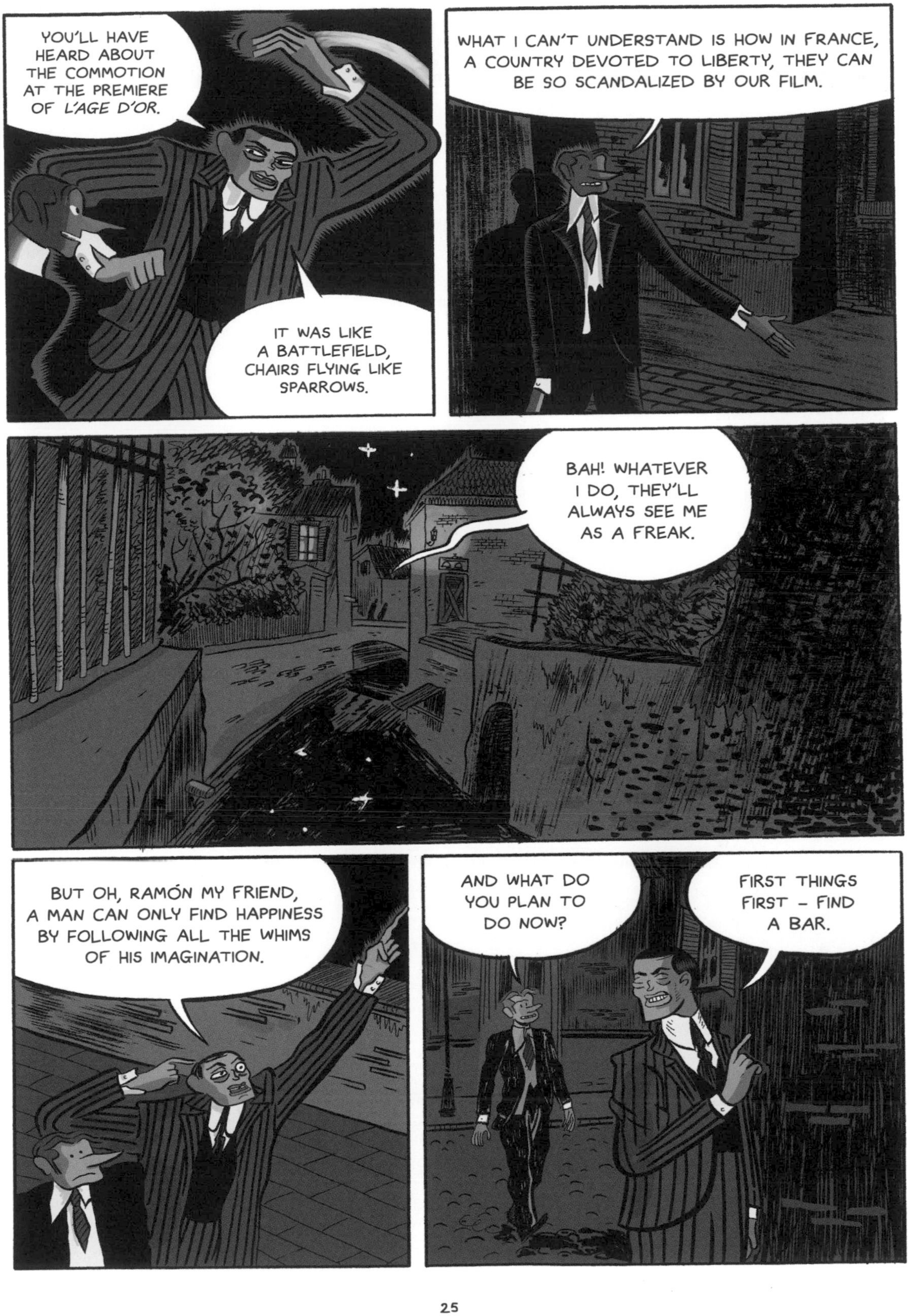
YOU'LL HAVE HEARD ABOUT THE COMMOTION AT THE PREMIERE OF *L'AGE D'OR*.
IT WAS LIKE A BATTLEFIELD, CHAIRS FLYING LIKE SPARROWS.
WHAT I CAN'T UNDERSTAND IS HOW IN FRANCE, A COUNTRY DEVOTED TO LIBERTY, THEY CAN BE SO SCANDALIZED BY OUR FILM.
BAH! WHATEVER I DO, THEY'LL ALWAYS SEE ME AS A FREAK.
BUT OH, RAMÓN MY FRIEND, A MAN CAN ONLY FIND HAPPINESS BY FOLLOWING ALL THE WHIMS OF HIS IMAGINATION.
AND WHAT DO YOU PLAN TO DO NOW?
FIRST THINGS FIRST – FIND A BAR.

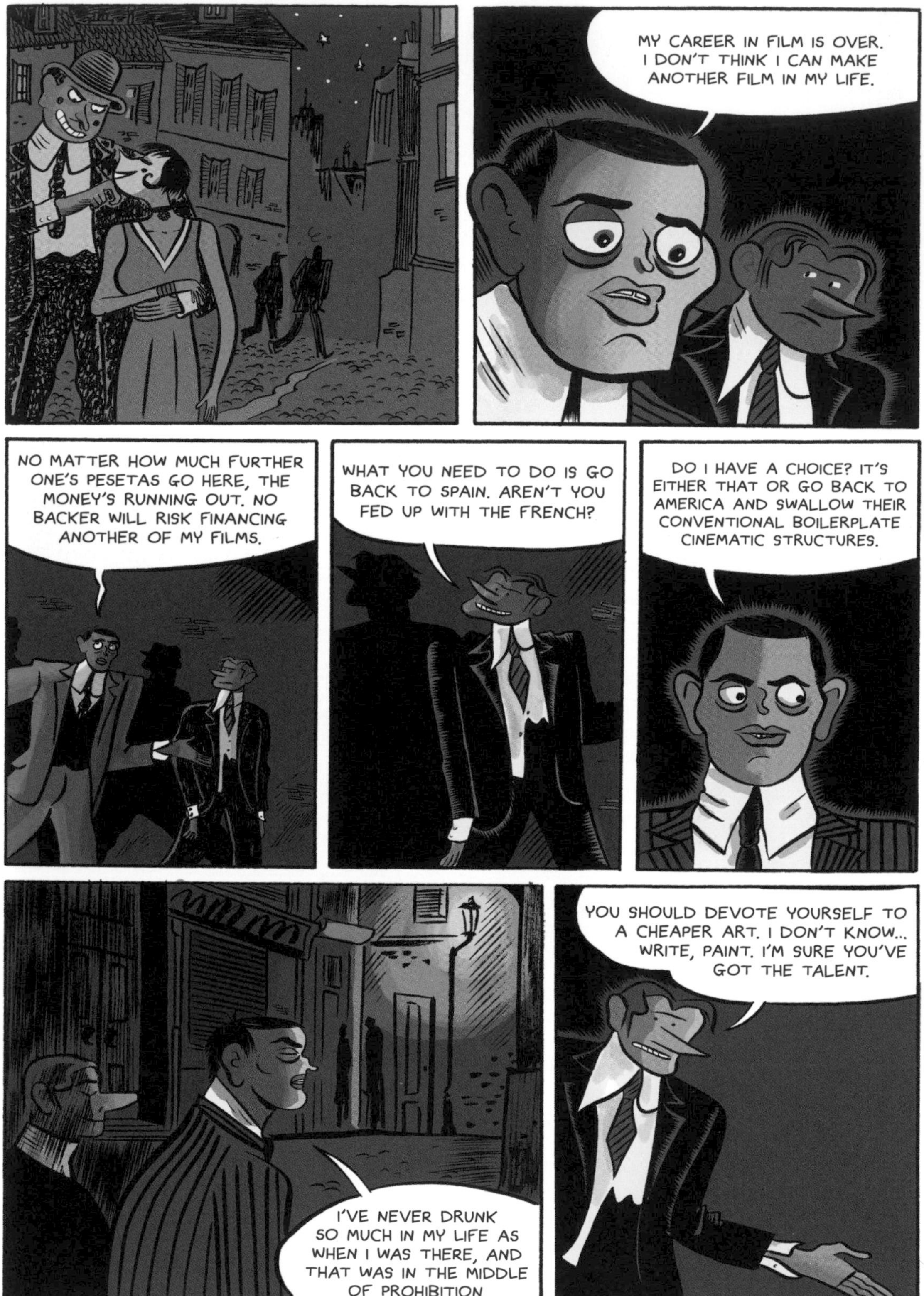
MY CAREER IN FILM IS OVER. I DON'T THINK I CAN MAKE ANOTHER FILM IN MY LIFE.
NO MATTER HOW MUCH FURTHER ONE'S PESETAS GO HERE, THE MONEY'S RUNNING OUT. NO BACKER WILL RISK FINANCING ANOTHER OF MY FILMS.
WHAT YOU NEED TO DO IS GO BACK TO SPAIN. AREN'T YOU FED UP WITH THE FRENCH?
DO I HAVE A CHOICE? IT'S EITHER THAT OR GO BACK TO AMERICA AND SWALLOW THEIR CONVENTIONAL BOILERPLATE CINEMATIC STRUCTURES.
I'VE NEVER DRUNK SO MUCH IN MY LIFE AS WHEN I WAS THERE, AND THAT WAS IN THE MIDDLE OF PROHIBITION.
YOU SHOULD DEVOTE YOURSELF TO A CHEAPER ART. I DON'T KNOW... WRITE, PAINT. I'M SURE YOU'VE GOT THE TALENT.

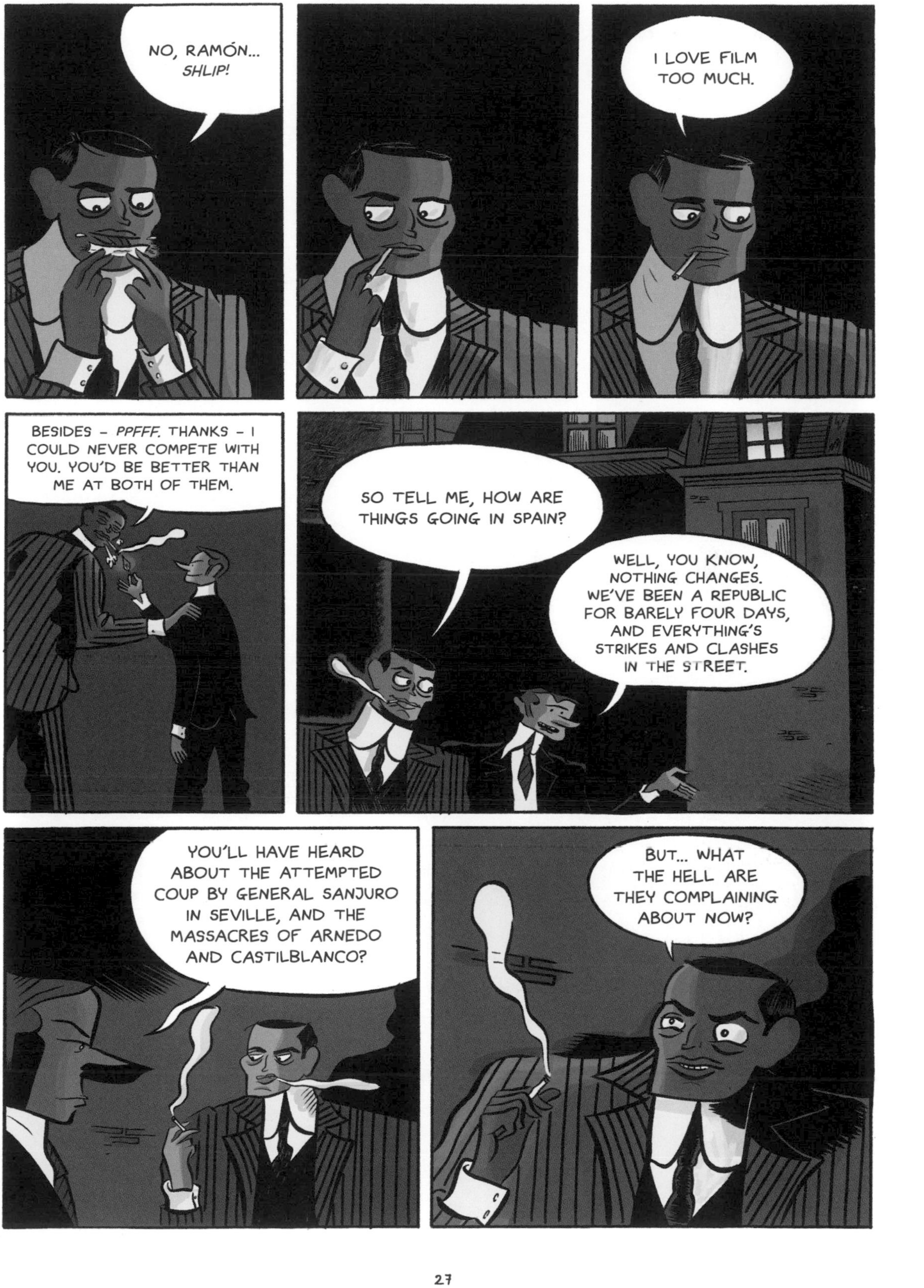
NO, RAMÓN... *SHLIP!*
I LOVE FILM TOO MUCH.
BESIDES – *PPFFF.* THANKS – I COULD NEVER COMPETE WITH YOU. YOU'D BE BETTER THAN ME AT BOTH OF THEM.
SO TELL ME, HOW ARE THINGS GOING IN SPAIN?
WELL, YOU KNOW, NOTHING CHANGES. WE'VE BEEN A REPUBLIC FOR BARELY FOUR DAYS, AND EVERYTHING'S STRIKES AND CLASHES IN THE STREET.
YOU'LL HAVE HEARD ABOUT THE ATTEMPTED COUP BY GENERAL SANJURO IN SEVILLE, AND THE MASSACRES OF ARNEDO AND CASTILBLANCO?
BUT... WHAT THE HELL ARE THEY COMPLAINING ABOUT NOW?

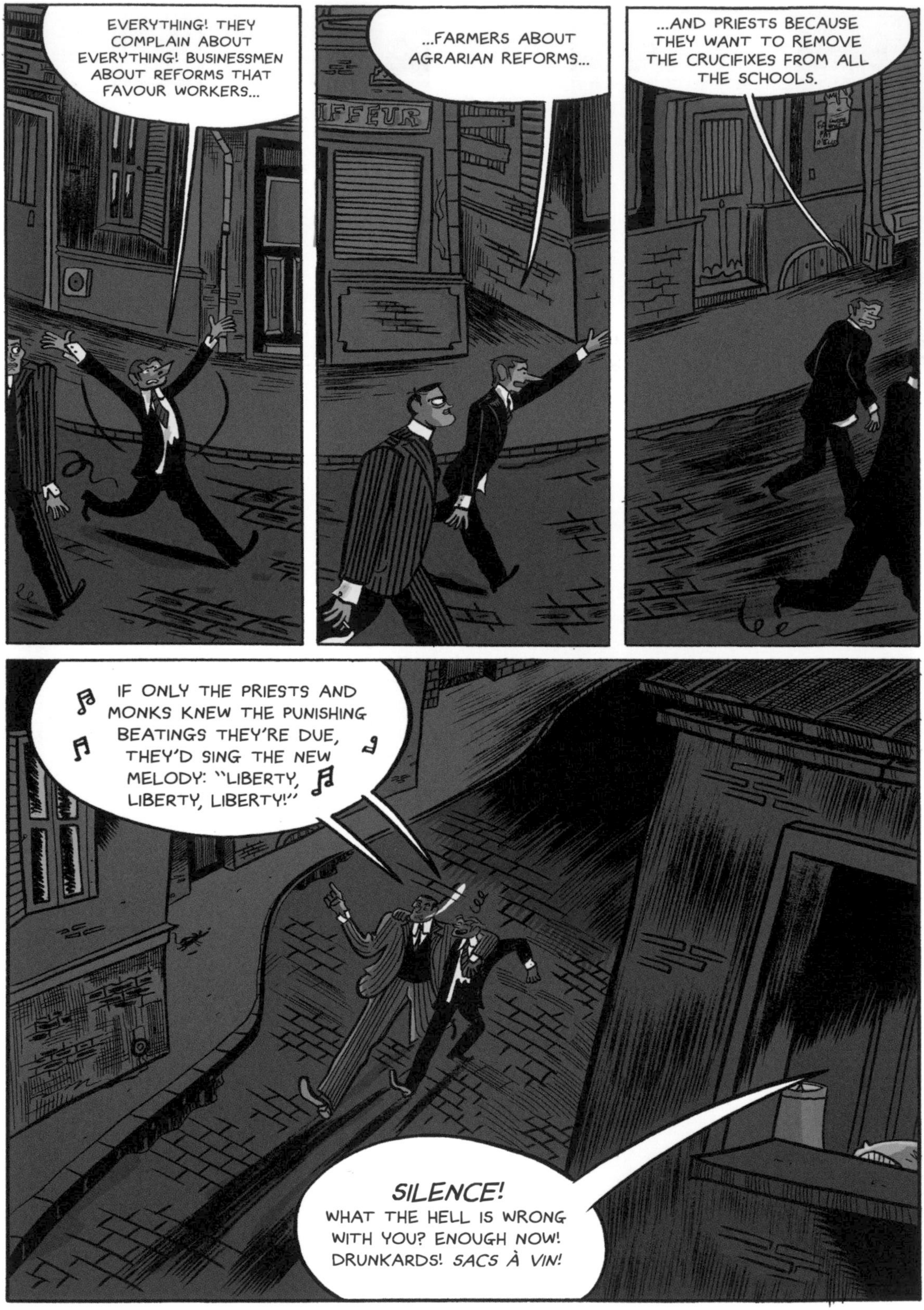
EVERYTHING! THEY COMPLAIN ABOUT EVERYTHING! BUSINESSMEN ABOUT REFORMS THAT FAVOUR WORKERS...
...FARMERS ABOUT AGRARIAN REFORMS...
...AND PRIESTS BECAUSE THEY WANT TO REMOVE THE CRUCIFIXES FROM ALL THE SCHOOLS.
IF ONLY THE PRIESTS AND MONKS KNEW THE PUNISHING BEATINGS THEY'RE DUE, THEY'D SING THE NEW MELODY: "LIBERTY, LIBERTY, LIBERTY!"
SILENCE! WHAT THE HELL IS WRONG WITH YOU? ENOUGH NOW! DRUNKARDS! *SACS À VIN!*

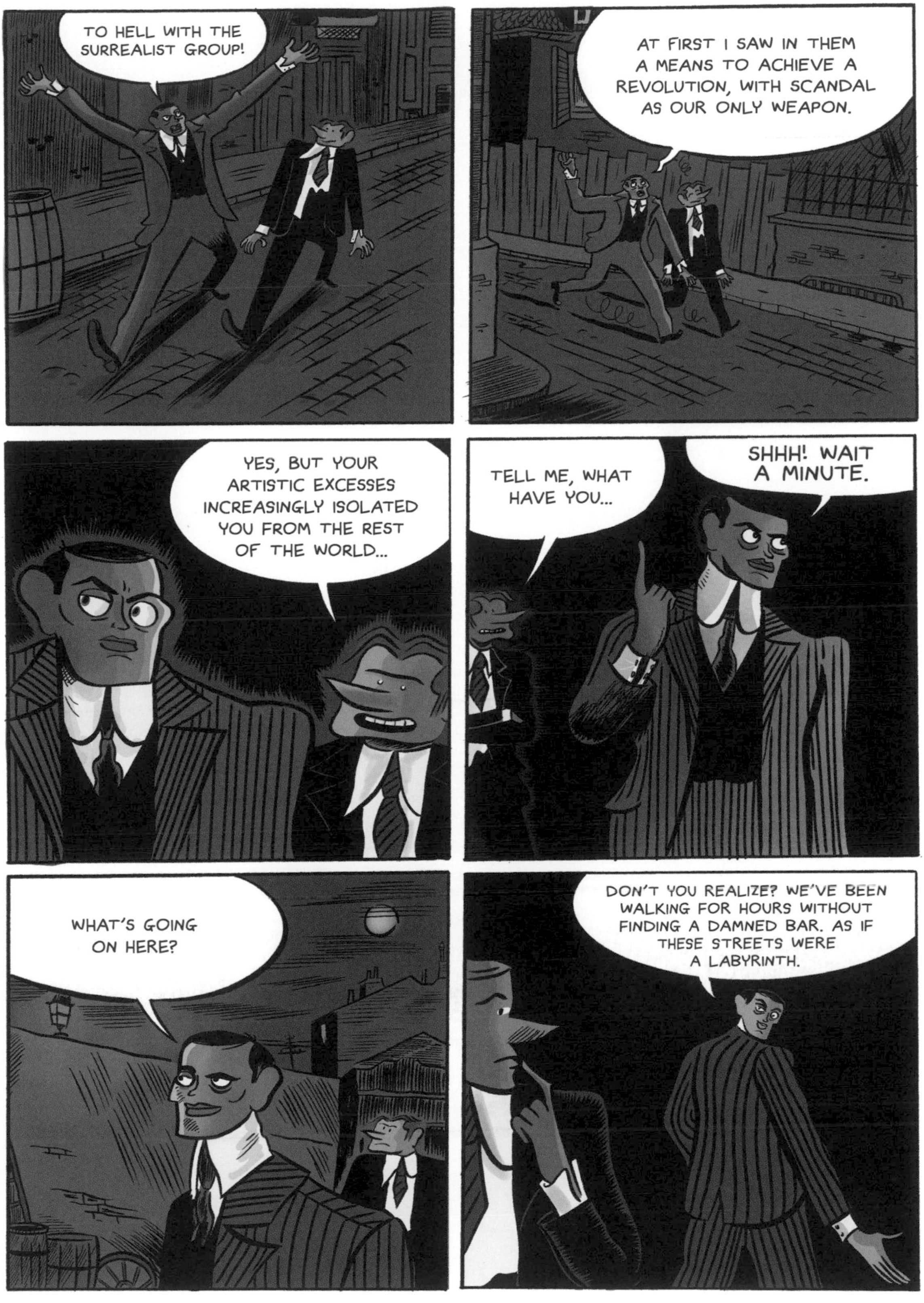
TO HELL WITH THE SURREALIST GROUP!
AT FIRST I SAW IN THEM A MEANS TO ACHIEVE A REVOLUTION, WITH SCANDAL AS OUR ONLY WEAPON.
YES, BUT YOUR ARTISTIC EXCESSES INCREASINGLY ISOLATED YOU FROM THE REST OF THE WORLD...
TELL ME, WHAT HAVE YOU...
SHHH! WAIT A MINUTE.
WHAT'S GOING ON HERE?
DON'T YOU REALIZE? WE'VE BEEN WALKING FOR HOURS WITHOUT FINDING A DAMNED BAR. AS IF THESE STREETS WERE A LABYRINTH.

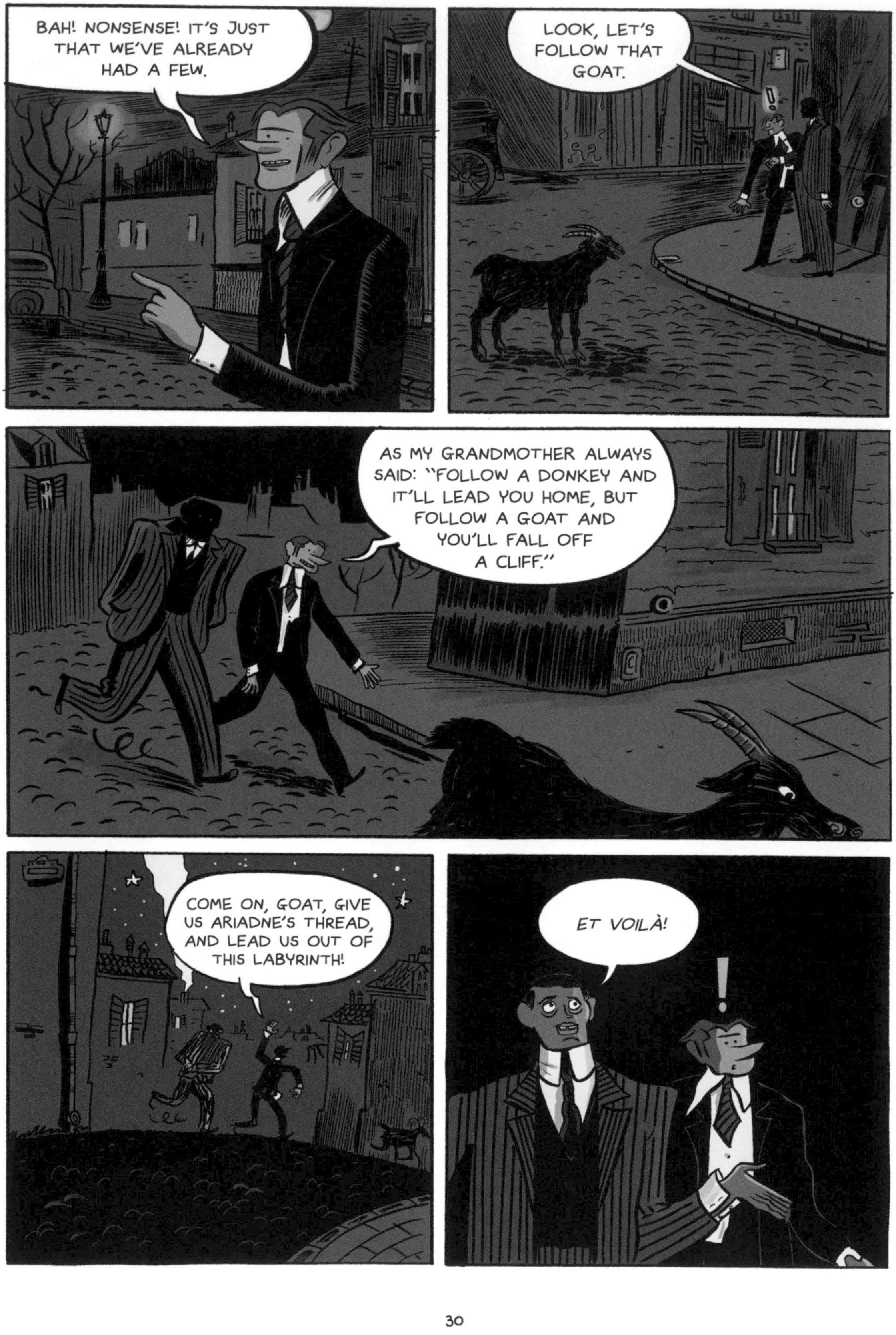
BAH! NONSENSE! IT'S JUST THAT WE'VE ALREADY HAD A FEW.
LOOK, LET'S FOLLOW THAT GOAT.
!
AS MY GRANDMOTHER ALWAYS SAID: "FOLLOW A DONKEY AND IT'LL LEAD YOU HOME, BUT FOLLOW A GOAT AND YOU'LL FALL OFF A CLIFF."
COME ON, GOAT, GIVE US ARIADNE'S THREAD, AND LEAD US OUT OF THIS LABYRINTH!
ET VOILÀ!
!

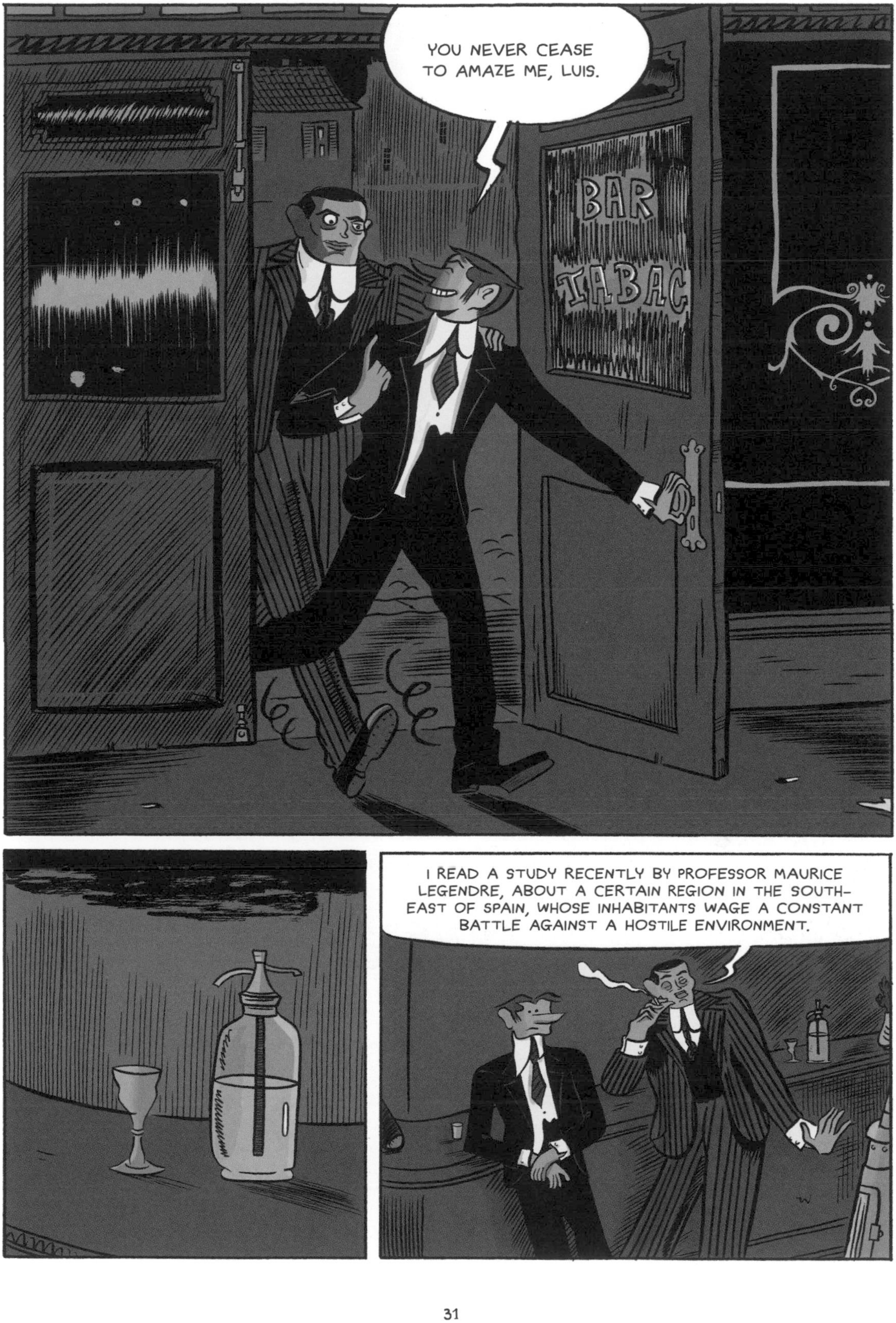
YOU NEVER CEASE TO AMAZE ME, LUIS.
BAR TABAC
I READ A STUDY RECENTLY BY PROFESSOR MAURICE LEGENDRE, ABOUT A CERTAIN REGION IN THE SOUTH-EAST OF SPAIN, WHOSE INHABITANTS WAGE A CONSTANT BATTLE AGAINST A HOSTILE ENVIRONMENT.

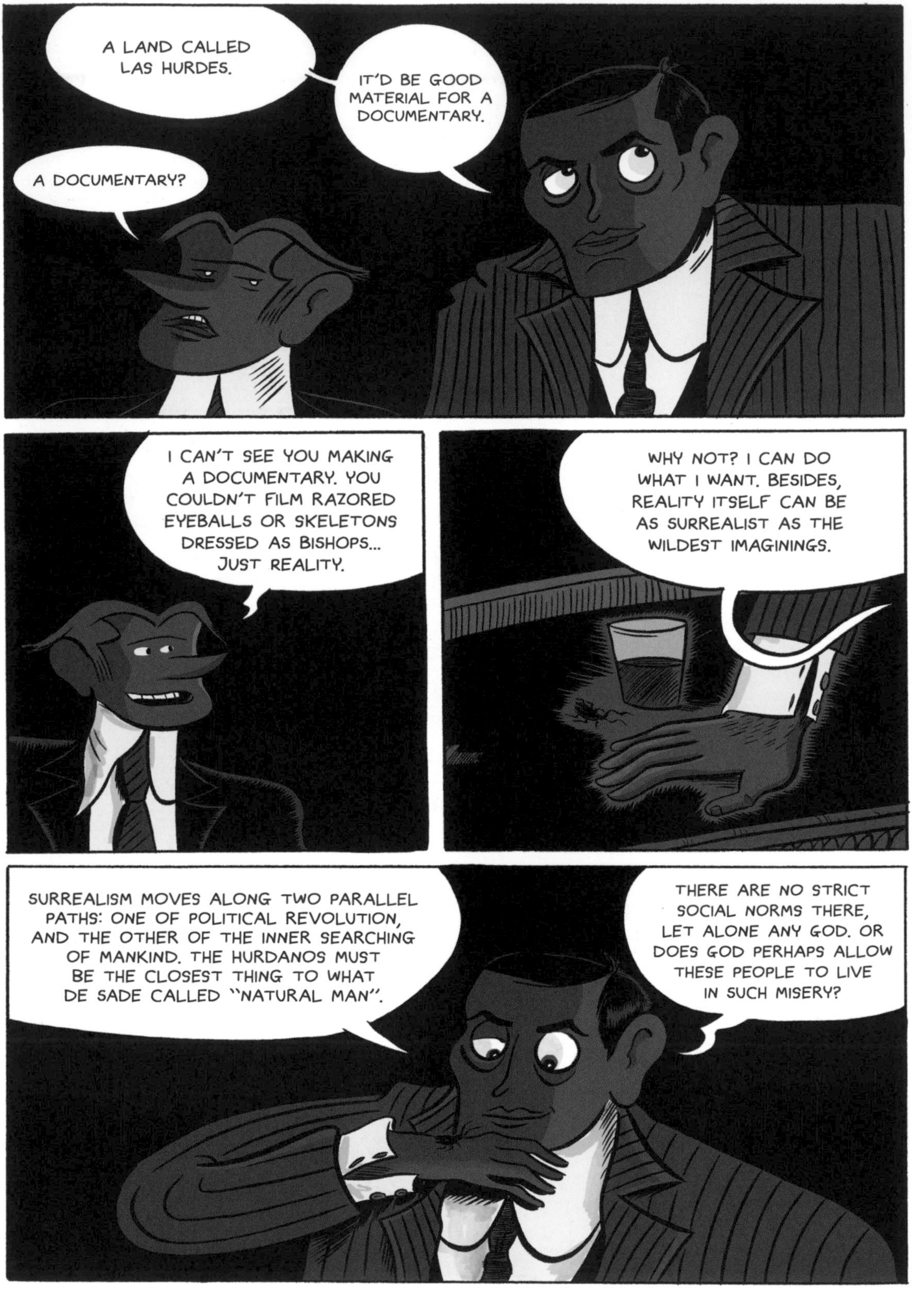
A LAND CALLED LAS HURDES.
IT'D BE GOOD MATERIAL FOR A DOCUMENTARY.
A DOCUMENTARY?
I CAN'T SEE YOU MAKING A DOCUMENTARY. YOU COULDN'T FILM RAZORED EYEBALLS OR SKELETONS DRESSED AS BISHOPS... JUST REALITY.
WHY NOT? I CAN DO WHAT I WANT. BESIDES, REALITY ITSELF CAN BE AS SURREALIST AS THE WILDEST IMAGININGS.
SURREALISM MOVES ALONG TWO PARALLEL PATHS: ONE OF POLITICAL REVOLUTION, AND THE OTHER OF THE INNER SEARCHING OF MANKIND. THE HURDANOS MUST BE THE CLOSEST THING TO WHAT DE SADE CALLED "NATURAL MAN".
THERE ARE NO STRICT SOCIAL NORMS THERE, LET ALONE ANY GOD. OR DOES GOD PERHAPS ALLOW THESE PEOPLE TO LIVE IN SUCH MISERY?

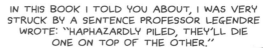

THE ONLY LAW THAT EXISTS THERE IS THE LAW OF NATURE. A HOSTILE NATURE THAT IMPOSES ITSELF FEROCIOUSLY UPON THE PEOPLE.

IN THIS BOOK I TOLD YOU ABOUT, I WAS VERY STRUCK BY A SENTENCE PROFESSOR LEGENDRE WROTE: "HAPHAZARDLY PILED, THEY'LL DIE ONE ON TOP OF THE OTHER."

ARE YOU LISTENING TO ME, RAMÓN?

WHAT? OH... YES, OF COURSE.

BE RIGHT BACK.

WHY, YOU...

WAIT! LET ME HAVE HER! YOU'RE TOO DRUNK. I WANT TO TRY OUT MY HYPNOTIC POWERS.

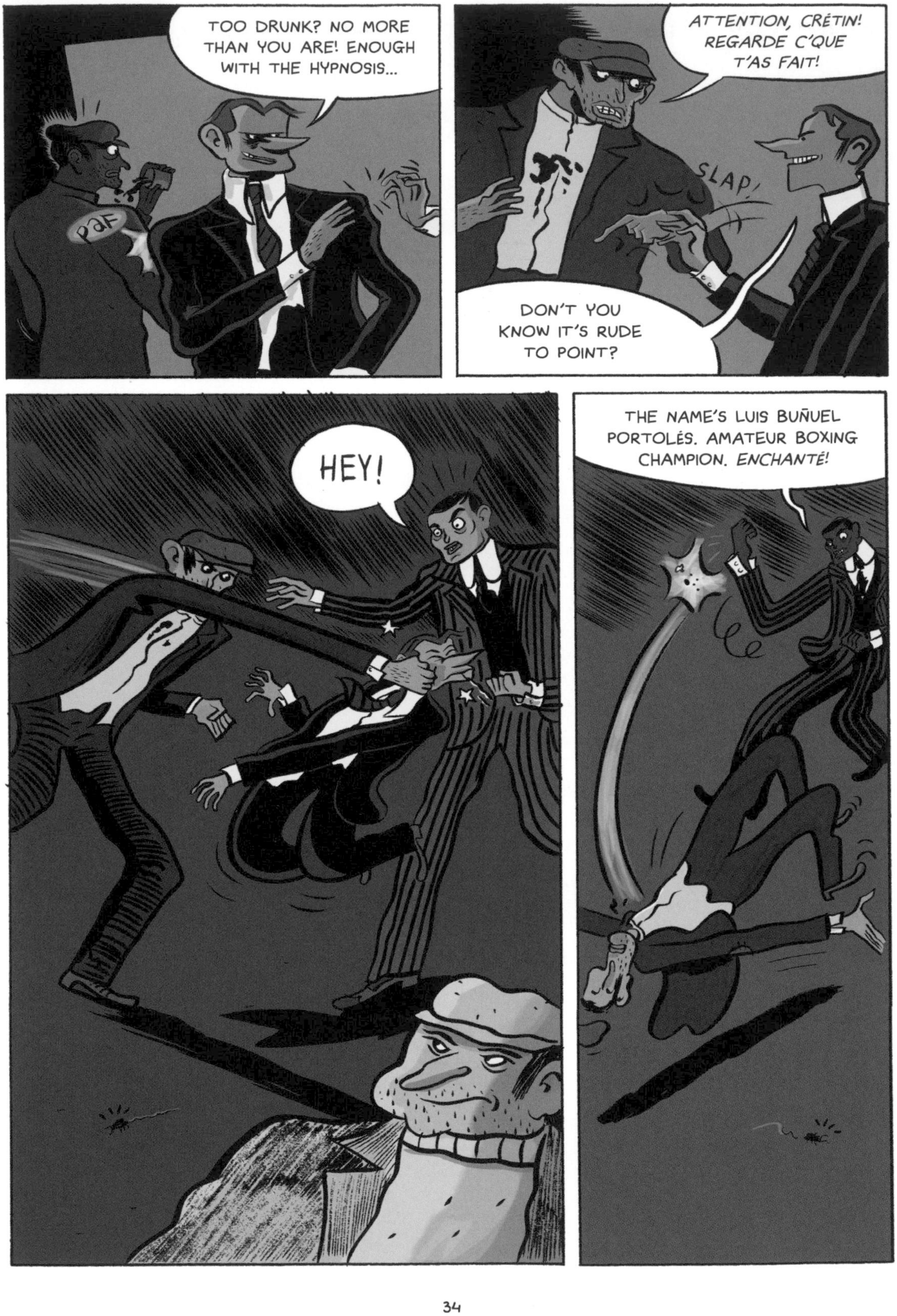
TOO DRUNK? NO MORE THAN YOU ARE! ENOUGH WITH THE HYPNOSIS...
PAF
ATTENTION, CRÉTIN! REGARDE C'QUE T'AS FAIT!
SLAP!
DON'T YOU KNOW IT'S RUDE TO POINT?
HEY!
THE NAME'S LUIS BUÑUEL PORTOLÉS. AMATEUR BOXING CHAMPION. *ENCHANTÉ!*

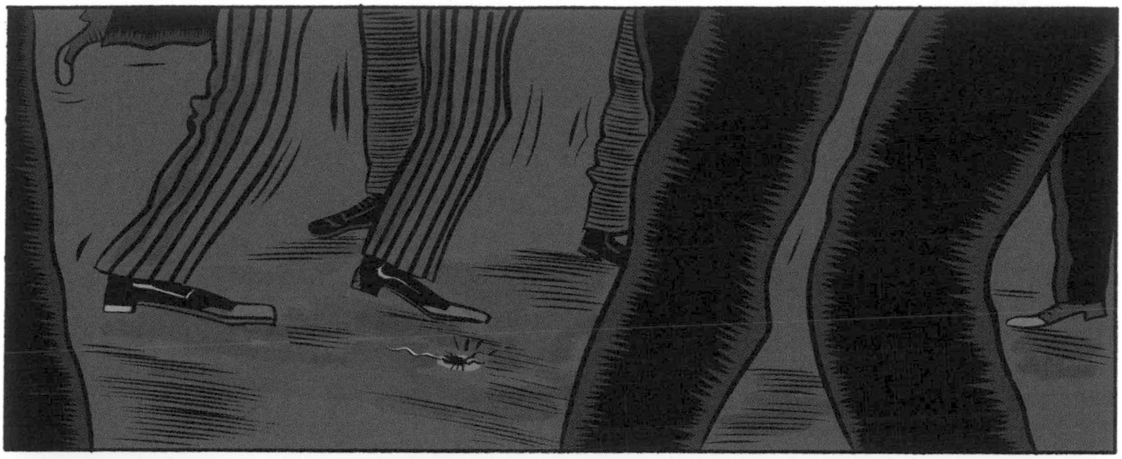

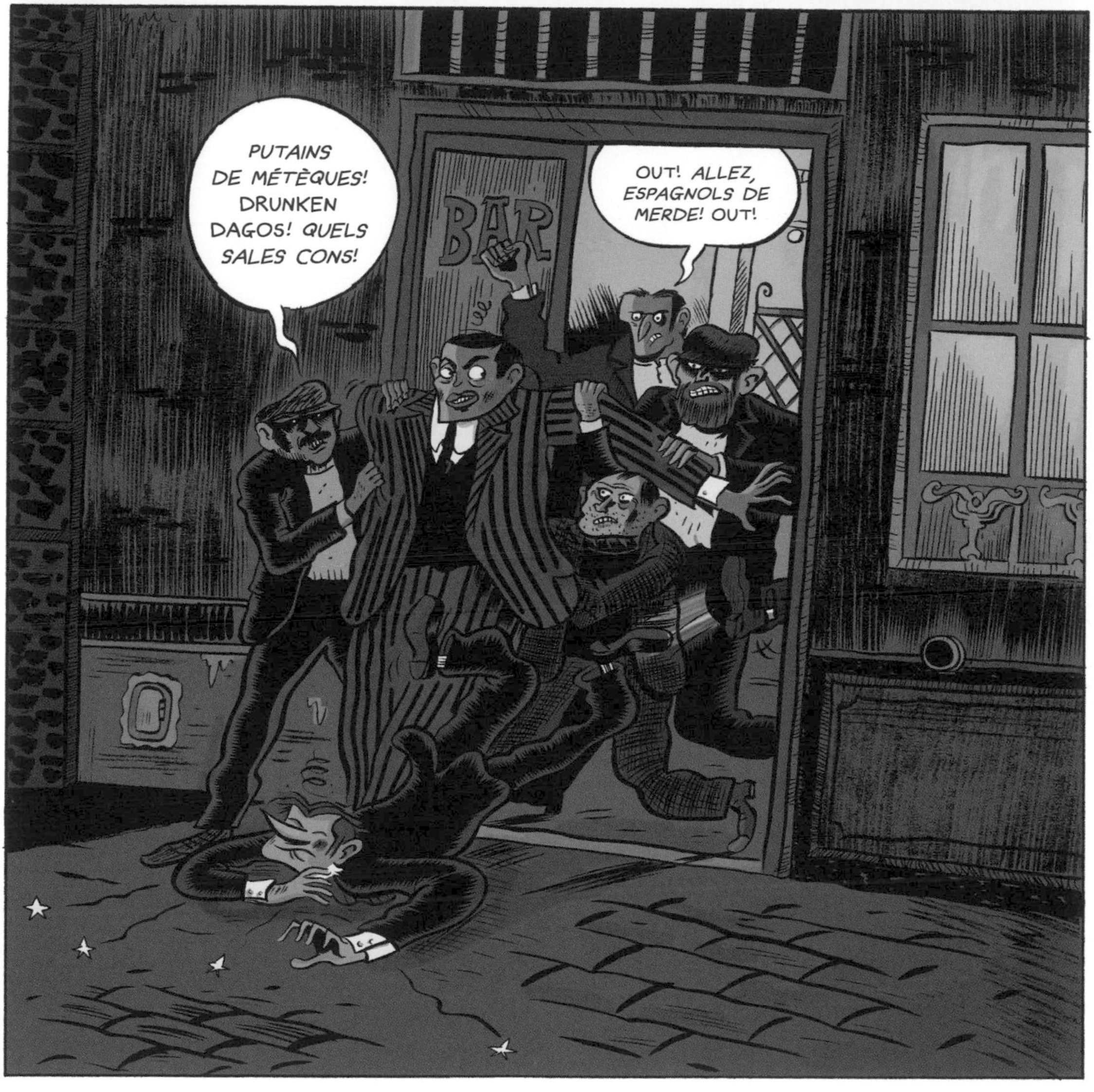
PUTAINS DE MÉTÈQUES! DRUNKEN DAGOS! QUELS SALES CONS!
BAR
OUT! ALLEZ, ESPAGNOLS DE MERDE! OUT!

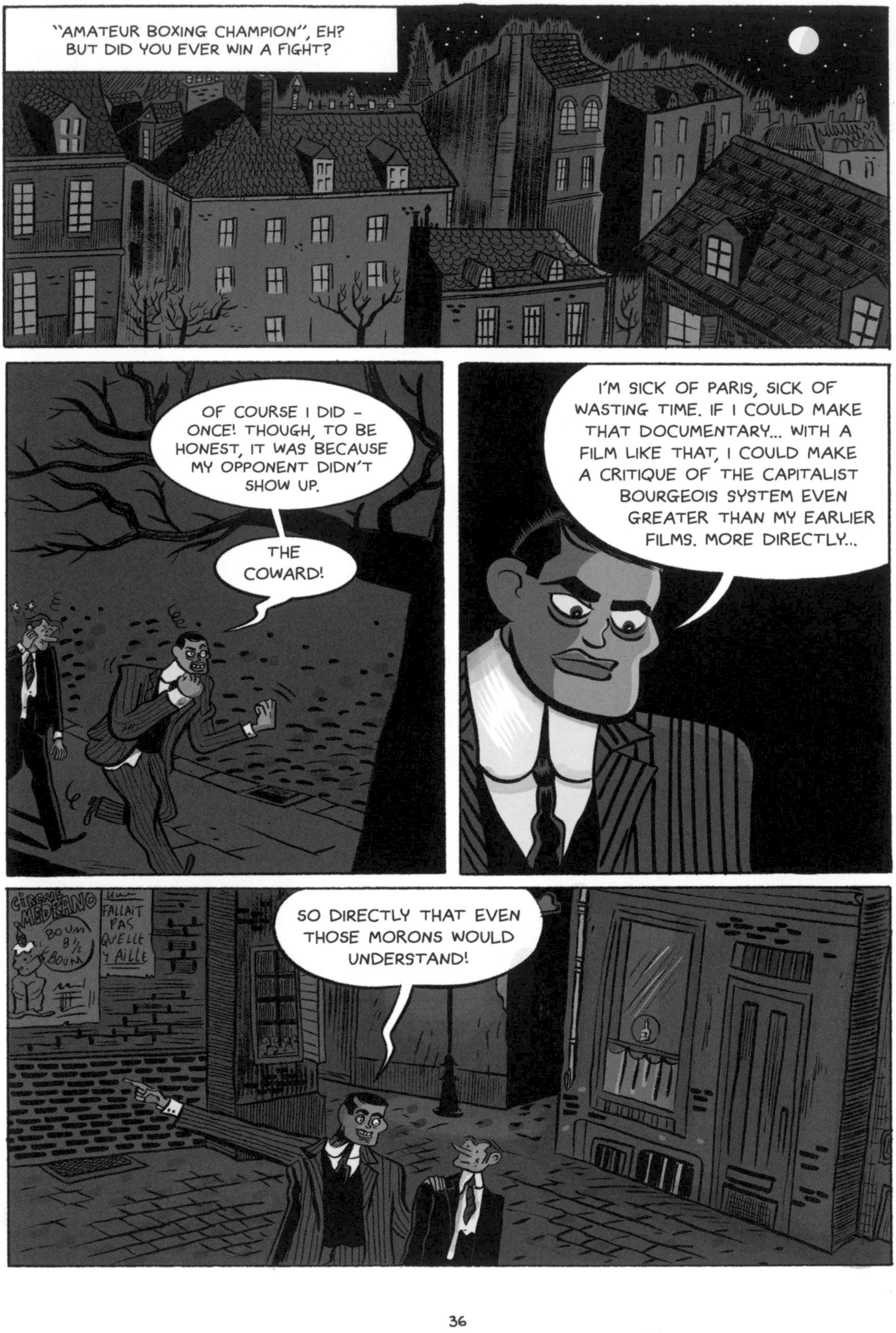

"AMATEUR BOXING CHAMPION", EH? BUT DID YOU EVER WIN A FIGHT?
OF COURSE I DID – ONCE! THOUGH, TO BE HONEST, IT WAS BECAUSE MY OPPONENT DIDN'T SHOW UP.
THE COWARD!
I'M SICK OF PARIS, SICK OF WASTING TIME. IF I COULD MAKE THAT DOCUMENTARY... WITH A FILM LIKE THAT, I COULD MAKE A CRITIQUE OF THE CAPITALIST BOURGEOIS SYSTEM EVEN GREATER THAN MY EARLIER FILMS. MORE DIRECTLY...
CIRQUE MEDRANO
FALLAIT PAS QUELLE Y AILLE
SO DIRECTLY THAT EVEN THOSE MORONS WOULD UNDERSTAND!

SO WHAT'S STOPPING YOU FROM MAKING THIS BLOODY FILM? MONEY?

YES! MONEY, RAMÓN. ALWAYS THE FILTHY LUCRE.

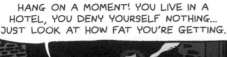

HANG ON A MOMENT! YOU LIVE IN A HOTEL, YOU DENY YOURSELF NOTHING... JUST LOOK AT HOW FAT YOU'RE GETTING.

I STILL HAVE A LITTLE OF THE MONEY MY MOTHER LENT ME, PLUS SOME FROM THE JOB IN AMERICA.

AS FOR MY PHYSICAL APPEARANCE...

I'LL HAVE YOU KNOW THAT HERE IN PARIS I MET THE POET PABLO NERUDA, AND HE TOLD ME THAT TO SUCCEED IN LIFE ONE HAD TO BE FAT. EVERY MONDAY HE WOULD STOP IN FRONT OF THE WINDOW OF THE QUAI VOLTAIRE BOOKSHOP, WHERE THE COMPLETE WORKS OF VICTOR HUGO WERE ON DISPLAY, AND MEASURE HIS BELLY. "I AM NOW UP TO VOLUME FIVE," HE SAID...

ISN'T A FAT BELLY A SYNONYM FOR BEING BOURGEOIS? LIKE THE BISHOPS AND BAKERS?

OH, MY DEAR FRIEND, SOME DAY YOU'LL EXPLAIN TO ME WHY A PETIT BOURGEOIS LIKE YOU HAS THIS YEARNING TO FOMENT A REVOLUTION.

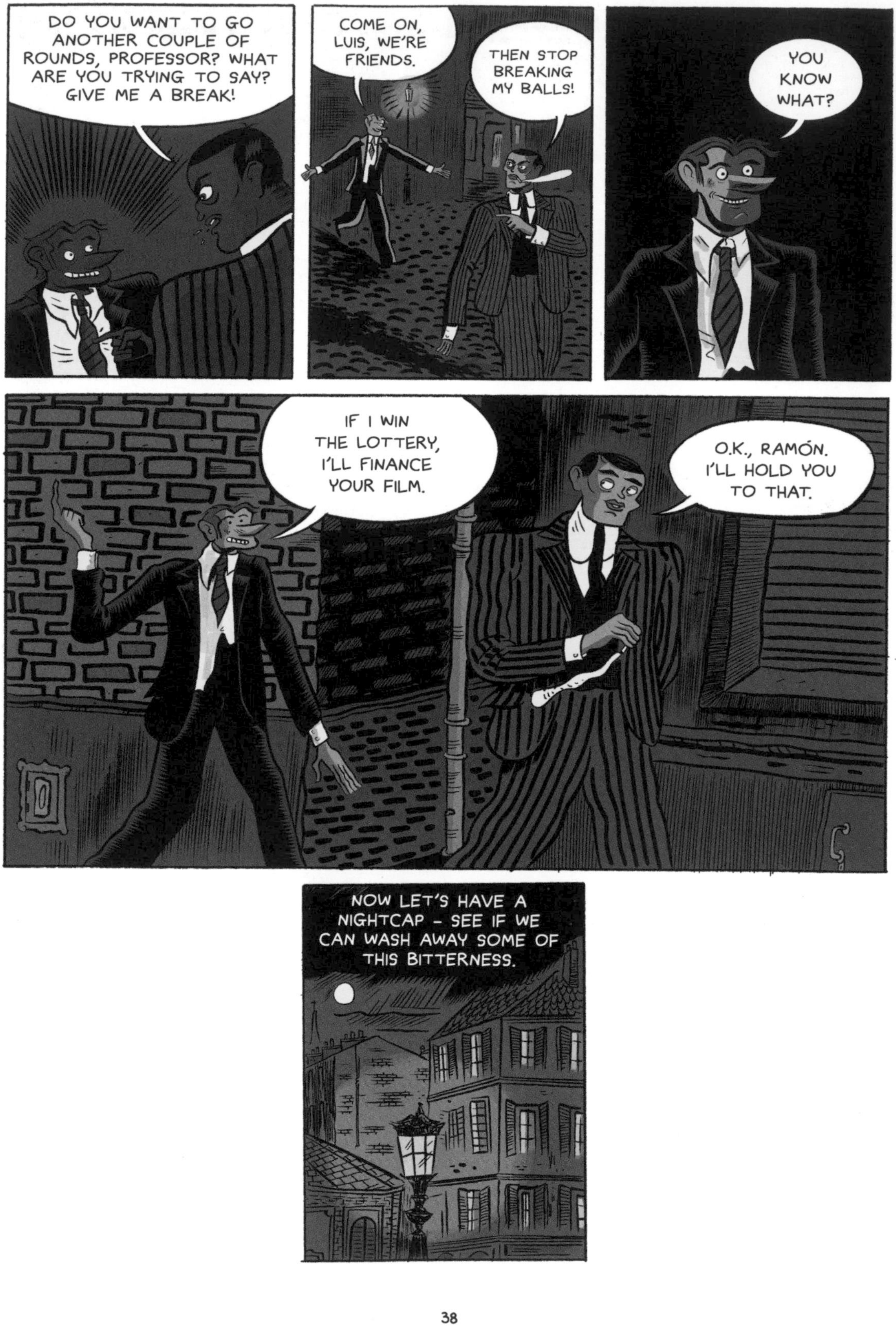
DO YOU WANT TO GO ANOTHER COUPLE OF ROUNDS, PROFESSOR? WHAT ARE YOU TRYING TO SAY? GIVE ME A BREAK!
COME ON, LUIS, WE'RE FRIENDS.
THEN STOP BREAKING MY BALLS!
YOU KNOW WHAT?
IF I WIN THE LOTTERY, I'LL FINANCE YOUR FILM.
O.K., RAMÓN. I'LL HOLD YOU TO THAT.
NOW LET'S HAVE A NIGHTCAP - SEE IF WE CAN WASH AWAY SOME OF THIS BITTERNESS.

3

TEN HOURS FROM PARIS

"THESE MISCREANTS, WHO NEVER WERE ALIVE,
WERE NAKED, AND WERE STUNG EXCEEDINGLY
BY GADFLIES AND BY HORNETS THAT WERE THERE."
– DANTE, *INFERNO*, III, 64–6 (TRANS. LONGFELLOW)

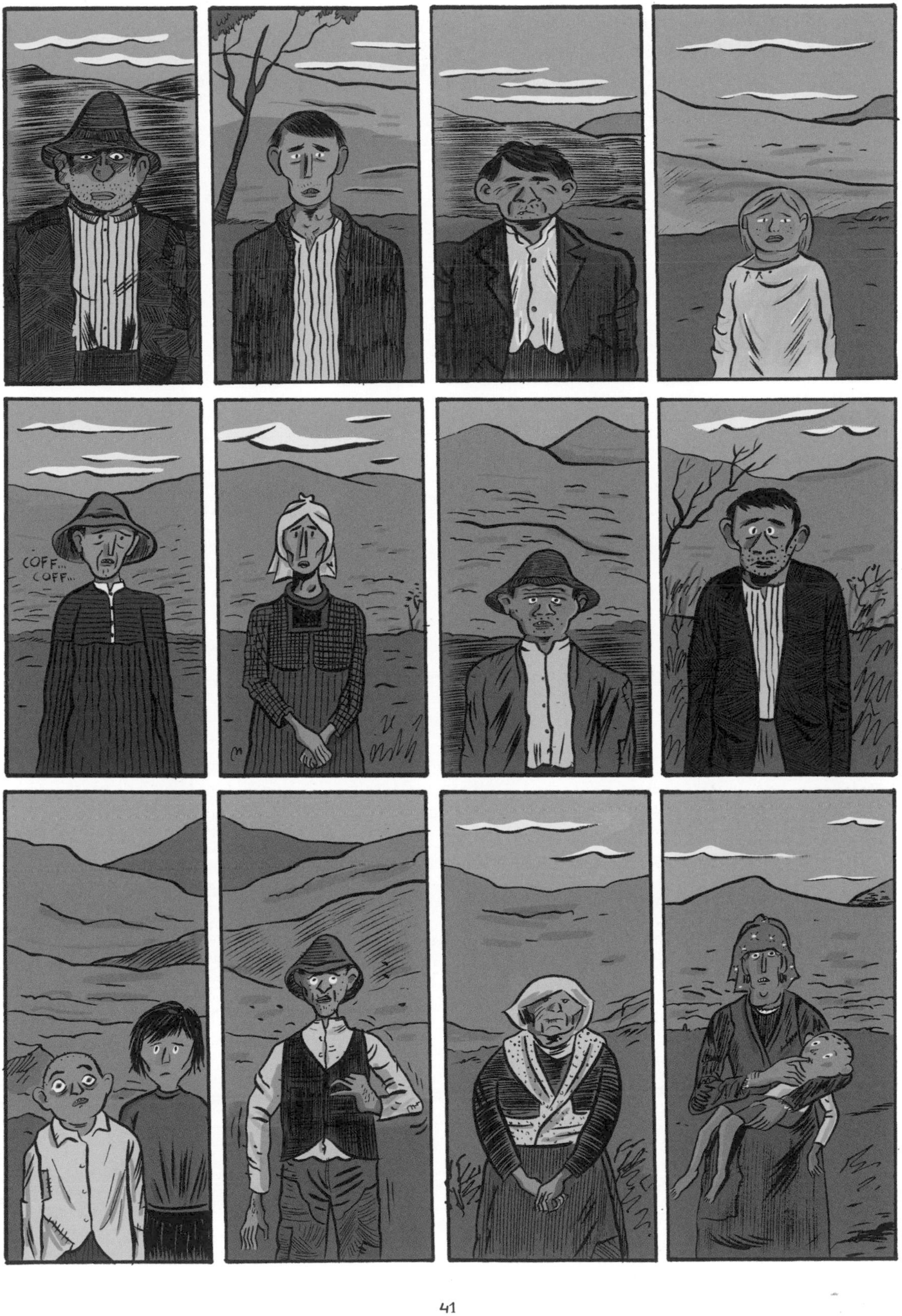
COFF... COFF...

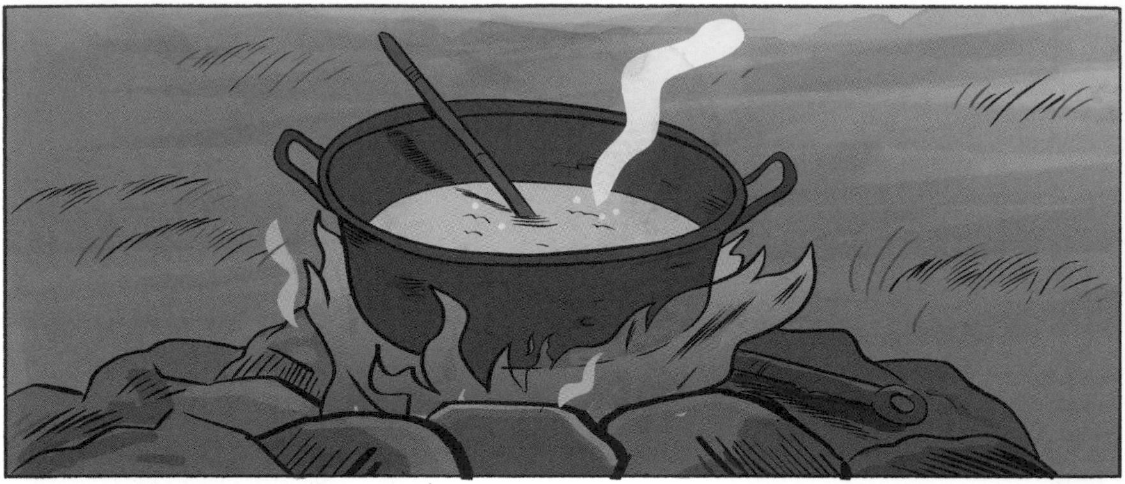

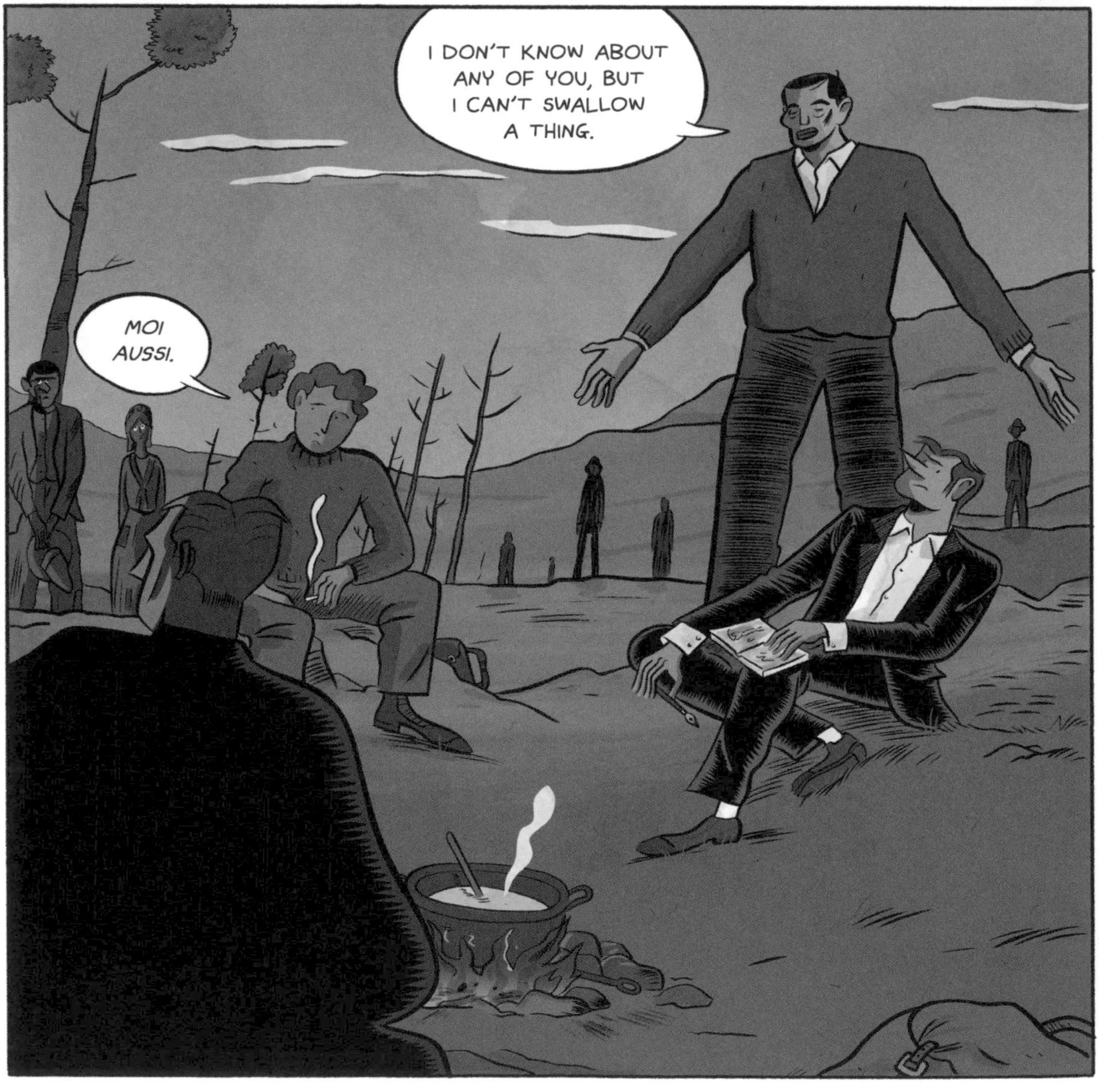
I DON'T KNOW ABOUT ANY OF YOU, BUT I CAN'T SWALLOW A THING.
MOI AUSSI.

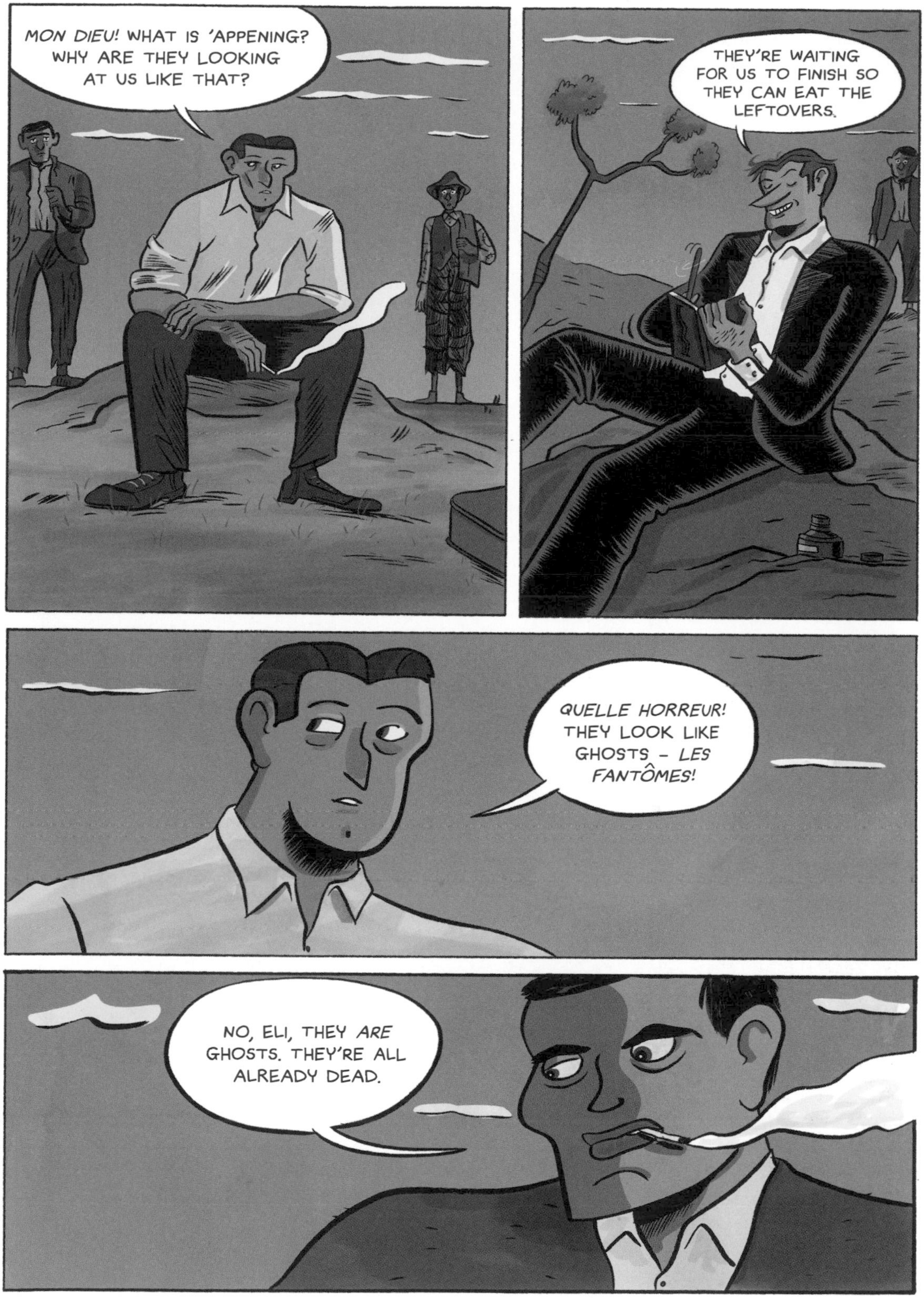
MON DIEU! WHAT IS 'APPENING? WHY ARE THEY LOOKING AT US LIKE THAT?
THEY'RE WAITING FOR US TO FINISH SO THEY CAN EAT THE LEFTOVERS.
QUELLE HORREUR! THEY LOOK LIKE GHOSTS – *LES FANTÔMES!*
NO, ELI, THEY *ARE* GHOSTS. THEY'RE ALL ALREADY DEAD.

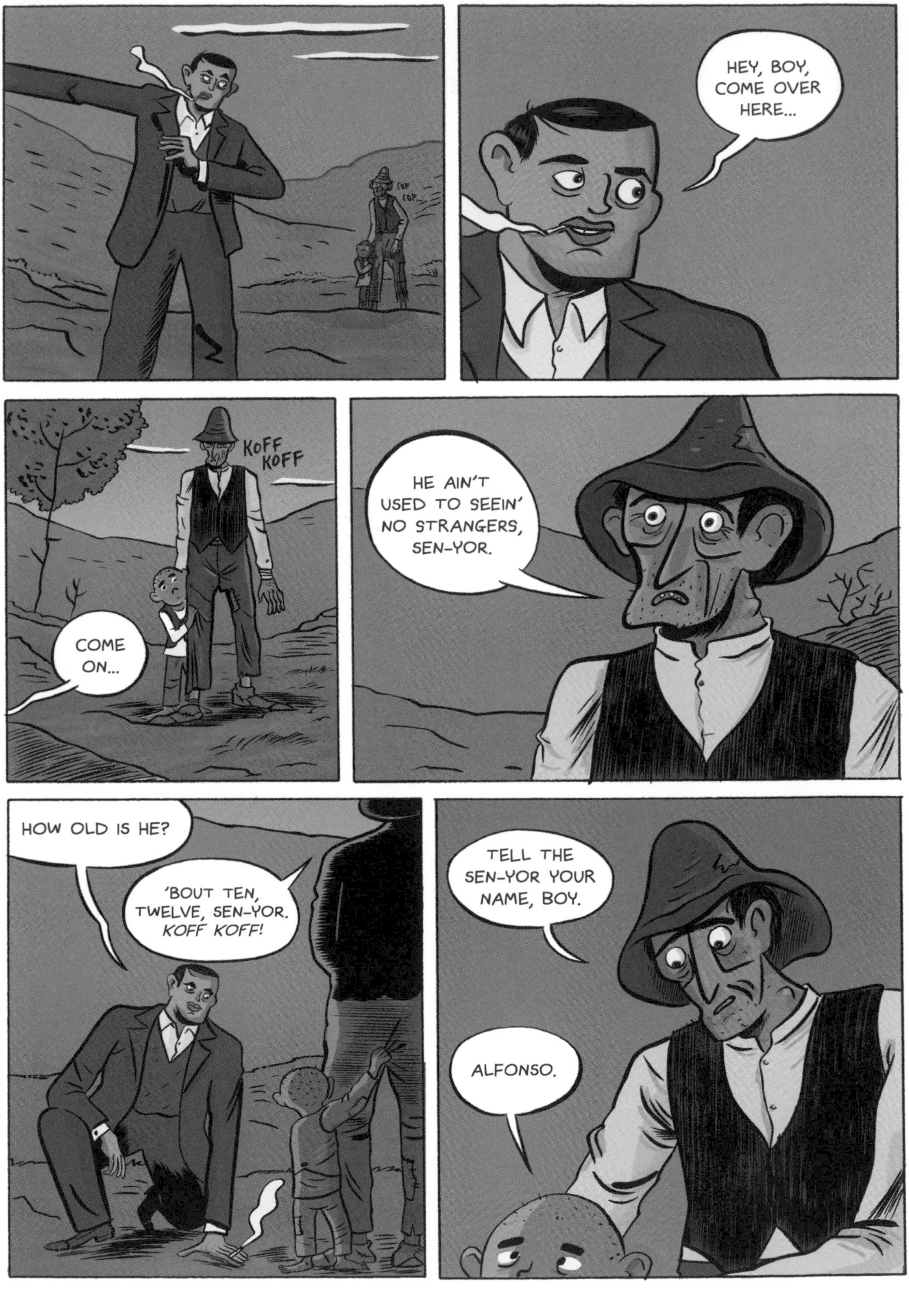
HEY, BOY, COME OVER HERE...
KOFF KOFF
COME ON...
HE AIN'T USED TO SEEIN' NO STRANGERS, SEN-YOR.
HOW OLD IS HE?
'BOUT TEN, TWELVE, SEN-YOR. KOFF KOFF!
TELL THE SEN-YOR YOUR NAME, BOY.
ALFONSO.

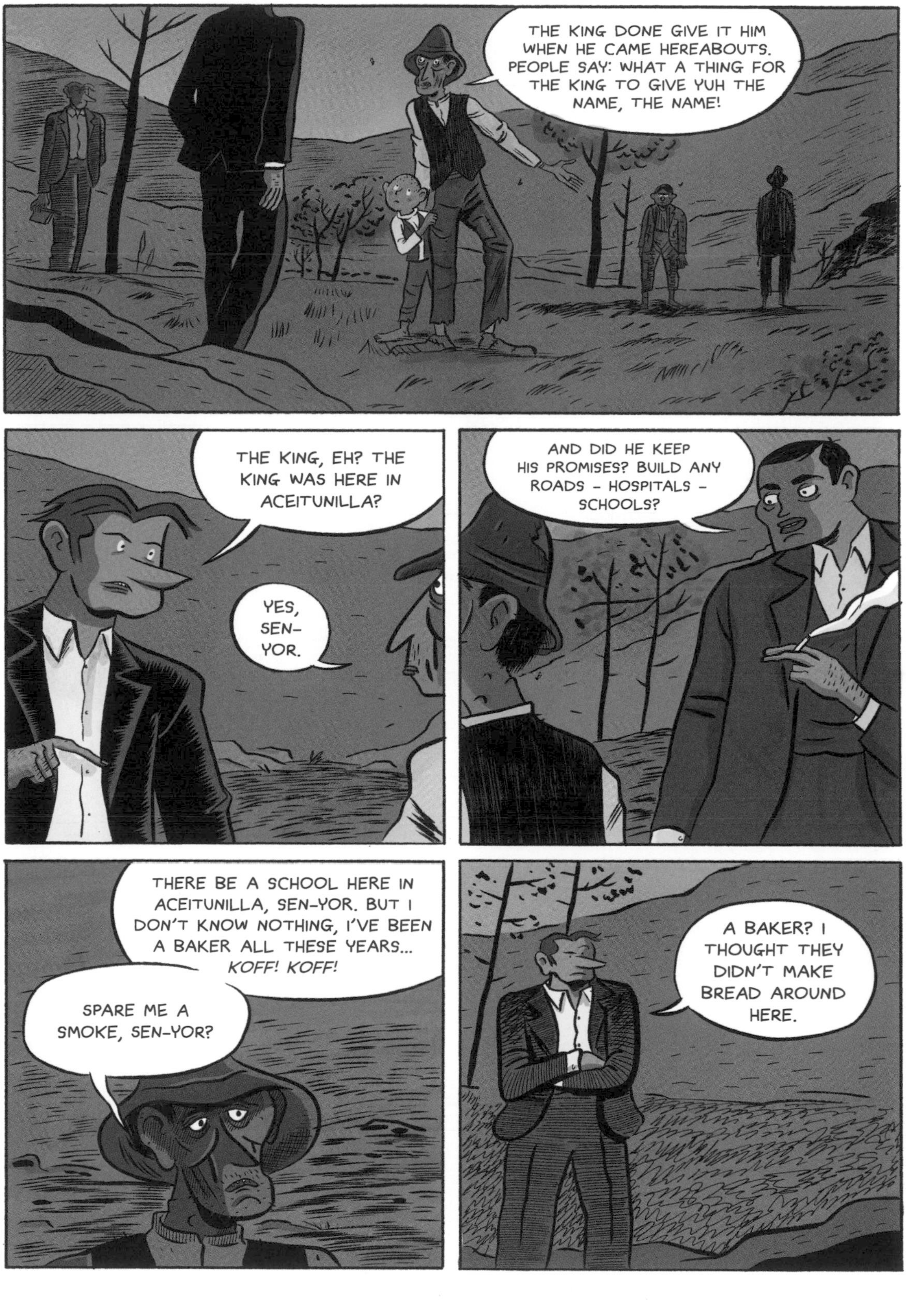
THE KING DONE GIVE IT HIM WHEN HE CAME HEREABOUTS. PEOPLE SAY: WHAT A THING FOR THE KING TO GIVE YUH THE NAME, THE NAME!
THE KING, EH? THE KING WAS HERE IN ACEITUNILLA?
YES, SEN-YOR.
AND DID HE KEEP HIS PROMISES? BUILD ANY ROADS - HOSPITALS - SCHOOLS?
THERE BE A SCHOOL HERE IN ACEITUNILLA, SEN-YOR. BUT I DON'T KNOW NOTHING, I'VE BEEN A BAKER ALL THESE YEARS... *KOFF! KOFF!*
SPARE ME A SMOKE, SEN-YOR?
A BAKER? I THOUGHT THEY DIDN'T MAKE BREAD AROUND HERE.

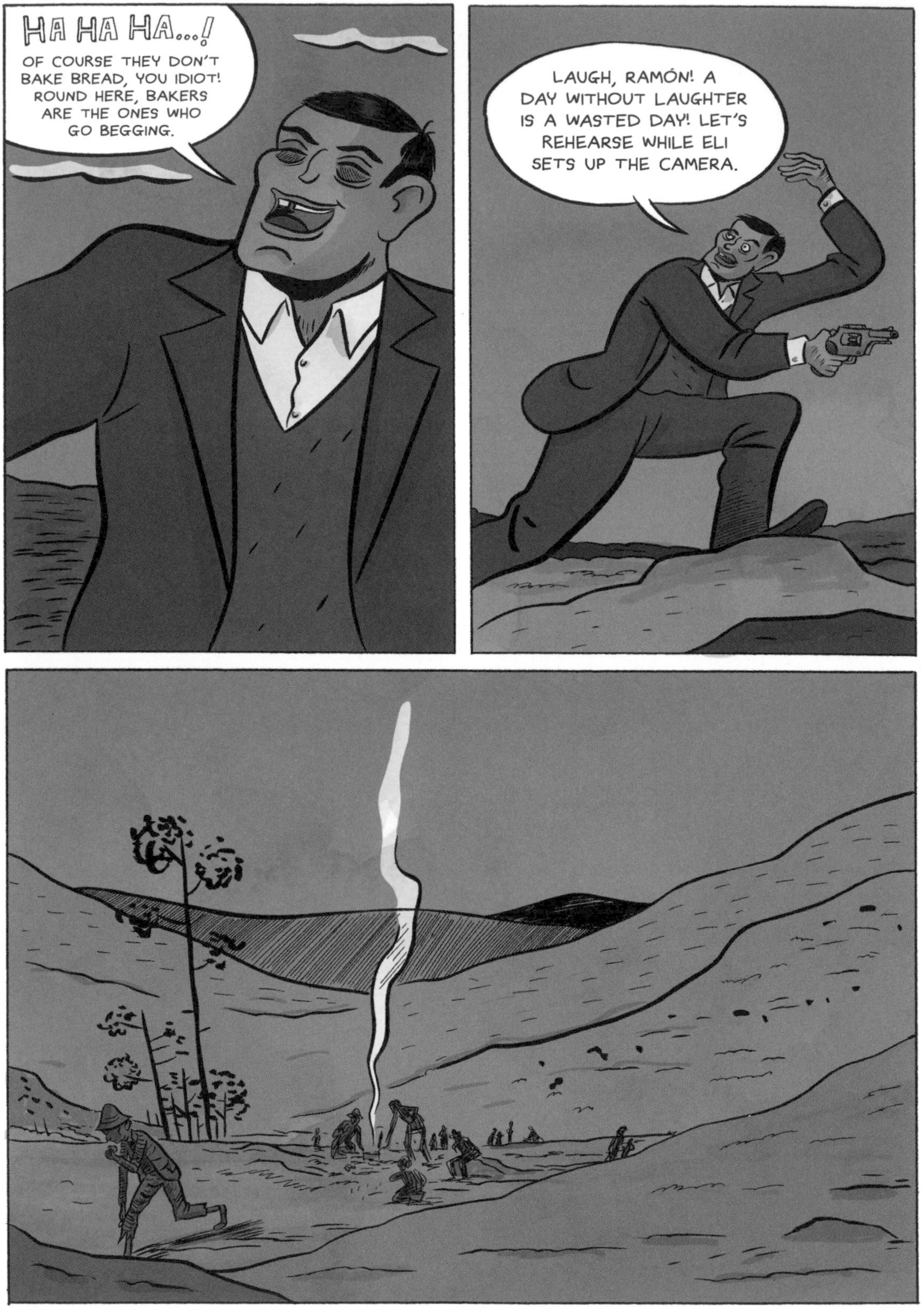
HA HA HA...!
OF COURSE THEY DON'T BAKE BREAD, YOU IDIOT! ROUND HERE, BAKERS ARE THE ONES WHO GO BEGGING.
LAUGH, RAMÓN! A DAY WITHOUT LAUGHTER IS A WASTED DAY! LET'S REHEARSE WHILE ELI SETS UP THE CAMERA.

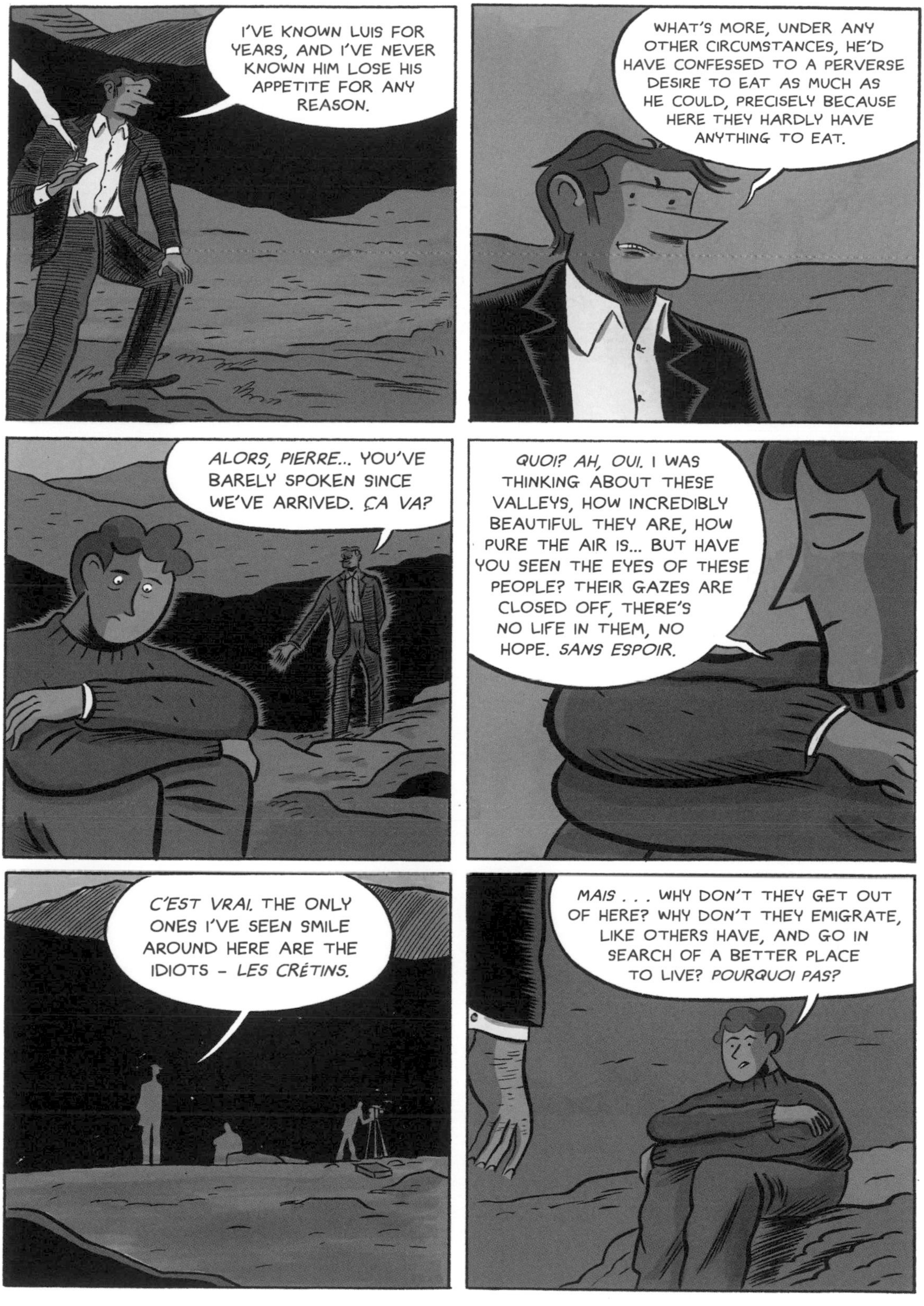
I'VE KNOWN LUIS FOR YEARS, AND I'VE NEVER KNOWN HIM LOSE HIS APPETITE FOR ANY REASON.
WHAT'S MORE, UNDER ANY OTHER CIRCUMSTANCES, HE'D HAVE CONFESSED TO A PERVERSE DESIRE TO EAT AS MUCH AS HE COULD, PRECISELY BECAUSE HERE THEY HARDLY HAVE ANYTHING TO EAT.
ALORS, PIERRE... YOU'VE BARELY SPOKEN SINCE WE'VE ARRIVED. *ÇA VA?*
QUOI? AH, OUI. I WAS THINKING ABOUT THESE VALLEYS, HOW INCREDIBLY BEAUTIFUL THEY ARE, HOW PURE THE AIR IS... BUT HAVE YOU SEEN THE EYES OF THESE PEOPLE? THEIR GAZES ARE CLOSED OFF, THERE'S NO LIFE IN THEM, NO HOPE. *SANS ESPOIR.*
C'EST VRAI. THE ONLY ONES I'VE SEEN SMILE AROUND HERE ARE THE IDIOTS – *LES CRÉTINS.*
MAIS . . . WHY DON'T THEY GET OUT OF HERE? WHY DON'T THEY EMIGRATE, LIKE OTHERS HAVE, AND GO IN SEARCH OF A BETTER PLACE TO LIVE? *POURQUOI PAS?*

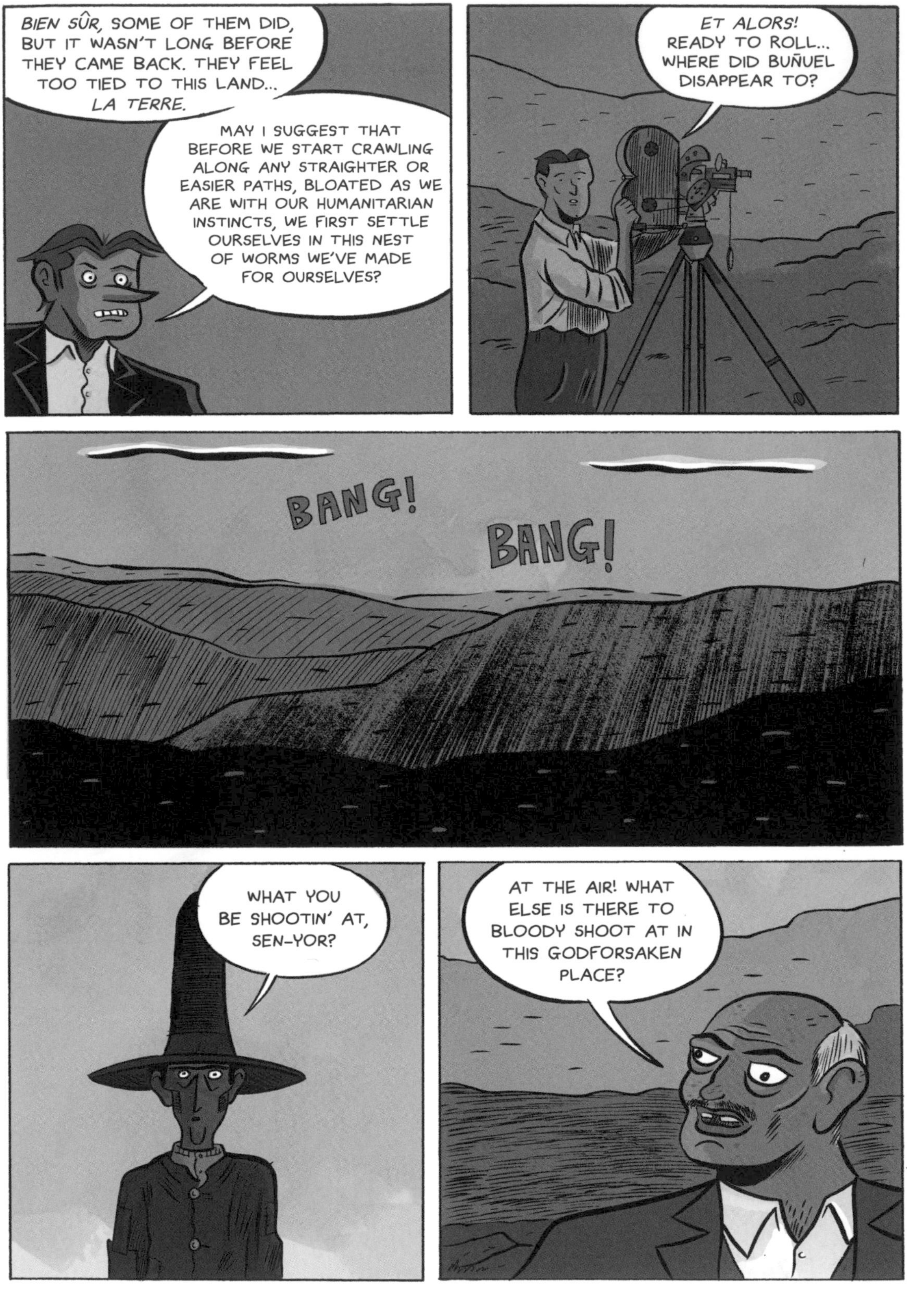
BIEN SÛR, SOME OF THEM DID, BUT IT WASN'T LONG BEFORE THEY CAME BACK. THEY FEEL TOO TIED TO THIS LAND... *LA TERRE.*
MAY I SUGGEST THAT BEFORE WE START CRAWLING ALONG ANY STRAIGHTER OR EASIER PATHS, BLOATED AS WE ARE WITH OUR HUMANITARIAN INSTINCTS, WE FIRST SETTLE OURSELVES IN THIS NEST OF WORMS WE'VE MADE FOR OURSELVES?
ET ALORS! READY TO ROLL... WHERE DID BUÑUEL DISAPPEAR TO?
BANG!
BANG!
WHAT YOU BE SHOOTIN' AT, SEN-YOR?
AT THE AIR! WHAT ELSE IS THERE TO BLOODY SHOOT AT IN THIS GODFORSAKEN PLACE?

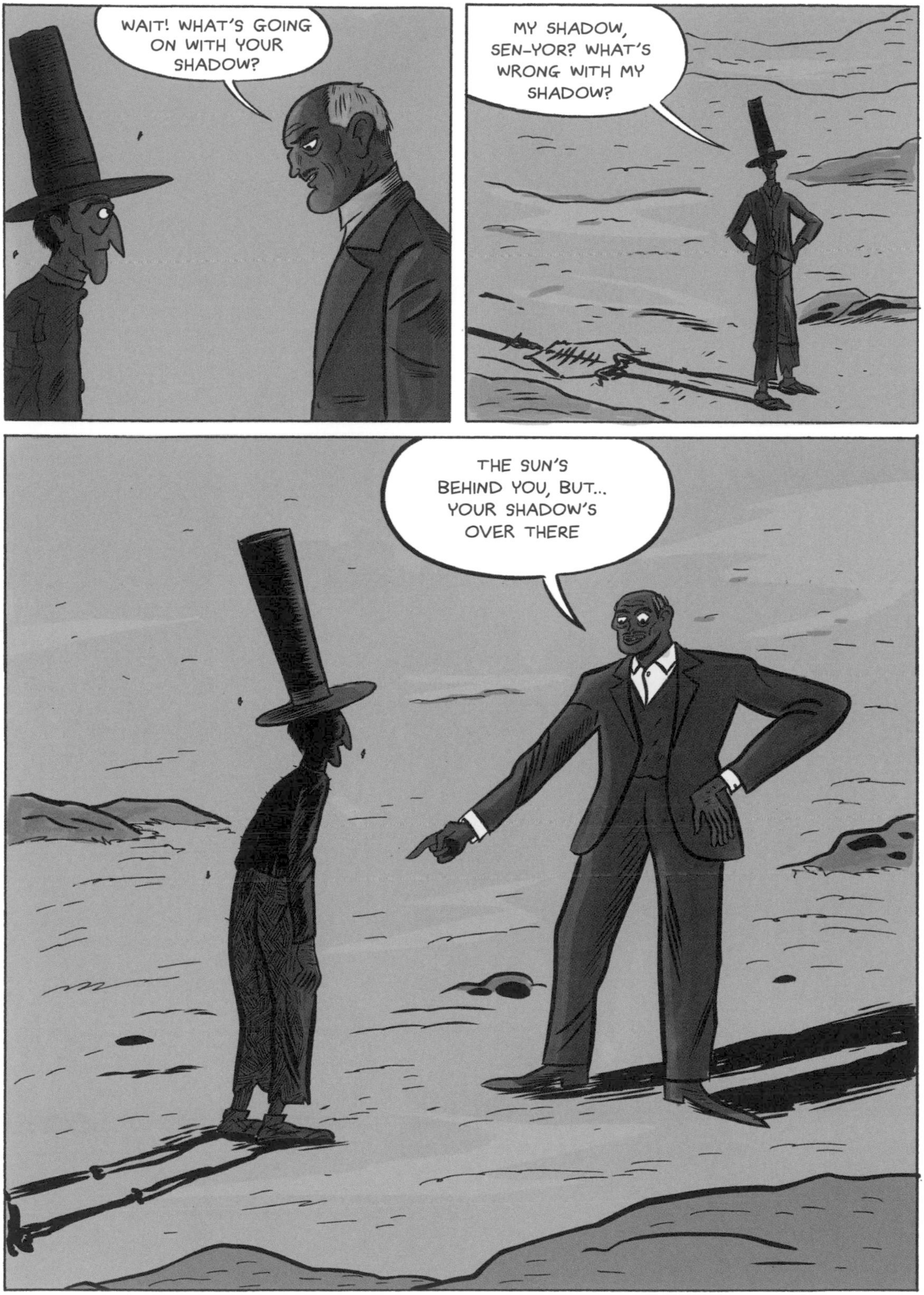
WAIT! WHAT'S GOING ON WITH YOUR SHADOW?
MY SHADOW, SEN-YOR? WHAT'S WRONG WITH MY SHADOW?
THE SUN'S BEHIND YOU, BUT... YOUR SHADOW'S OVER THERE

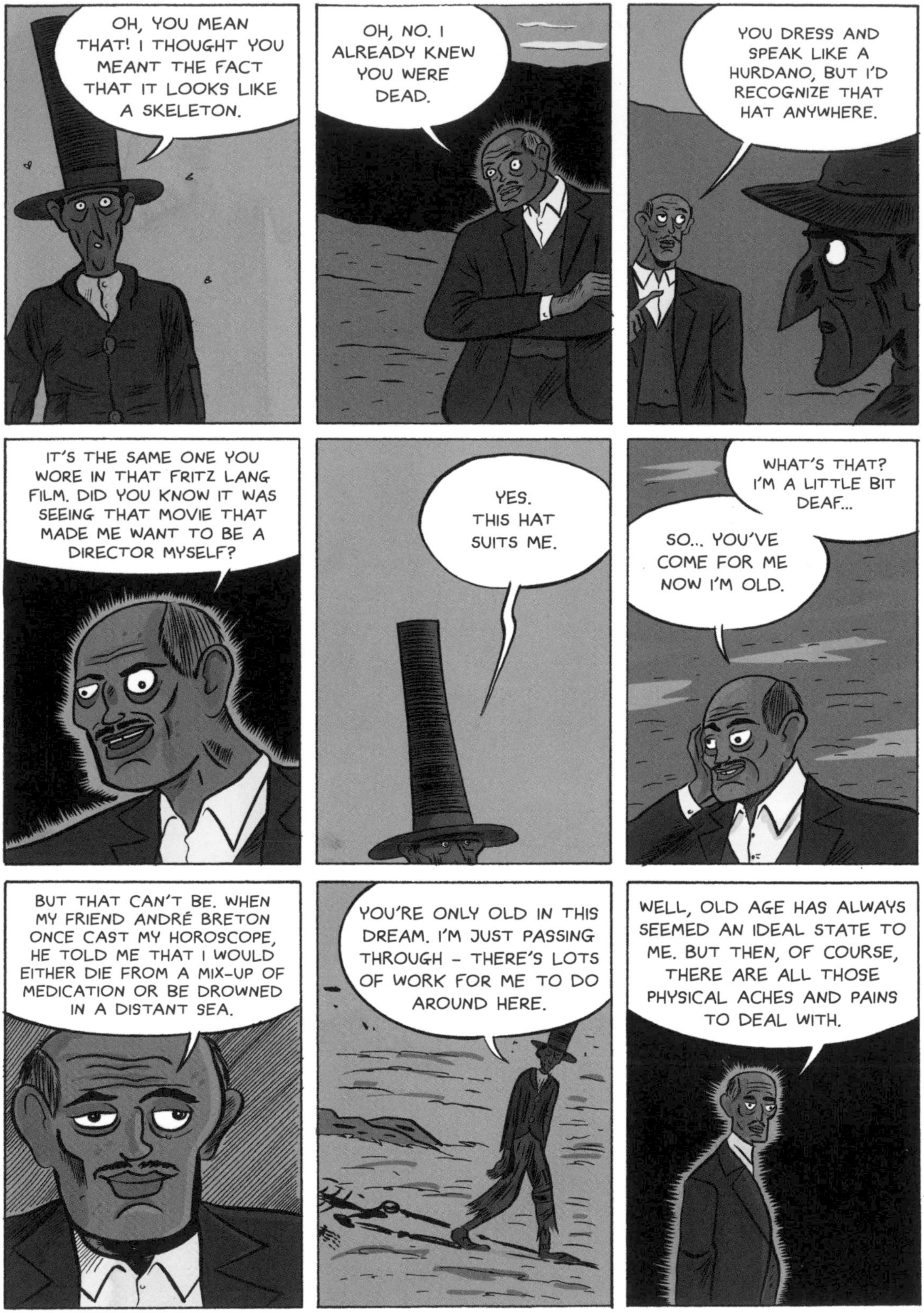
OH, YOU MEAN THAT! I THOUGHT YOU MEANT THE FACT THAT IT LOOKS LIKE A SKELETON.
OH, NO. I ALREADY KNEW YOU WERE DEAD.
YOU DRESS AND SPEAK LIKE A HURDANO, BUT I'D RECOGNIZE THAT HAT ANYWHERE.
IT'S THE SAME ONE YOU WORE IN THAT FRITZ LANG FILM. DID YOU KNOW IT WAS SEEING THAT MOVIE THAT MADE ME WANT TO BE A DIRECTOR MYSELF?
YES. THIS HAT SUITS ME.
SO... YOU'VE COME FOR ME NOW I'M OLD.
WHAT'S THAT? I'M A LITTLE BIT DEAF...
BUT THAT CAN'T BE. WHEN MY FRIEND ANDRÉ BRETON ONCE CAST MY HOROSCOPE, HE TOLD ME THAT I WOULD EITHER DIE FROM A MIX-UP OF MEDICATION OR BE DROWNED IN A DISTANT SEA.
YOU'RE ONLY OLD IN THIS DREAM. I'M JUST PASSING THROUGH - THERE'S LOTS OF WORK FOR ME TO DO AROUND HERE.
WELL, OLD AGE HAS ALWAYS SEEMED AN IDEAL STATE TO ME. BUT THEN, OF COURSE, THERE ARE ALL THOSE PHYSICAL ACHES AND PAINS TO DEAL WITH.

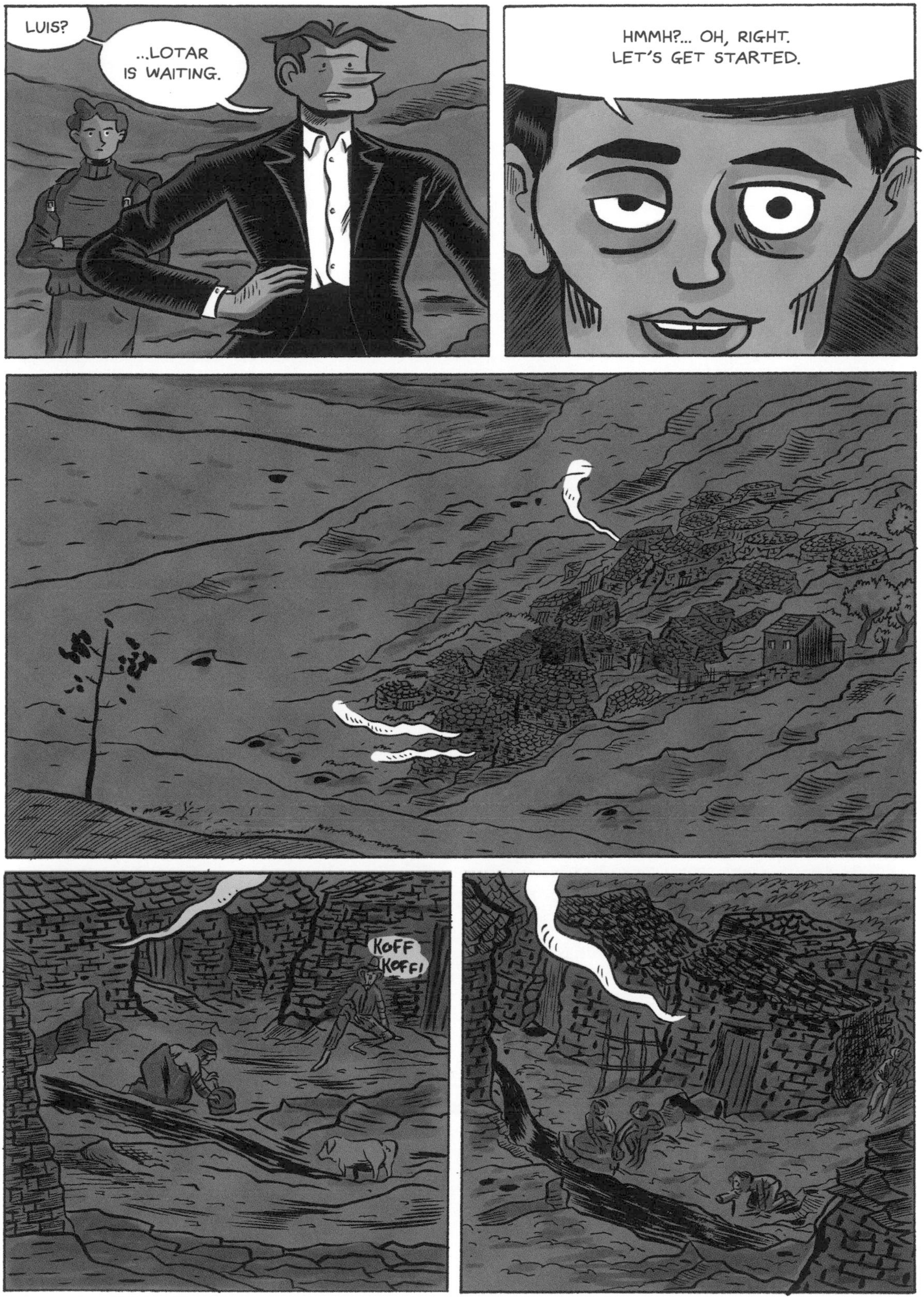
LUIS?
...LOTAR IS WAITING.
HMMH?... OH, RIGHT. LET'S GET STARTED.
KOFF KOFF!

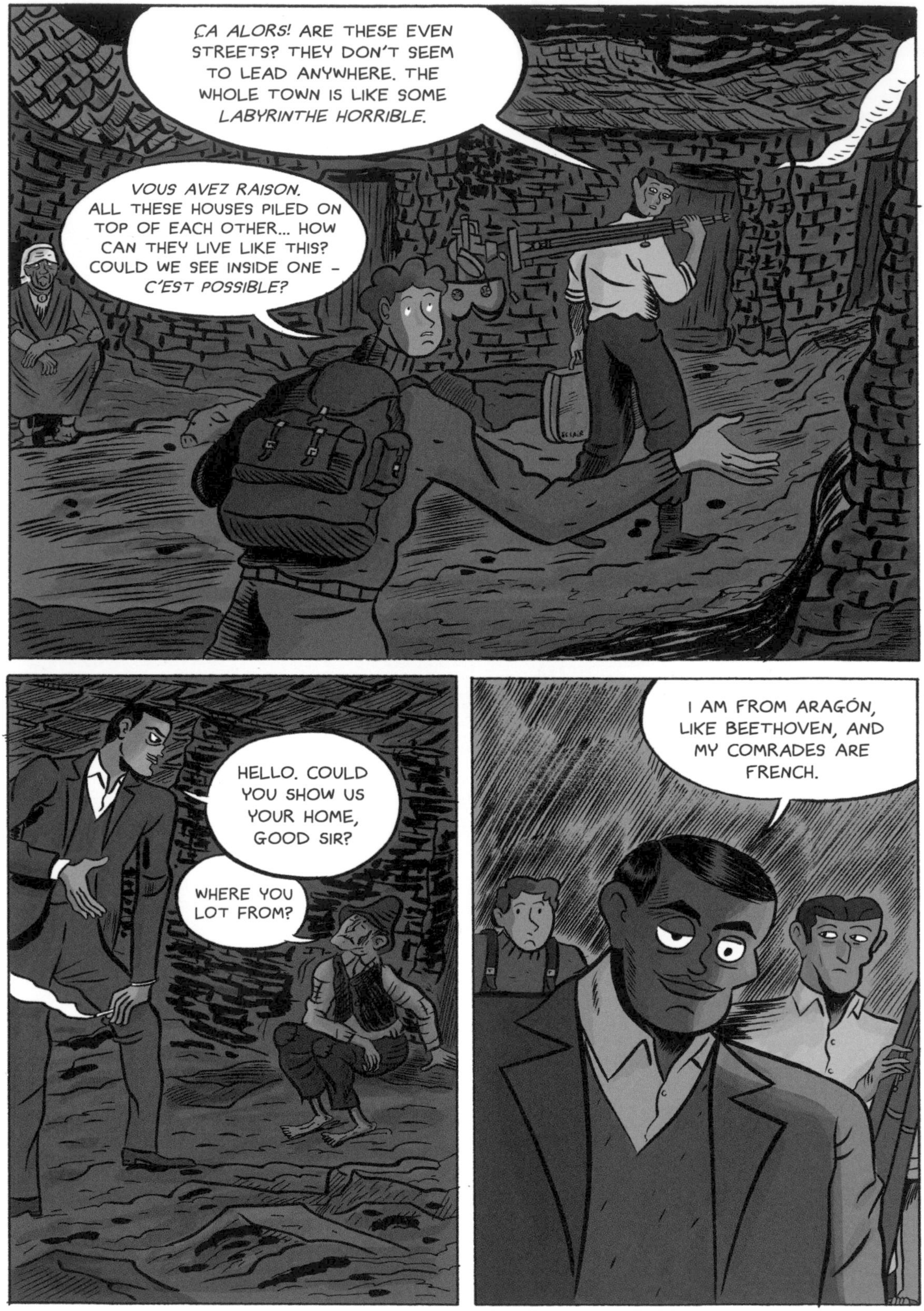
ÇA ALORS! ARE THESE EVEN STREETS? THEY DON'T SEEM TO LEAD ANYWHERE. THE WHOLE TOWN IS LIKE SOME LABYRINTHE HORRIBLE.
VOUS AVEZ RAISON. ALL THESE HOUSES PILED ON TOP OF EACH OTHER... HOW CAN THEY LIVE LIKE THIS? COULD WE SEE INSIDE ONE - C'EST POSSIBLE?
HELLO. COULD YOU SHOW US YOUR HOME, GOOD SIR?
WHERE YOU LOT FROM?
I AM FROM ARAGÓN, LIKE BEETHOVEN, AND MY COMRADES ARE FRENCH.

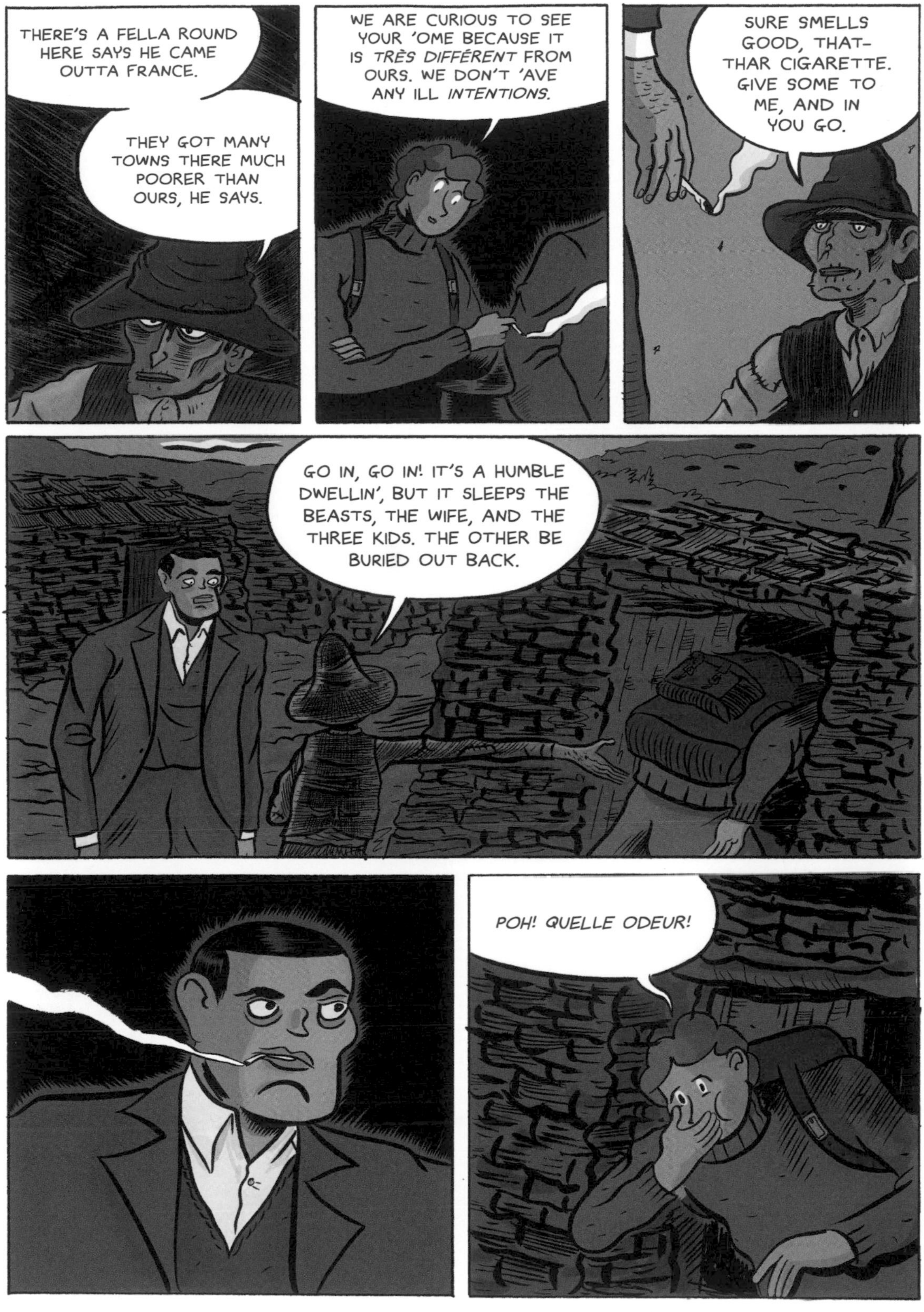
THERE'S A FELLA ROUND HERE SAYS HE CAME OUTTA FRANCE.
THEY GOT MANY TOWNS THERE MUCH POORER THAN OURS, HE SAYS.
WE ARE CURIOUS TO SEE YOUR 'OME BECAUSE IT IS *TRÈS DIFFÉRENT* FROM OURS. WE DON'T 'AVE ANY ILL *INTENTIONS*.
SURE SMELLS GOOD, THAT-THAR CIGARETTE. GIVE SOME TO ME, AND IN YOU GO.
GO IN, GO IN! IT'S A HUMBLE DWELLIN', BUT IT SLEEPS THE BEASTS, THE WIFE, AND THE THREE KIDS. THE OTHER BE BURIED OUT BACK.
POH! QUELLE ODEUR!

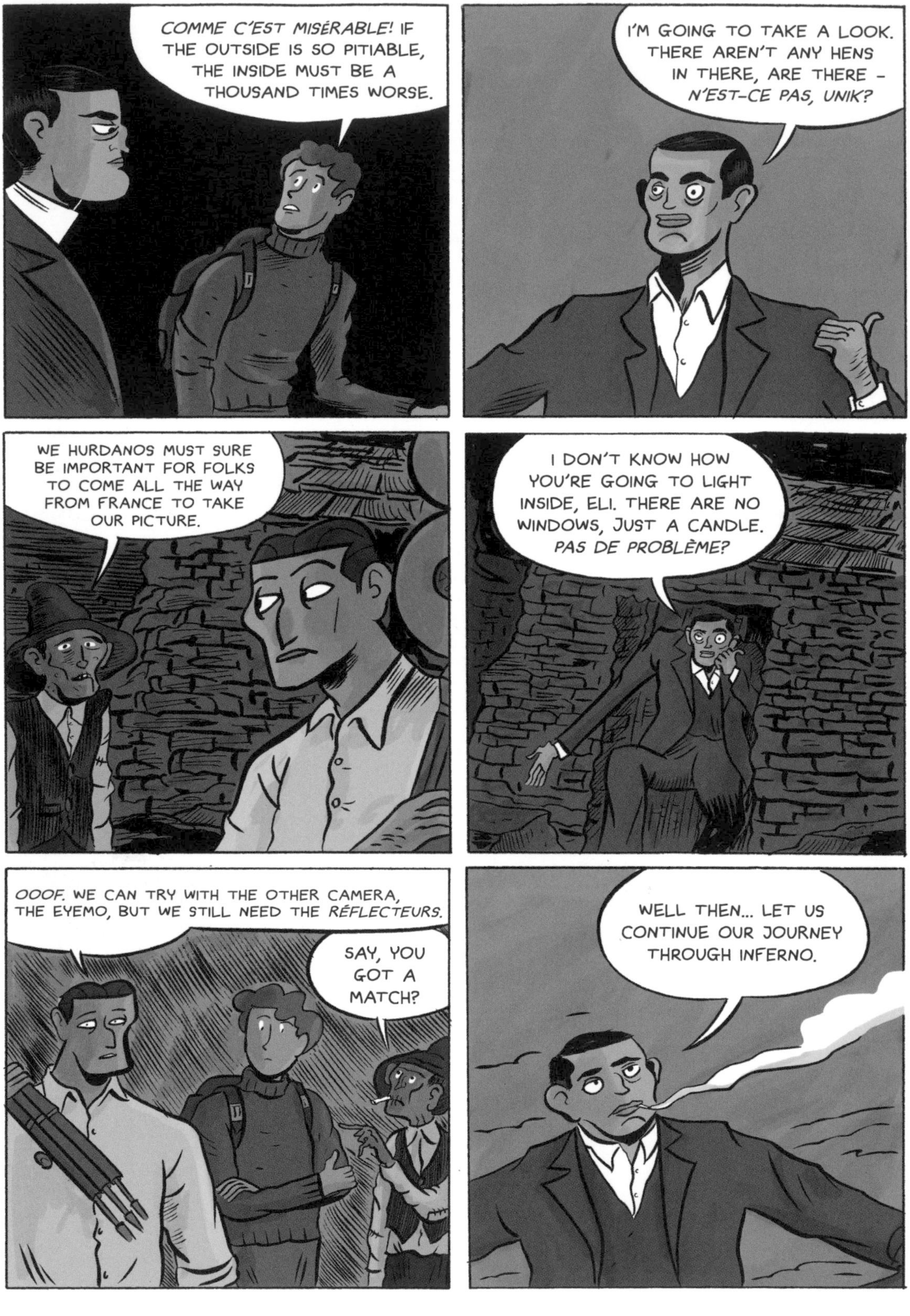

COMME C'EST MISÉRABLE! IF THE OUTSIDE IS SO PITIABLE, THE INSIDE MUST BE A THOUSAND TIMES WORSE.
I'M GOING TO TAKE A LOOK. THERE AREN'T ANY HENS IN THERE, ARE THERE – *N'EST-CE PAS, UNIK?*
WE HURDANOS MUST SURE BE IMPORTANT FOR FOLKS TO COME ALL THE WAY FROM FRANCE TO TAKE OUR PICTURE.
I DON'T KNOW HOW YOU'RE GOING TO LIGHT INSIDE, ELI. THERE ARE NO WINDOWS, JUST A CANDLE. *PAS DE PROBLÈME?*
OOOF. WE CAN TRY WITH THE OTHER CAMERA, THE EYEMO, BUT WE STILL NEED THE *RÉFLECTEURS.*
SAY, YOU GOT A MATCH?
WELL THEN... LET US CONTINUE OUR JOURNEY THROUGH INFERNO.

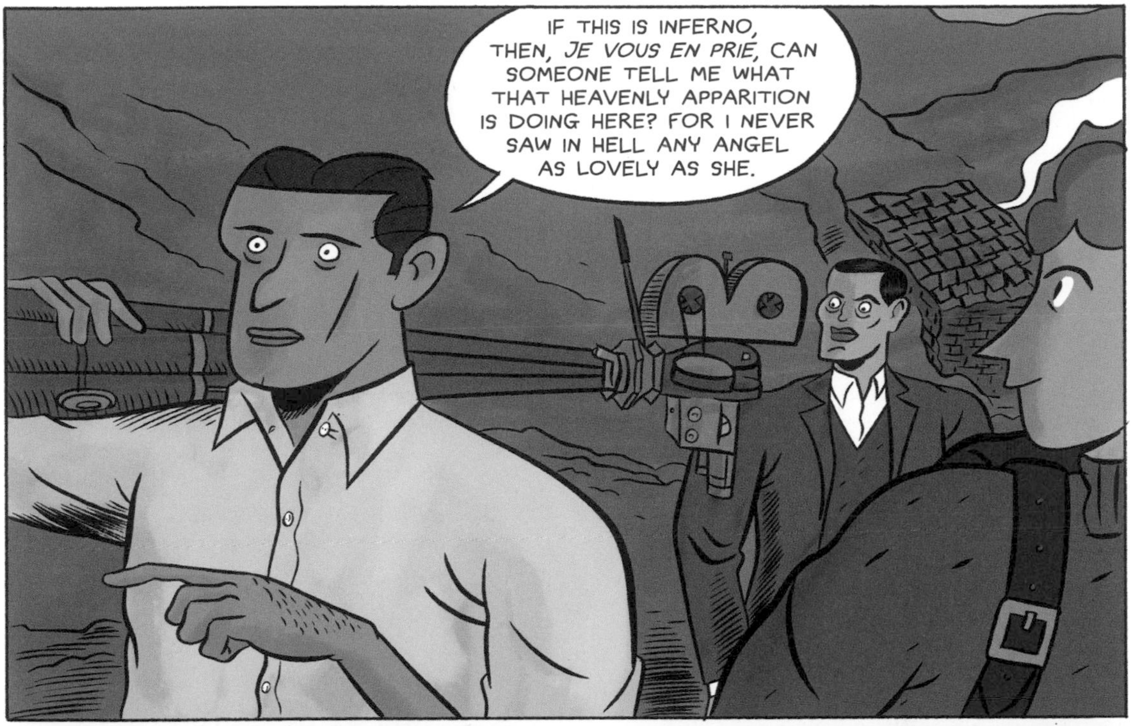
IF THIS IS INFERNO, THEN, *JE VOUS EN PRIE*, CAN SOMEONE TELL ME WHAT THAT HEAVENLY APPARITION IS DOING HERE? FOR I NEVER SAW IN HELL ANY ANGEL AS LOVELY AS SHE.

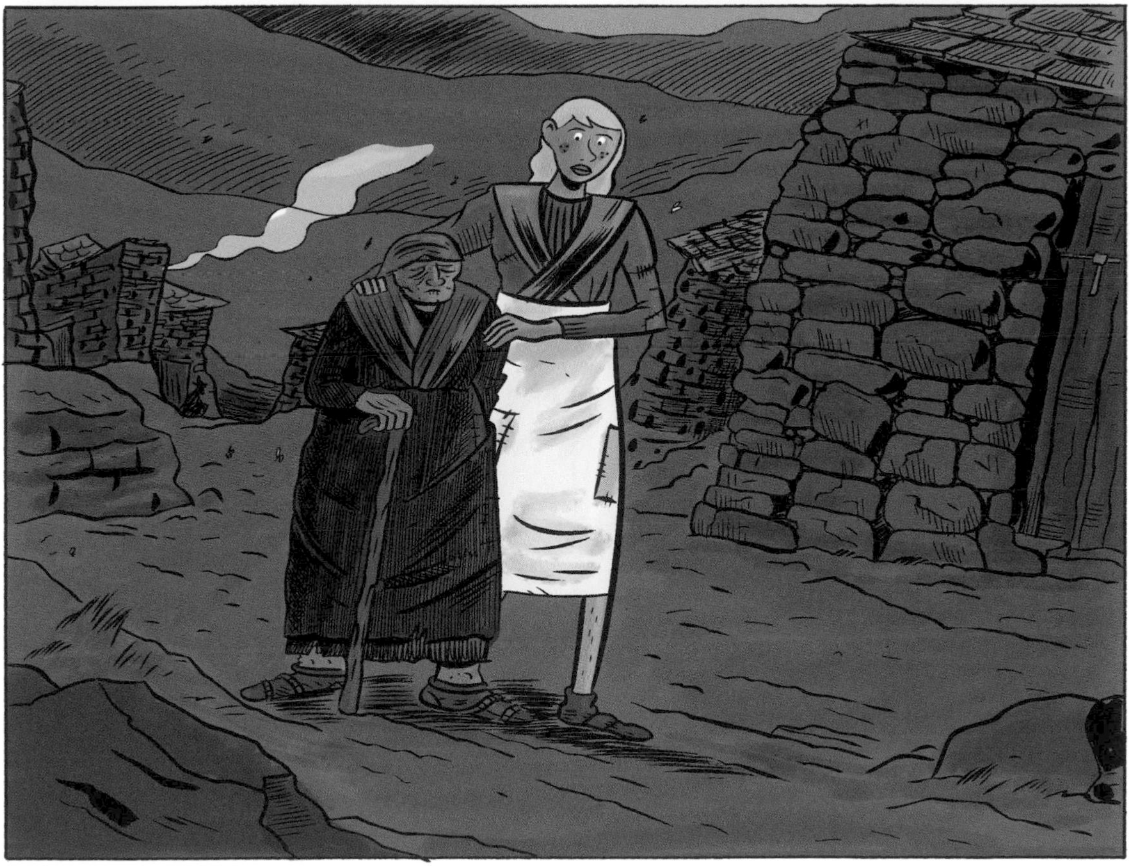

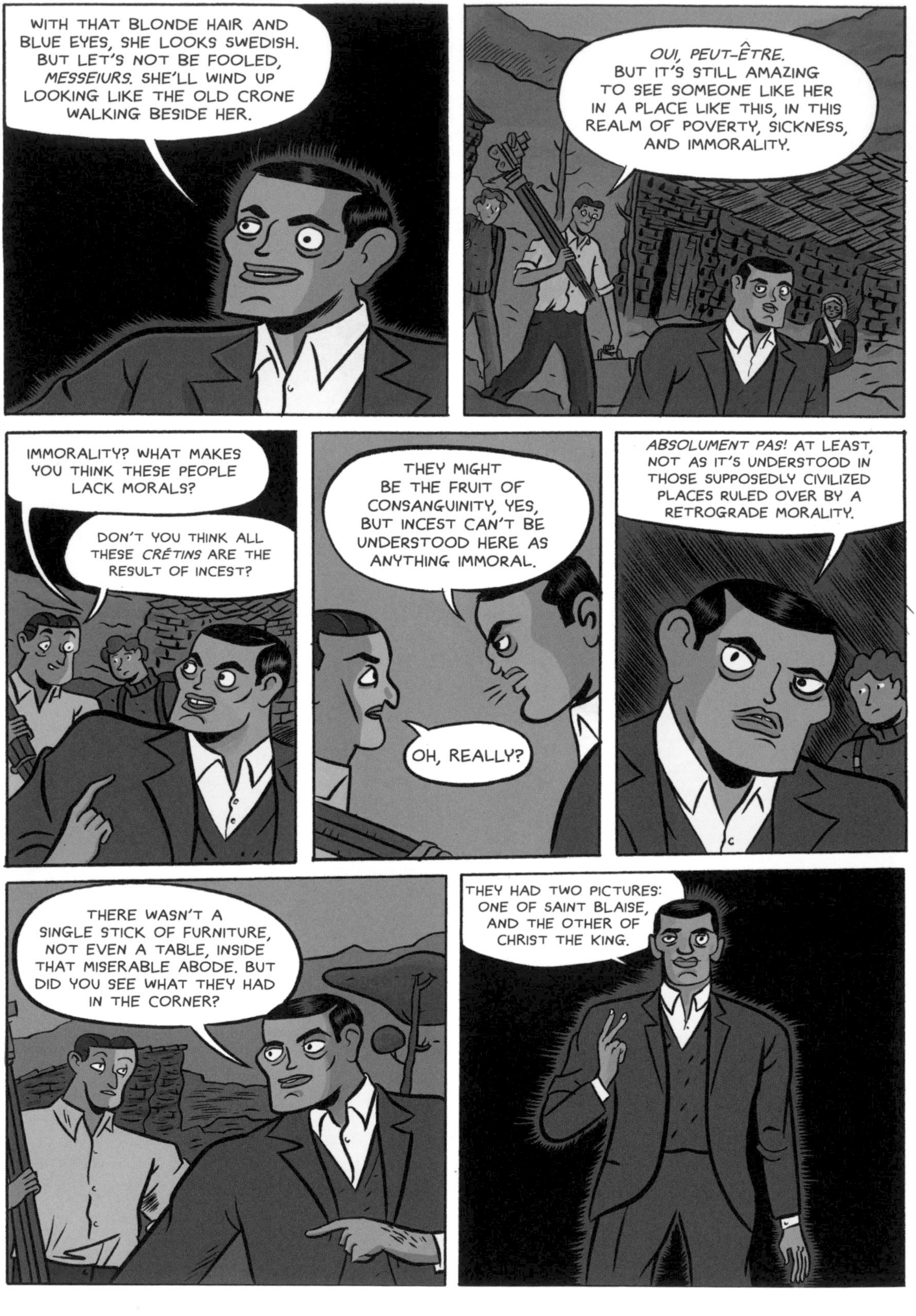
WITH THAT BLONDE HAIR AND BLUE EYES, SHE LOOKS SWEDISH. BUT LET'S NOT BE FOOLED, *MESSEIURS.* SHE'LL WIND UP LOOKING LIKE THE OLD CRONE WALKING BESIDE HER.
OUI, PEUT-ÊTRE. BUT IT'S STILL AMAZING TO SEE SOMEONE LIKE HER IN A PLACE LIKE THIS, IN THIS REALM OF POVERTY, SICKNESS, AND IMMORALITY.
IMMORALITY? WHAT MAKES YOU THINK THESE PEOPLE LACK MORALS?
DON'T YOU THINK ALL THESE *CRÉTINS* ARE THE RESULT OF INCEST?
THEY MIGHT BE THE FRUIT OF CONSANGUINITY, YES, BUT INCEST CAN'T BE UNDERSTOOD HERE AS ANYTHING IMMORAL.
OH, REALLY?
ABSOLUMENT PAS! AT LEAST, NOT AS IT'S UNDERSTOOD IN THOSE SUPPOSEDLY CIVILIZED PLACES RULED OVER BY A RETROGRADE MORALITY.
THERE WASN'T A SINGLE STICK OF FURNITURE, NOT EVEN A TABLE, INSIDE THAT MISERABLE ABODE. BUT DID YOU SEE WHAT THEY HAD IN THE CORNER?
THEY HAD TWO PICTURES: ONE OF SAINT BLAISE, AND THE OTHER OF CHRIST THE KING.

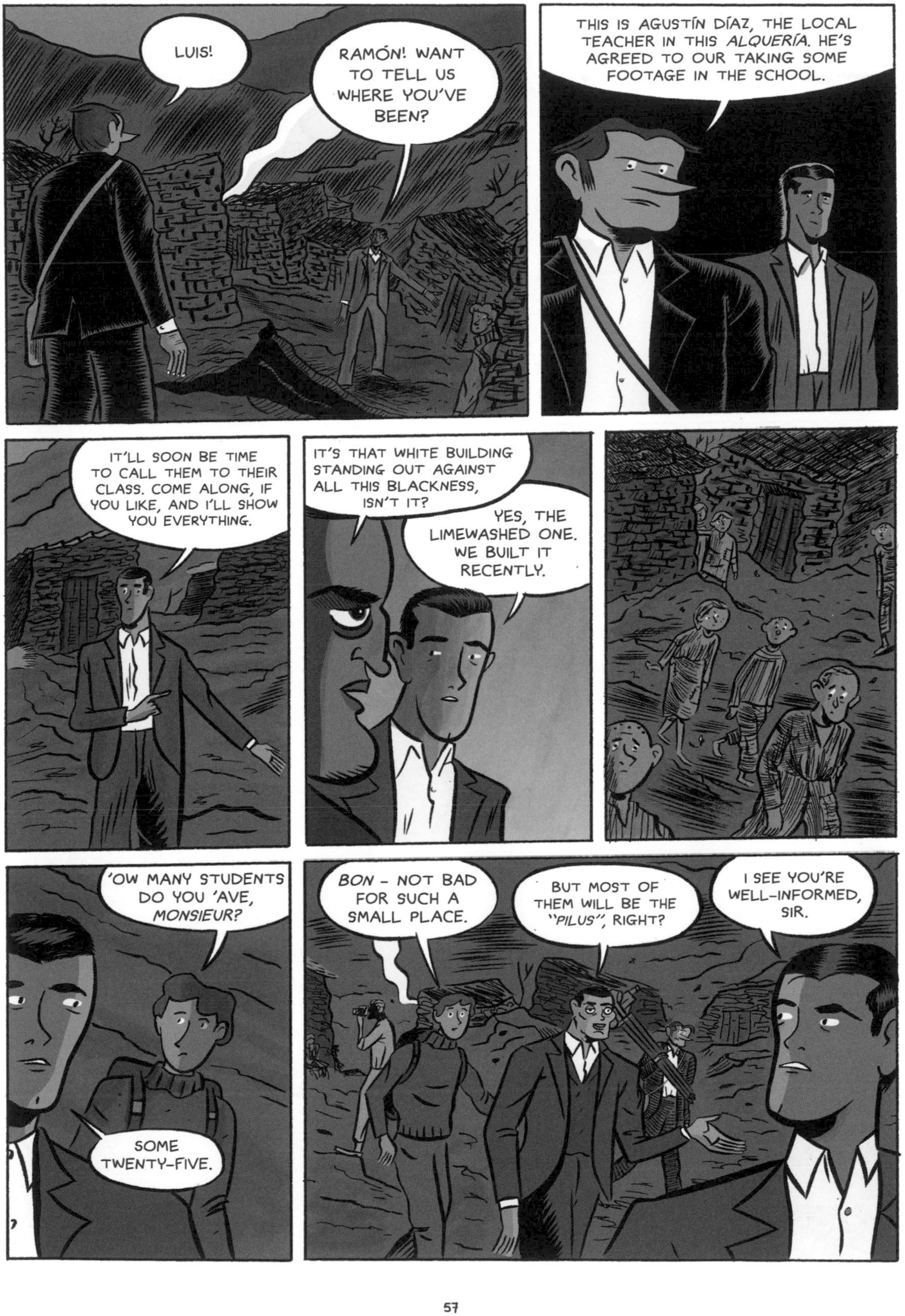
LUIS!
RAMÓN! WANT TO TELL US WHERE YOU'VE BEEN?
THIS IS AGUSTÍN DÍAZ, THE LOCAL TEACHER IN THIS *ALQUERÍA*. HE'S AGREED TO OUR TAKING SOME FOOTAGE IN THE SCHOOL.
IT'LL SOON BE TIME TO CALL THEM TO THEIR CLASS. COME ALONG, IF YOU LIKE, AND I'LL SHOW YOU EVERYTHING.
IT'S THAT WHITE BUILDING STANDING OUT AGAINST ALL THIS BLACKNESS, ISN'T IT?
YES, THE LIMEWASHED ONE. WE BUILT IT RECENTLY.
'OW MANY STUDENTS DO YOU 'AVE, *MONSIEUR*?
SOME TWENTY-FIVE.
BON - NOT BAD FOR SUCH A SMALL PLACE.
BUT MOST OF THEM WILL BE THE "*PILUS*", RIGHT?
I SEE YOU'RE WELL-INFORMED, SIR.

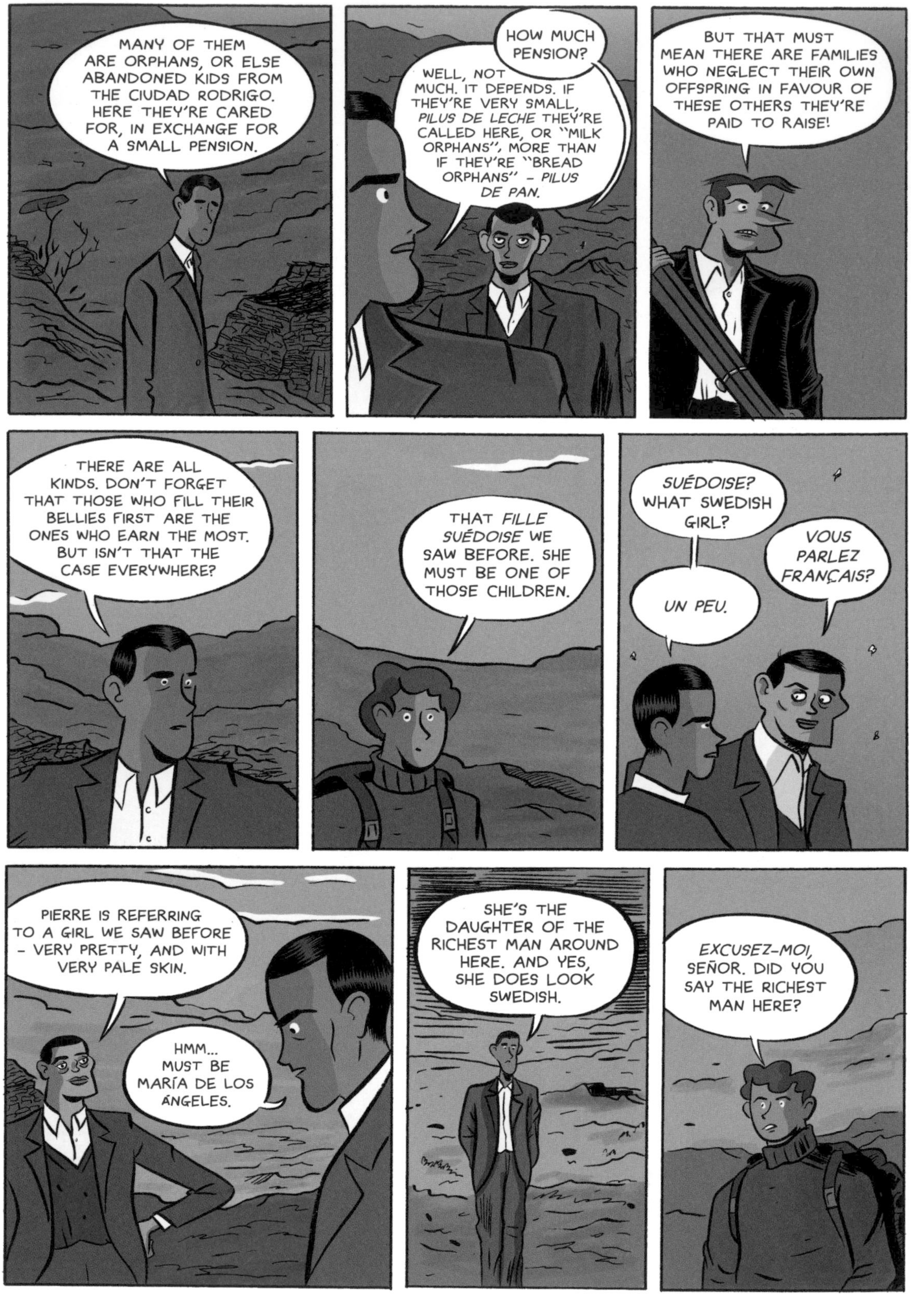
MANY OF THEM ARE ORPHANS, OR ELSE ABANDONED KIDS FROM THE CIUDAD RODRIGO. HERE THEY'RE CARED FOR, IN EXCHANGE FOR A SMALL PENSION.
HOW MUCH PENSION?
WELL, NOT MUCH. IT DEPENDS. IF THEY'RE VERY SMALL, *PILUS DE LECHE* THEY'RE CALLED HERE, OR "MILK ORPHANS", MORE THAN IF THEY'RE "BREAD ORPHANS" – *PILUS DE PAN*.
BUT THAT MUST MEAN THERE ARE FAMILIES WHO NEGLECT THEIR OWN OFFSPRING IN FAVOUR OF THESE OTHERS THEY'RE PAID TO RAISE!
THERE ARE ALL KINDS. DON'T FORGET THAT THOSE WHO FILL THEIR BELLIES FIRST ARE THE ONES WHO EARN THE MOST. BUT ISN'T THAT THE CASE EVERYWHERE?
THAT *FILLE SUÉDOISE* WE SAW BEFORE. SHE MUST BE ONE OF THOSE CHILDREN.
SUÉDOISE? WHAT SWEDISH GIRL?
VOUS PARLEZ FRANÇAIS?
UN PEU.
PIERRE IS REFERRING TO A GIRL WE SAW BEFORE – VERY PRETTY, AND WITH VERY PALE SKIN.
HMM... MUST BE MARÍA DE LOS ÁNGELES.
SHE'S THE DAUGHTER OF THE RICHEST MAN AROUND HERE. AND YES, SHE DOES LOOK SWEDISH.
EXCUSEZ-MOI, SEÑOR. DID YOU SAY THE RICHEST MAN HERE?

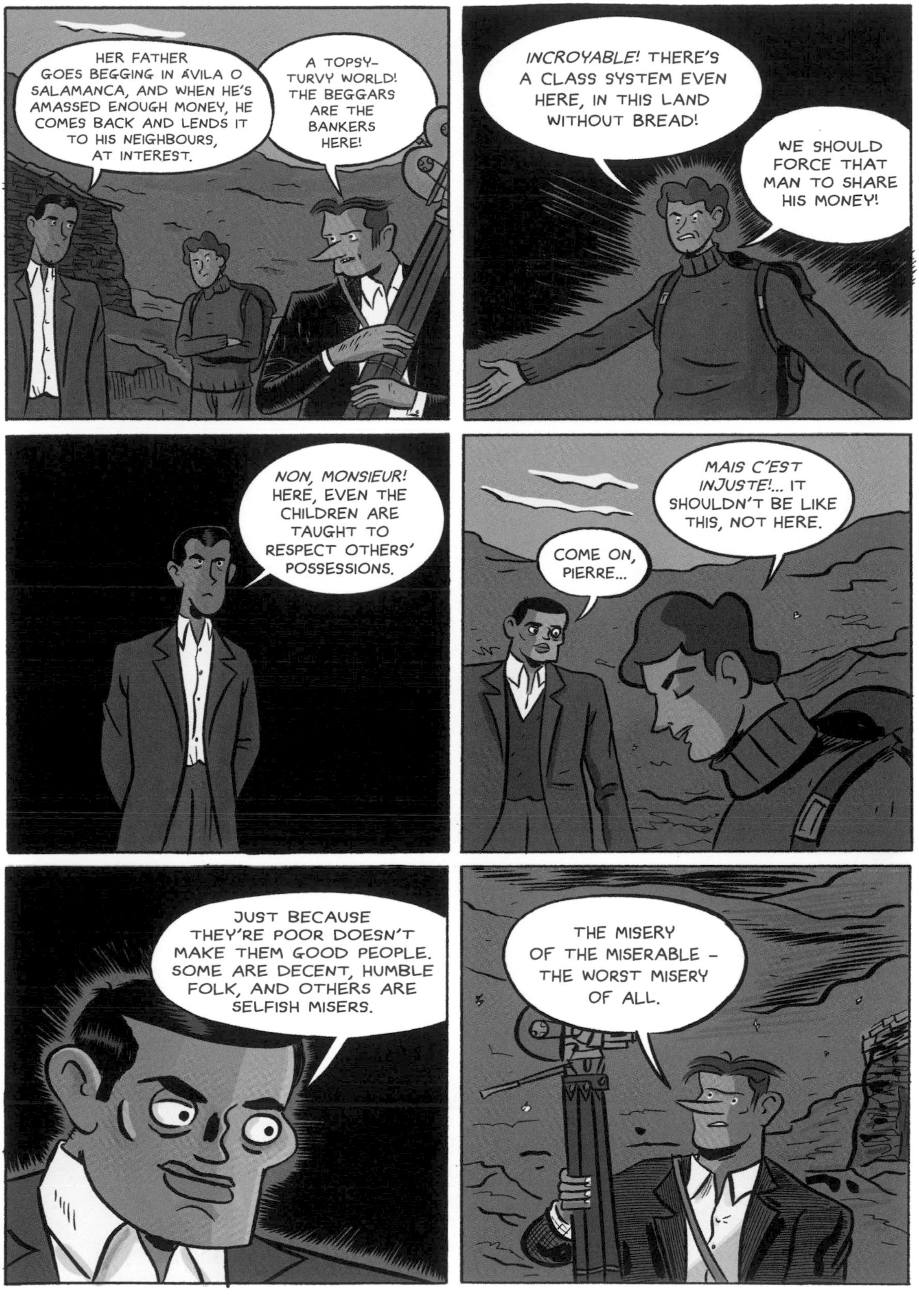
HER FATHER GOES BEGGING IN ÁVILA O SALAMANCA, AND WHEN HE'S AMASSED ENOUGH MONEY, HE COMES BACK AND LENDS IT TO HIS NEIGHBOURS, AT INTEREST.
A TOPSY-TURVY WORLD! THE BEGGARS ARE THE BANKERS HERE!
INCROYABLE! THERE'S A CLASS SYSTEM EVEN HERE, IN THIS LAND WITHOUT BREAD!
WE SHOULD FORCE THAT MAN TO SHARE HIS MONEY!
NON, MONSIEUR! HERE, EVEN THE CHILDREN ARE TAUGHT TO RESPECT OTHERS' POSSESSIONS.
MAIS C'EST INJUSTE!... IT SHOULDN'T BE LIKE THIS, NOT HERE.
COME ON, PIERRE...
JUST BECAUSE THEY'RE POOR DOESN'T MAKE THEM GOOD PEOPLE. SOME ARE DECENT, HUMBLE FOLK, AND OTHERS ARE SELFISH MISERS.
THE MISERY OF THE MISERABLE – THE WORST MISERY OF ALL.

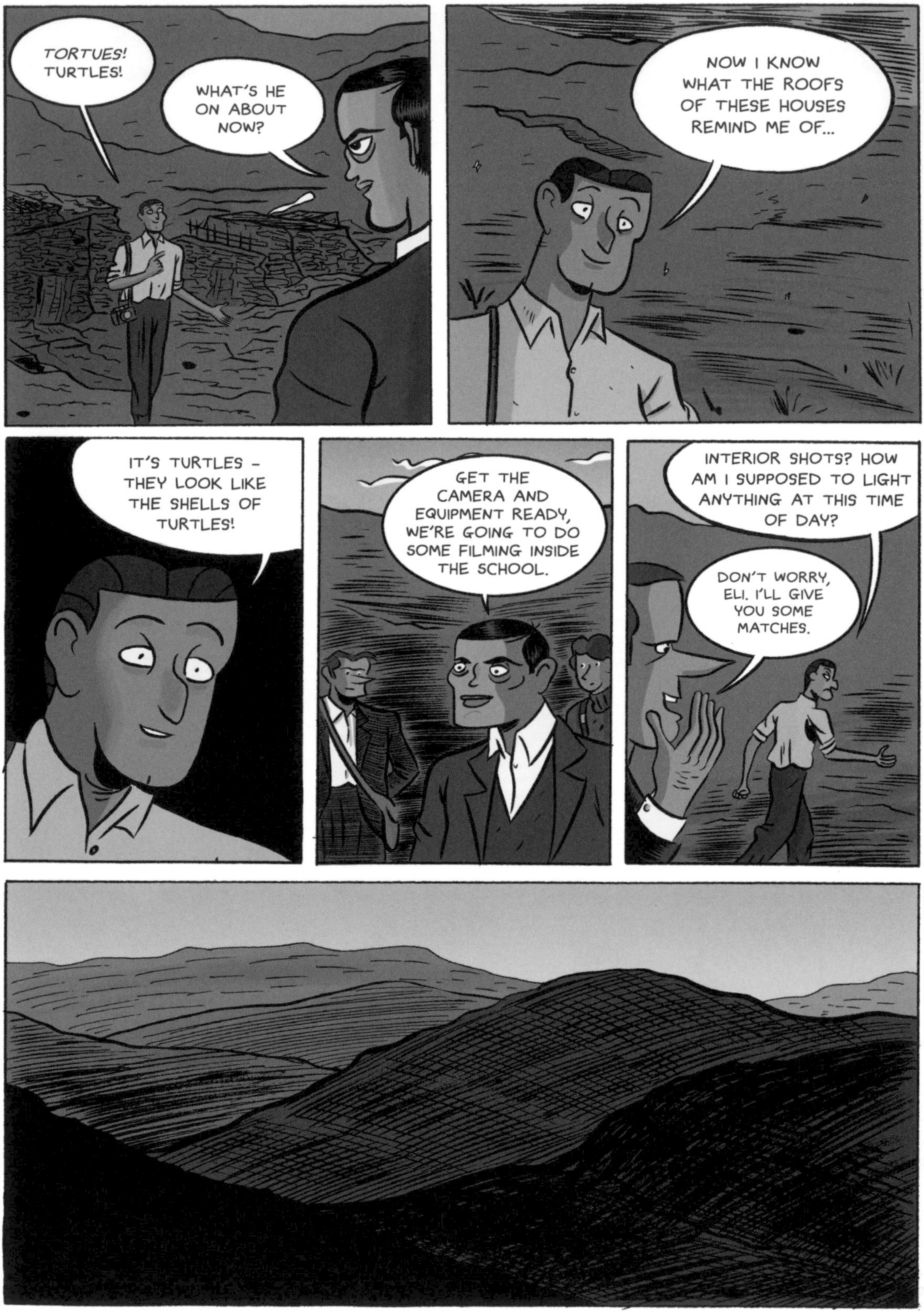
TORTUES! TURTLES!
WHAT'S HE ON ABOUT NOW?
NOW I KNOW WHAT THE ROOFS OF THESE HOUSES REMIND ME OF...
IT'S TURTLES – THEY LOOK LIKE THE SHELLS OF TURTLES!
GET THE CAMERA AND EQUIPMENT READY, WE'RE GOING TO DO SOME FILMING INSIDE THE SCHOOL.
INTERIOR SHOTS? HOW AM I SUPPOSED TO LIGHT ANYTHING AT THIS TIME OF DAY?
DON'T WORRY, ELI. I'LL GIVE YOU SOME MATCHES.

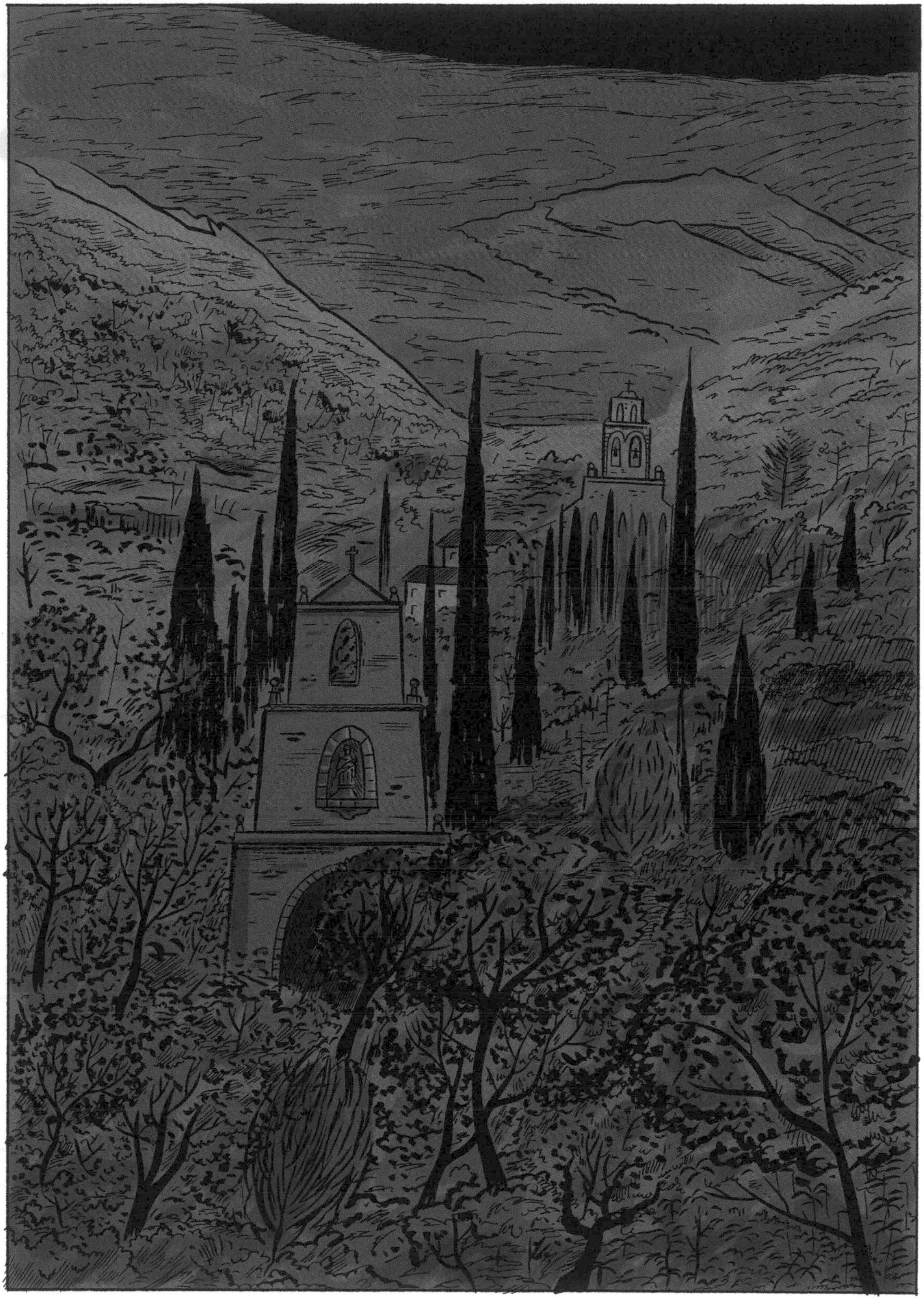

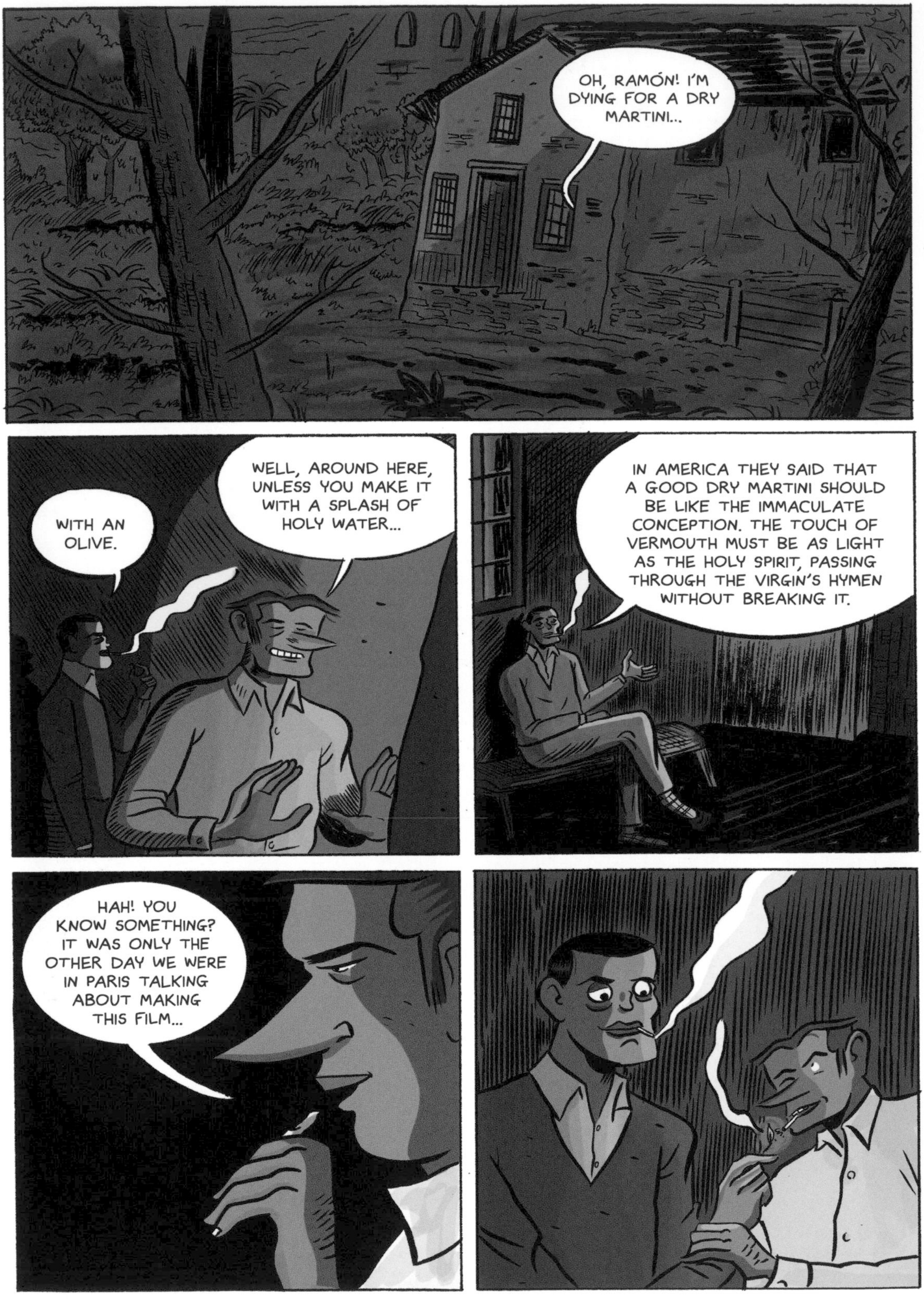
OH, RAMÓN! I'M DYING FOR A DRY MARTINI...
WITH AN OLIVE.
WELL, AROUND HERE, UNLESS YOU MAKE IT WITH A SPLASH OF HOLY WATER...
IN AMERICA THEY SAID THAT A GOOD DRY MARTINI SHOULD BE LIKE THE IMMACULATE CONCEPTION. THE TOUCH OF VERMOUTH MUST BE AS LIGHT AS THE HOLY SPIRIT, PASSING THROUGH THE VIRGIN'S HYMEN WITHOUT BREAKING IT.
HAH! YOU KNOW SOMETHING? IT WAS ONLY THE OTHER DAY WE WERE IN PARIS TALKING ABOUT MAKING THIS FILM...

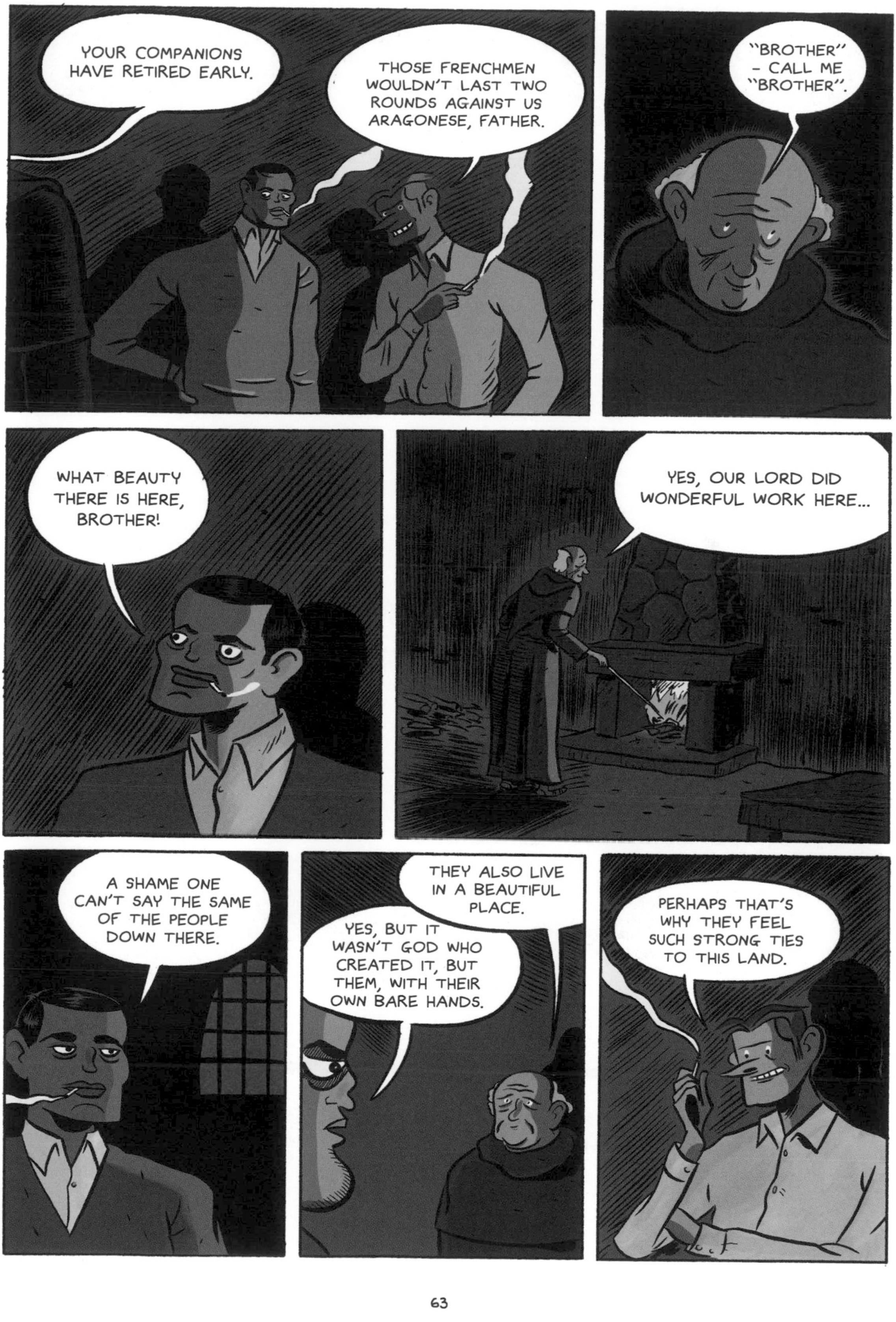
YOUR COMPANIONS HAVE RETIRED EARLY.
THOSE FRENCHMEN WOULDN'T LAST TWO ROUNDS AGAINST US ARAGONESE, FATHER.
"BROTHER" – CALL ME "BROTHER".
WHAT BEAUTY THERE IS HERE, BROTHER!
YES, OUR LORD DID WONDERFUL WORK HERE...
A SHAME ONE CAN'T SAY THE SAME OF THE PEOPLE DOWN THERE.
THEY ALSO LIVE IN A BEAUTIFUL PLACE.
YES, BUT IT WASN'T GOD WHO CREATED IT, BUT THEM, WITH THEIR OWN BARE HANDS.
PERHAPS THAT'S WHY THEY FEEL SUCH STRONG TIES TO THIS LAND.

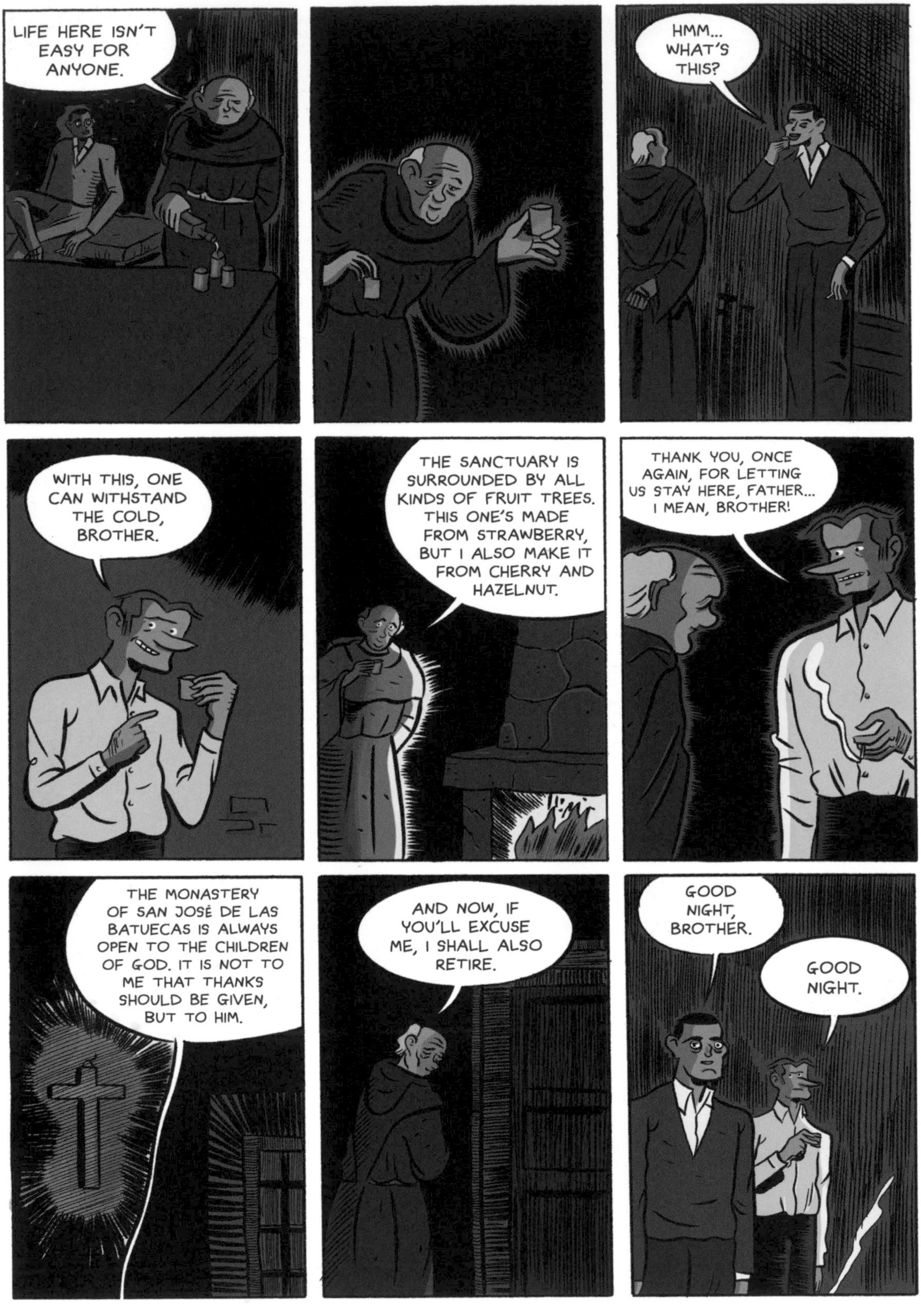
LIFE HERE ISN'T EASY FOR ANYONE.
HMM... WHAT'S THIS?
WITH THIS, ONE CAN WITHSTAND THE COLD, BROTHER.
THE SANCTUARY IS SURROUNDED BY ALL KINDS OF FRUIT TREES. THIS ONE'S MADE FROM STRAWBERRY, BUT I ALSO MAKE IT FROM CHERRY AND HAZELNUT.
THANK YOU, ONCE AGAIN, FOR LETTING US STAY HERE, FATHER... I MEAN, BROTHER!
THE MONASTERY OF SAN JOSÉ DE LAS BATUECAS IS ALWAYS OPEN TO THE CHILDREN OF GOD. IT IS NOT TO ME THAT THANKS SHOULD BE GIVEN, BUT TO HIM.
AND NOW, IF YOU'LL EXCUSE ME, I SHALL ALSO RETIRE.
GOOD NIGHT, BROTHER.
GOOD NIGHT.

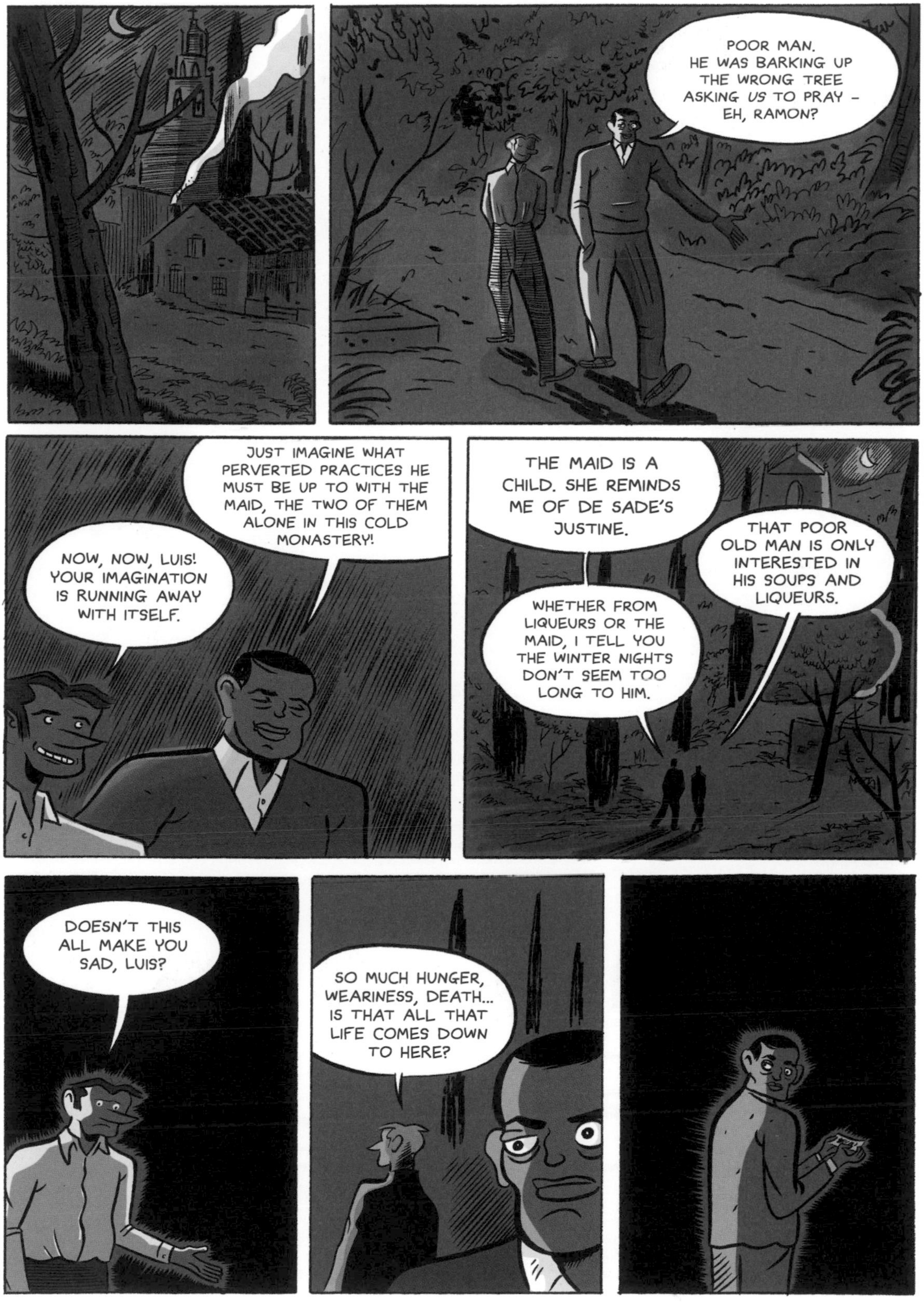
POOR MAN. HE WAS BARKING UP THE WRONG TREE ASKING *US* TO PRAY – EH, RAMON?
JUST IMAGINE WHAT PERVERTED PRACTICES HE MUST BE UP TO WITH THE MAID, THE TWO OF THEM ALONE IN THIS COLD MONASTERY!
NOW, NOW, LUIS! YOUR IMAGINATION IS RUNNING AWAY WITH ITSELF.
THE MAID IS A CHILD. SHE REMINDS ME OF DE SADE'S JUSTINE.
THAT POOR OLD MAN IS ONLY INTERESTED IN HIS SOUPS AND LIQUEURS.
WHETHER FROM LIQUEURS OR THE MAID, I TELL YOU THE WINTER NIGHTS DON'T SEEM TOO LONG TO HIM.
DOESN'T THIS ALL MAKE YOU SAD, LUIS?
SO MUCH HUNGER, WEARINESS, DEATH... IS THAT ALL THAT LIFE COMES DOWN TO HERE?

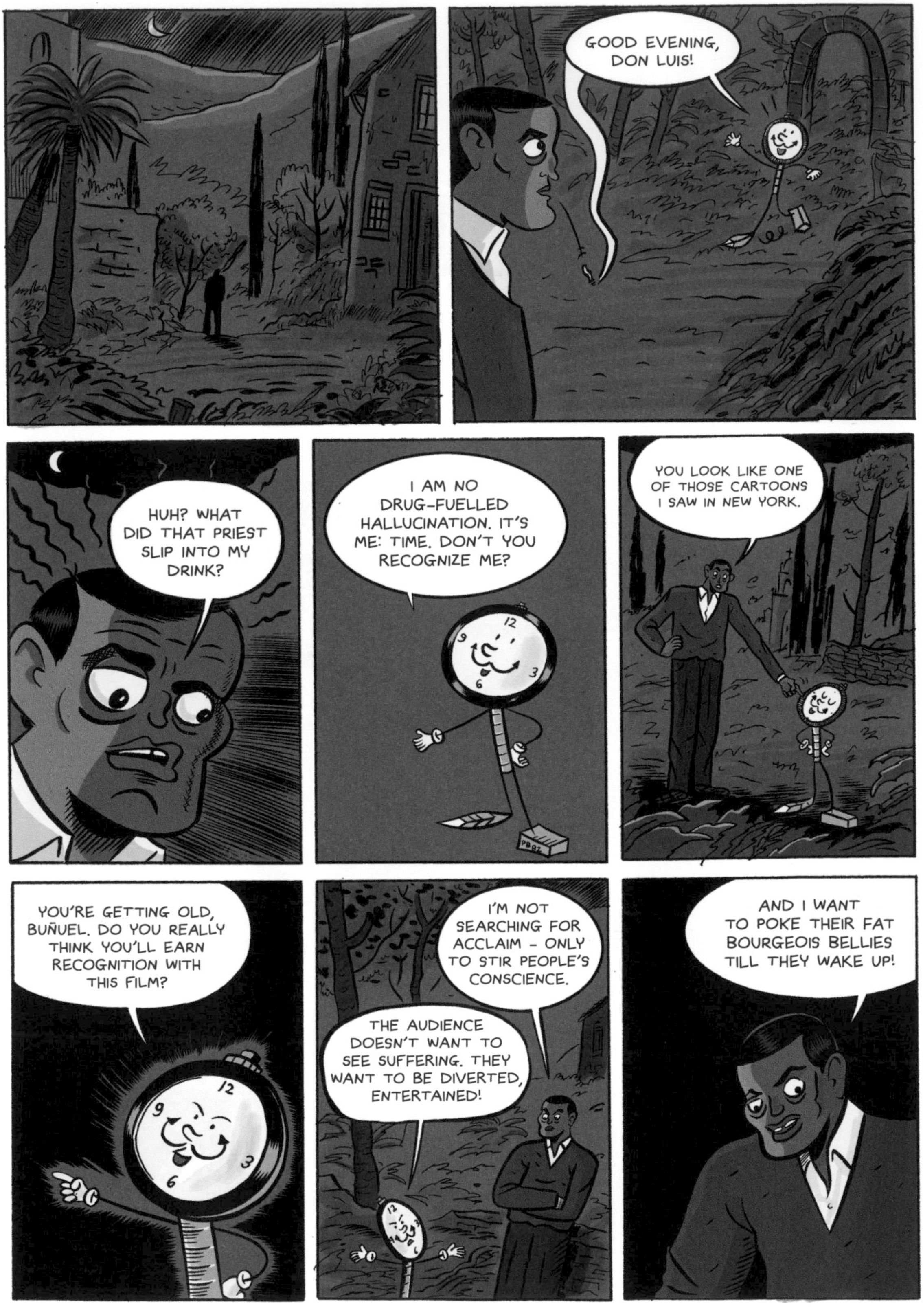
GOOD EVENING, DON LUIS!
HUH? WHAT DID THAT PRIEST SLIP INTO MY DRINK?
I AM NO DRUG-FUELLED HALLUCINATION. IT'S ME: TIME. DON'T YOU RECOGNIZE ME?
YOU LOOK LIKE ONE OF THOSE CARTOONS I SAW IN NEW YORK.
YOU'RE GETTING OLD, BUÑUEL. DO YOU REALLY THINK YOU'LL EARN RECOGNITION WITH THIS FILM?
THE AUDIENCE DOESN'T WANT TO SEE SUFFERING. THEY WANT TO BE DIVERTED, ENTERTAINED!
I'M NOT SEARCHING FOR ACCLAIM – ONLY TO STIR PEOPLE'S CONSCIENCE.
AND I WANT TO POKE THEIR FAT BOURGEOIS BELLIES TILL THEY WAKE UP!

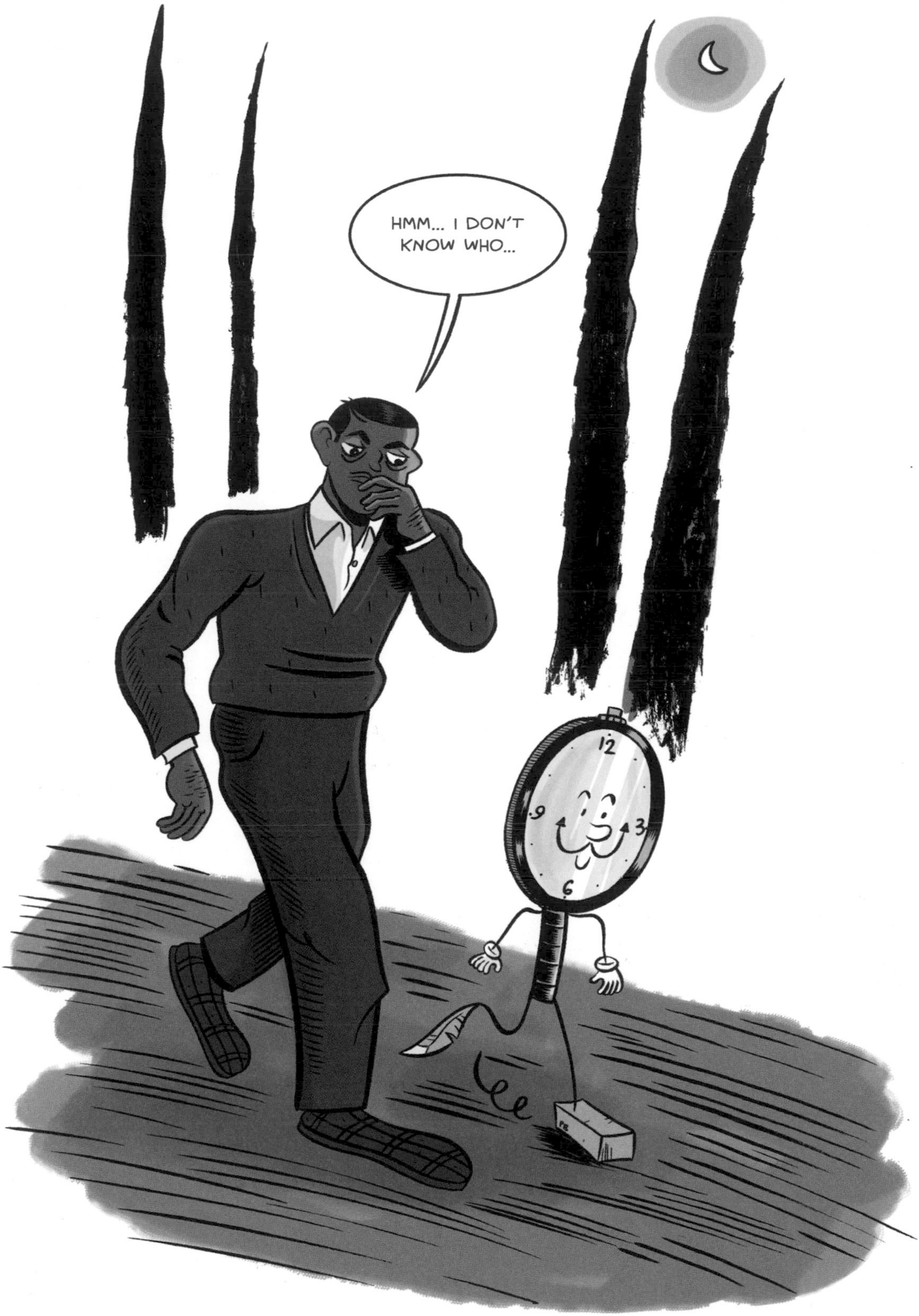
HMM... I DON'T KNOW WHO...

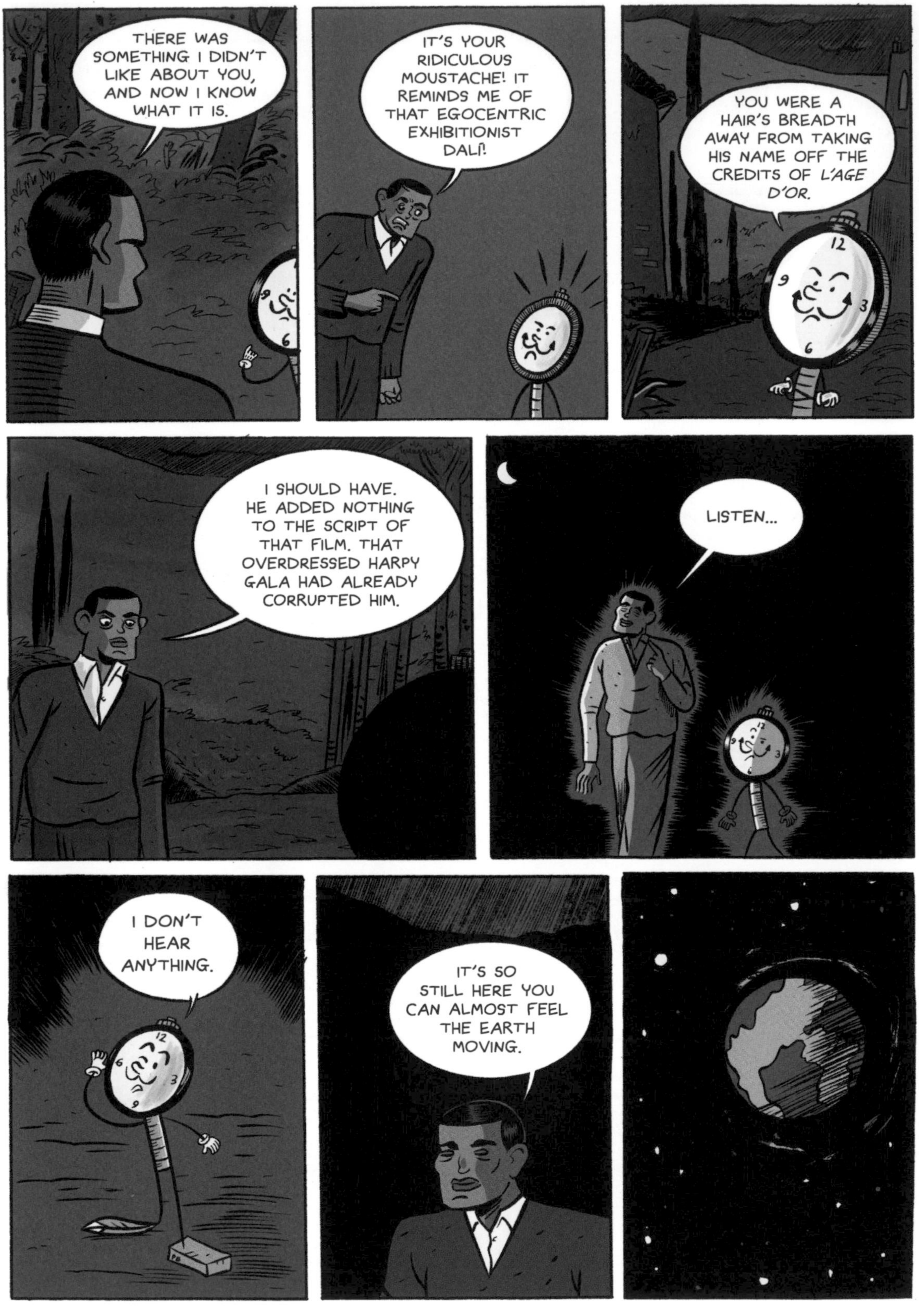
THERE WAS SOMETHING I DIDN'T LIKE ABOUT YOU, AND NOW I KNOW WHAT IT IS.
IT'S YOUR RIDICULOUS MOUSTACHE! IT REMINDS ME OF THAT EGOCENTRIC EXHIBITIONIST DALÍ!
YOU WERE A HAIR'S BREADTH AWAY FROM TAKING HIS NAME OFF THE CREDITS OF *L'AGE D'OR*.
I SHOULD HAVE. HE ADDED NOTHING TO THE SCRIPT OF THAT FILM. THAT OVERDRESSED HARPY GALA HAD ALREADY CORRUPTED HIM.
LISTEN...
I DON'T HEAR ANYTHING.
IT'S SO STILL HERE YOU CAN ALMOST FEEL THE EARTH MOVING.

PIERRE, PIERRE!

QU'Y A-T-IL? WHAT TIME IS IT?

IT'S FOUR A.M. LUIS WANTS TO TAKE ADVANTAGE OF THE MORNING LIGHT AND THEN COME BACK TO EAT.

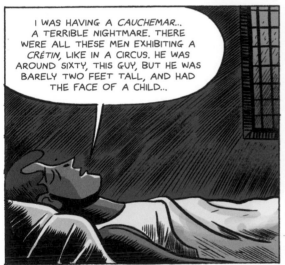

I WAS HAVING A *CAUCHEMAR...* A TERRIBLE NIGHTMARE. THERE WERE ALL THESE MEN EXHIBITING A *CRÉTIN*, LIKE IN A CIRCUS. HE WAS AROUND SIXTY, THIS GUY, BUT HE WAS BARELY TWO FEET TALL, AND HAD THE FACE OF A CHILD...

THEY HAD HIM TIED BY THE NECK WITH A LEAD, AS IF HE WERE AN ANIMAL, AND THEY MADE HIM WRITE ON A PIECE OF PAPER ON THE FLOOR, BECAUSE HIS HANDWRITING WAS SO FINE.

BUT THE CRUELLEST PART WAS THAT THEY FED HIM ON THE BONES OF DEAD BABIES.

IT'S THIS PLACE. IT'S DRIVING US ALL MAD... I'LL GO AND WAKE ELI.

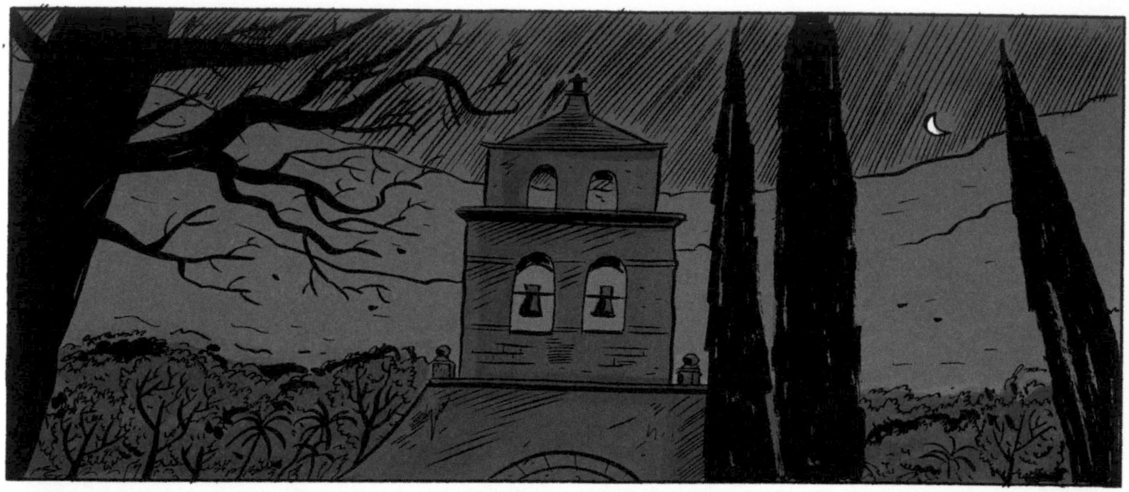

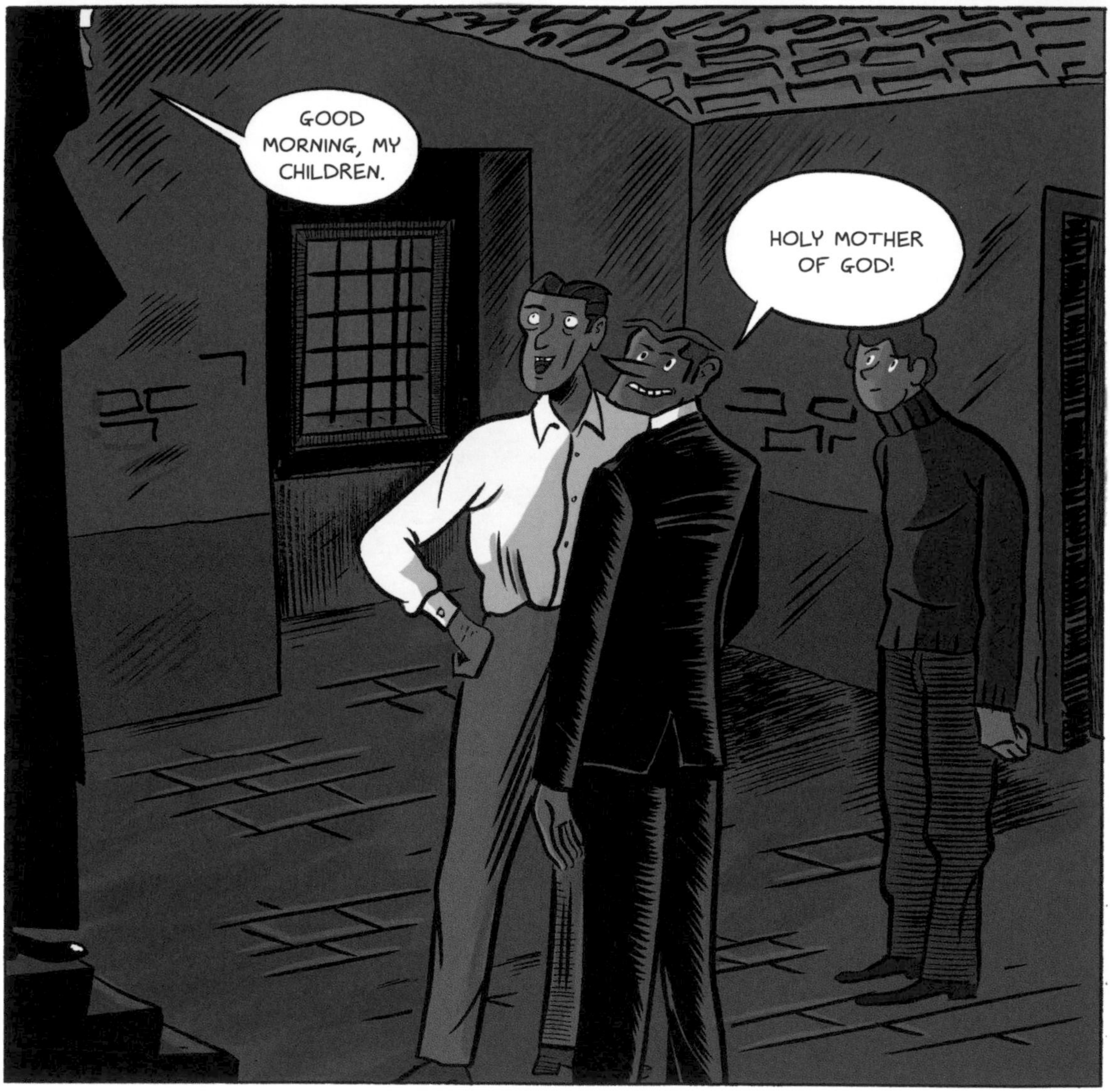
GOOD MORNING, MY CHILDREN.
HOLY MOTHER OF GOD!

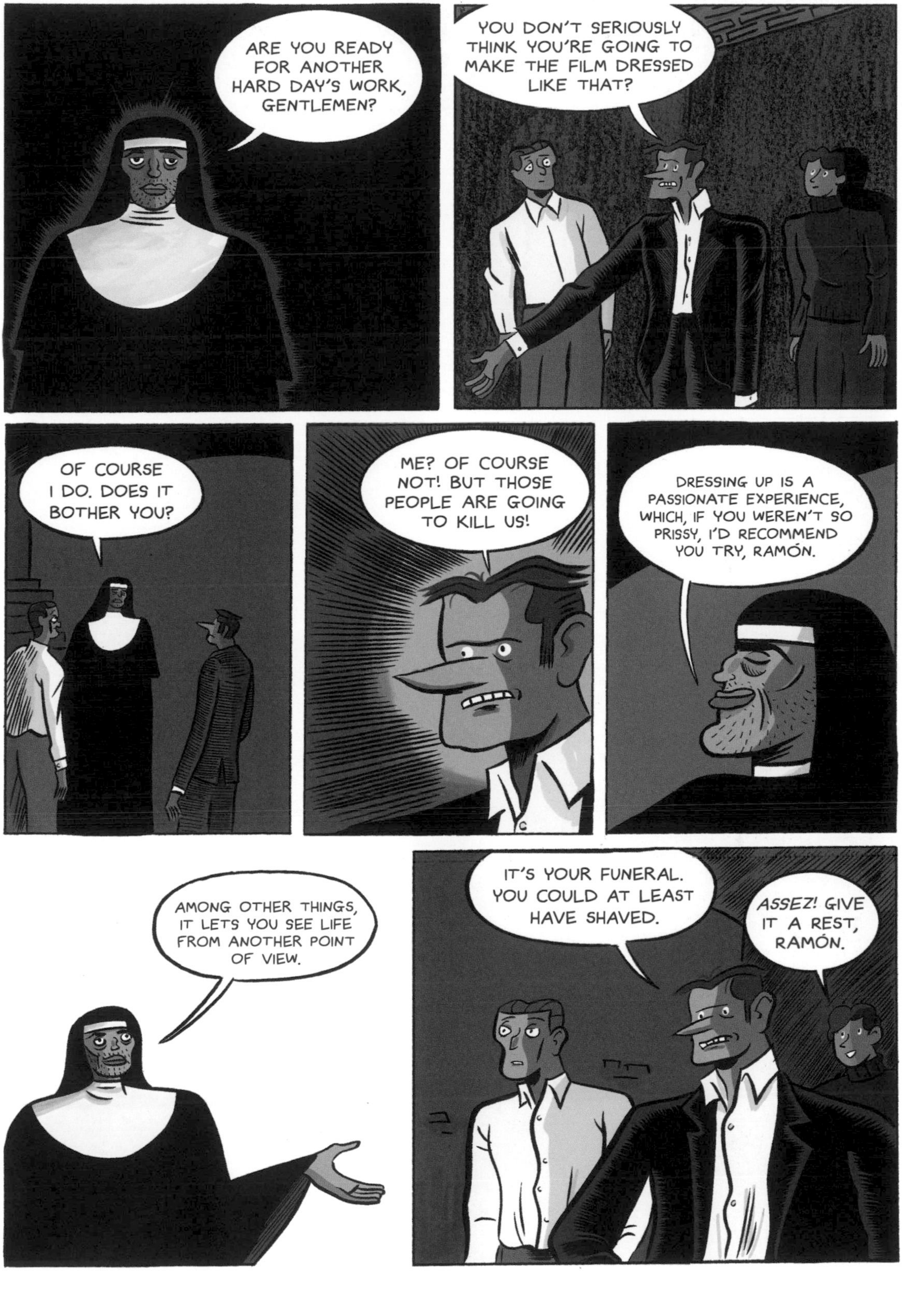

ARE YOU READY FOR ANOTHER HARD DAY'S WORK, GENTLEMEN?
YOU DON'T SERIOUSLY THINK YOU'RE GOING TO MAKE THE FILM DRESSED LIKE THAT?
OF COURSE I DO. DOES IT BOTHER YOU?
ME? OF COURSE NOT! BUT THOSE PEOPLE ARE GOING TO KILL US!
DRESSING UP IS A PASSIONATE EXPERIENCE, WHICH, IF YOU WEREN'T SO PRISSY, I'D RECOMMEND YOU TRY, RAMÓN.
AMONG OTHER THINGS, IT LETS YOU SEE LIFE FROM ANOTHER POINT OF VIEW.
IT'S YOUR FUNERAL. YOU COULD AT LEAST HAVE SHAVED.
ASSEZ! GIVE IT A REST, RAMÓN.

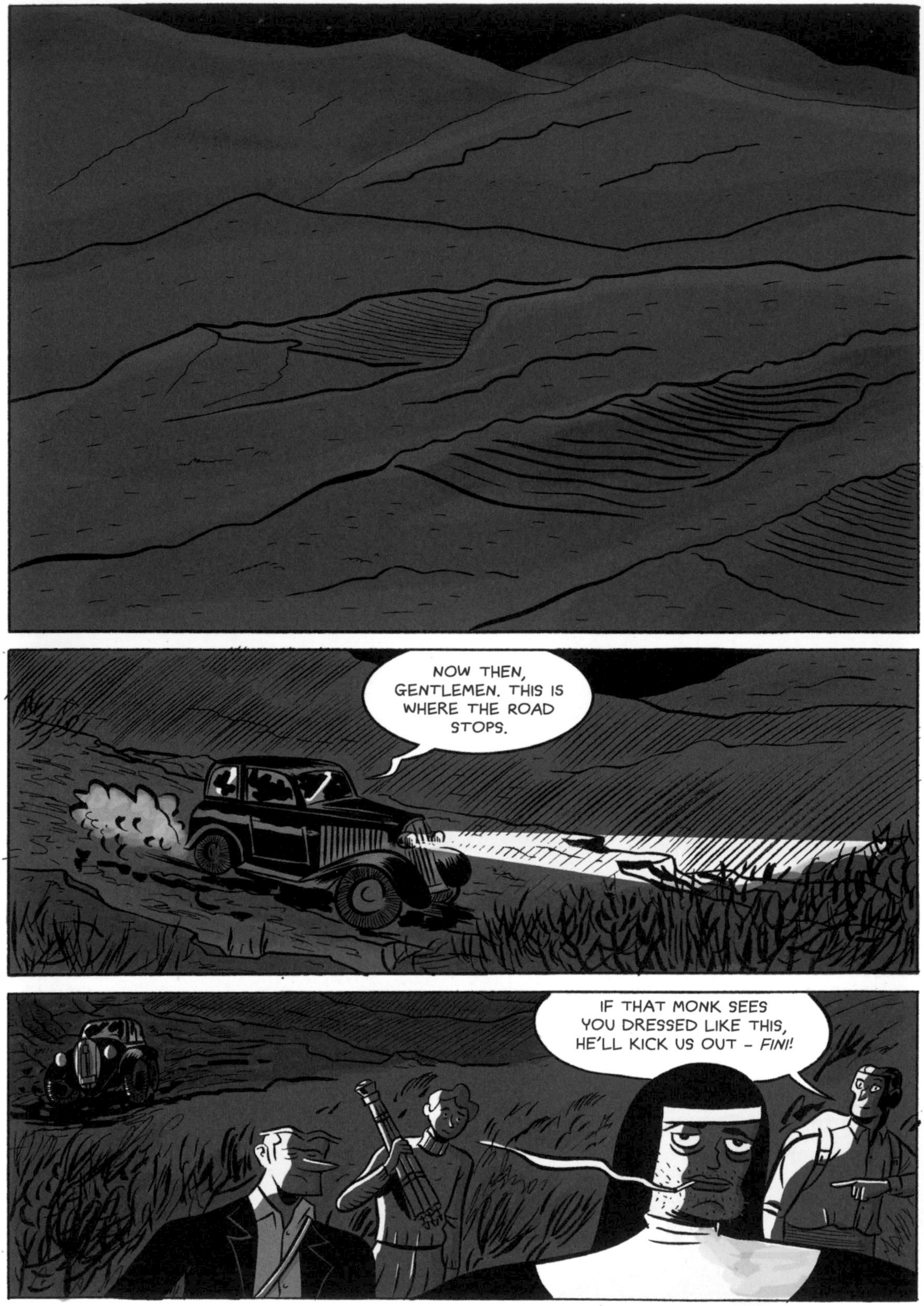
NOW THEN, GENTLEMEN. THIS IS WHERE THE ROAD STOPS.
IF THAT MONK SEES YOU DRESSED LIKE THIS, HE'LL KICK US OUT – *FINI!*

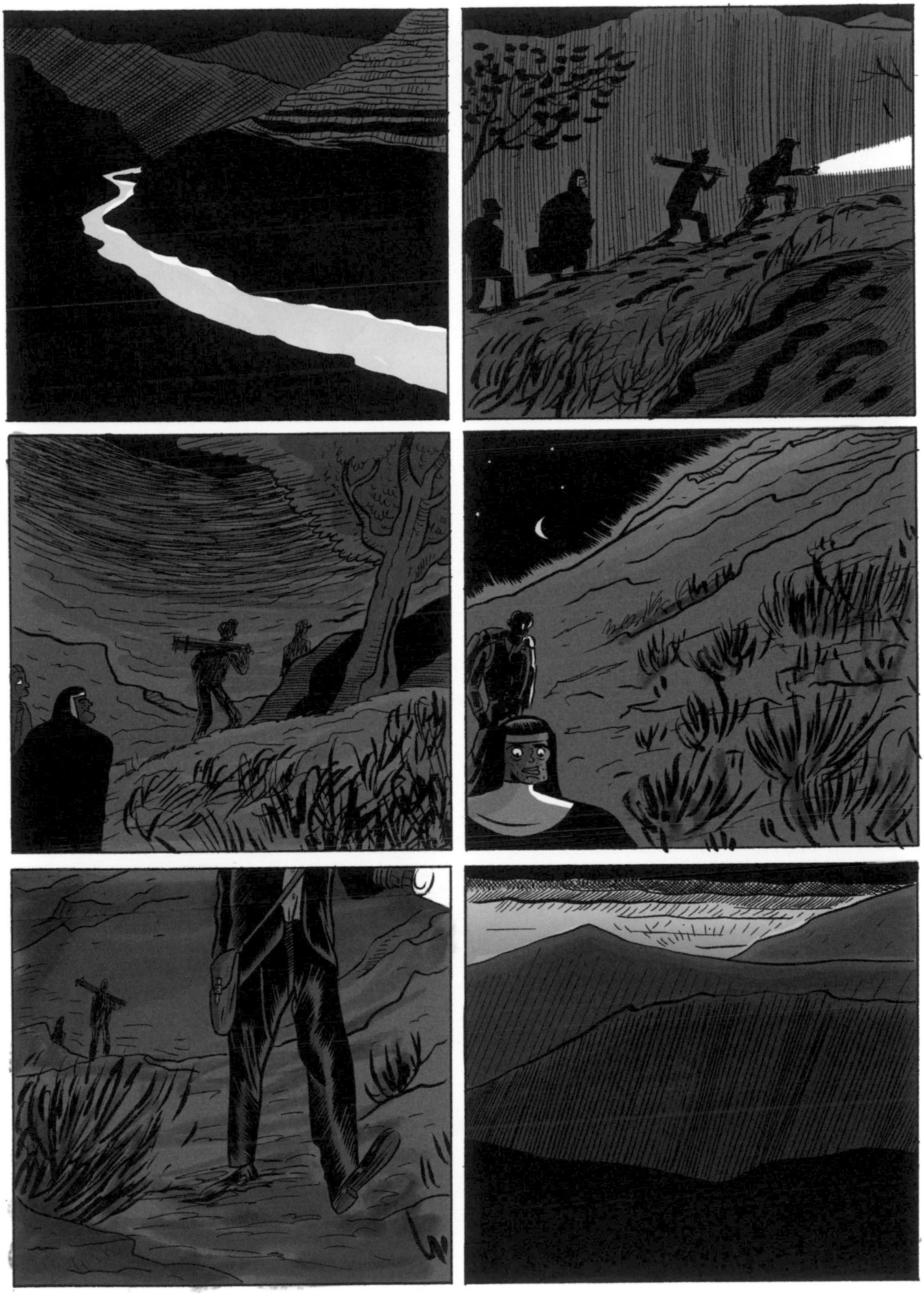

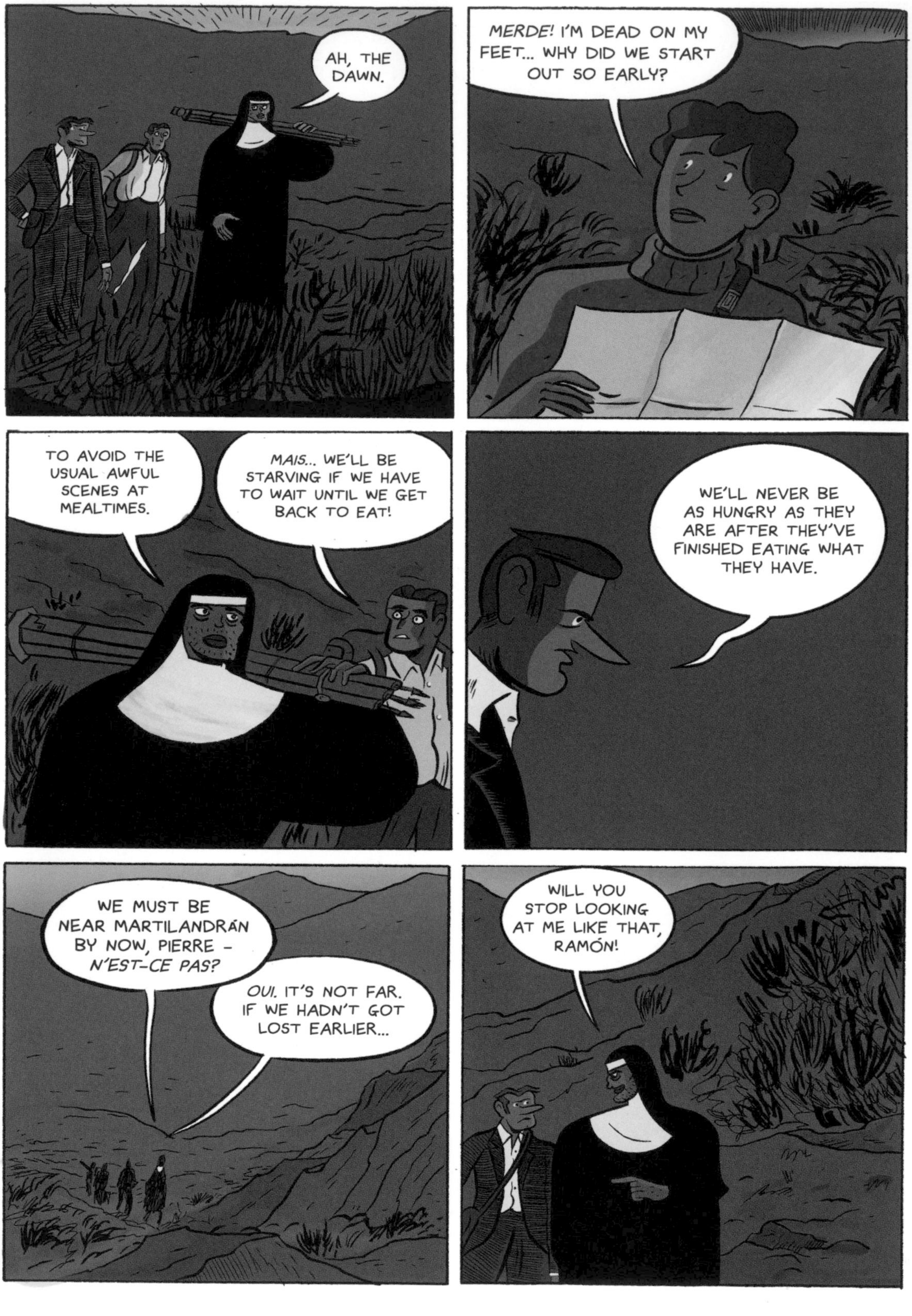
AH, THE DAWN.
MERDE! I'M DEAD ON MY FEET... WHY DID WE START OUT SO EARLY?
TO AVOID THE USUAL AWFUL SCENES AT MEALTIMES.
MAIS... WE'LL BE STARVING IF WE HAVE TO WAIT UNTIL WE GET BACK TO EAT!
WE'LL NEVER BE AS HUNGRY AS THEY ARE AFTER THEY'VE FINISHED EATING WHAT THEY HAVE.
WE MUST BE NEAR MARTILANDRÁN BY NOW, PIERRE – N'EST-CE PAS?
OUI. IT'S NOT FAR. IF WE HADN'T GOT LOST EARLIER...
WILL YOU STOP LOOKING AT ME LIKE THAT, RAMÓN!

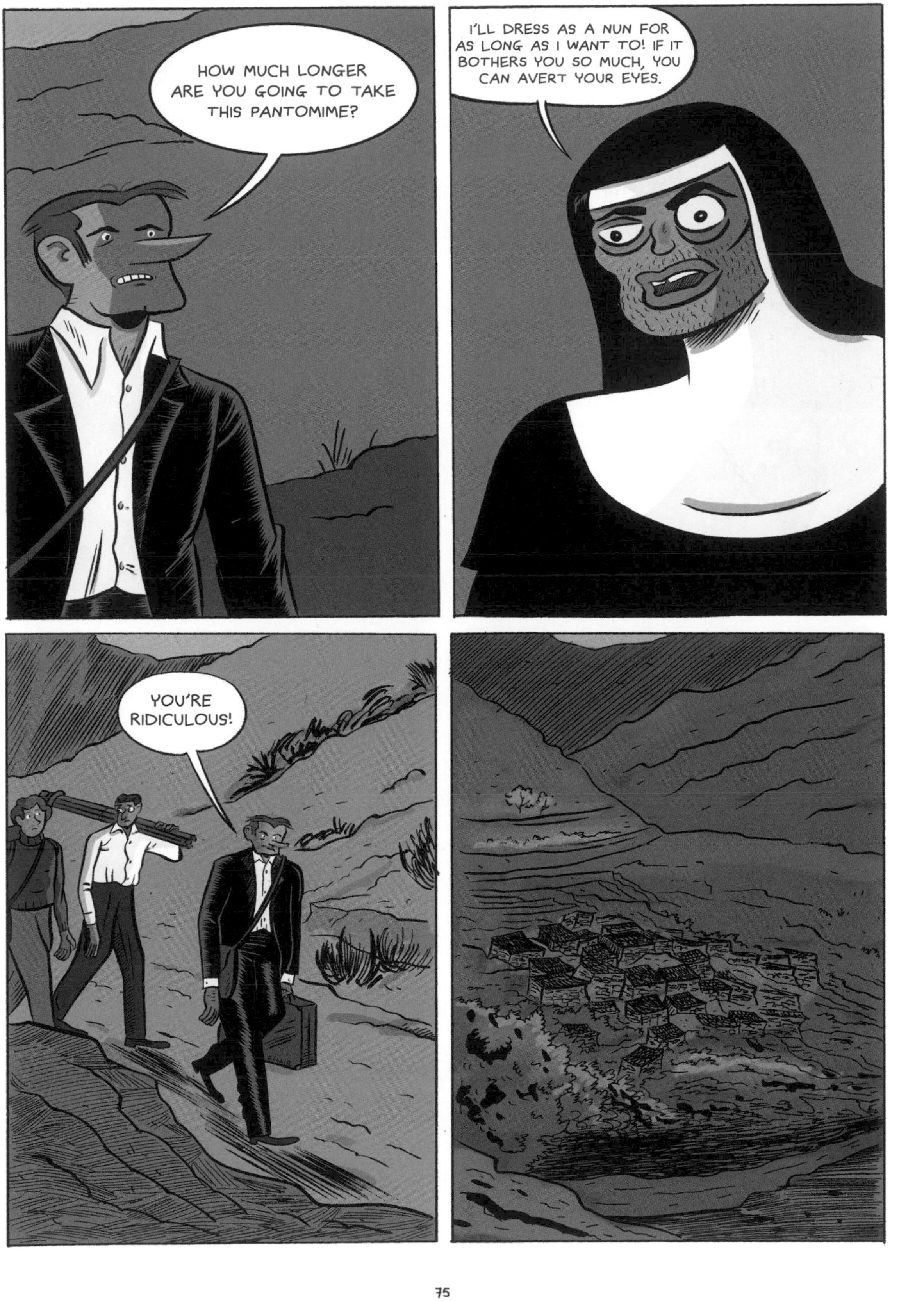
HOW MUCH LONGER ARE YOU GOING TO TAKE THIS PANTOMIME?
I'LL DRESS AS A NUN FOR AS LONG AS I WANT TO! IF IT BOTHERS YOU SO MUCH, YOU CAN AVERT YOUR EYES.
YOU'RE RIDICULOUS!

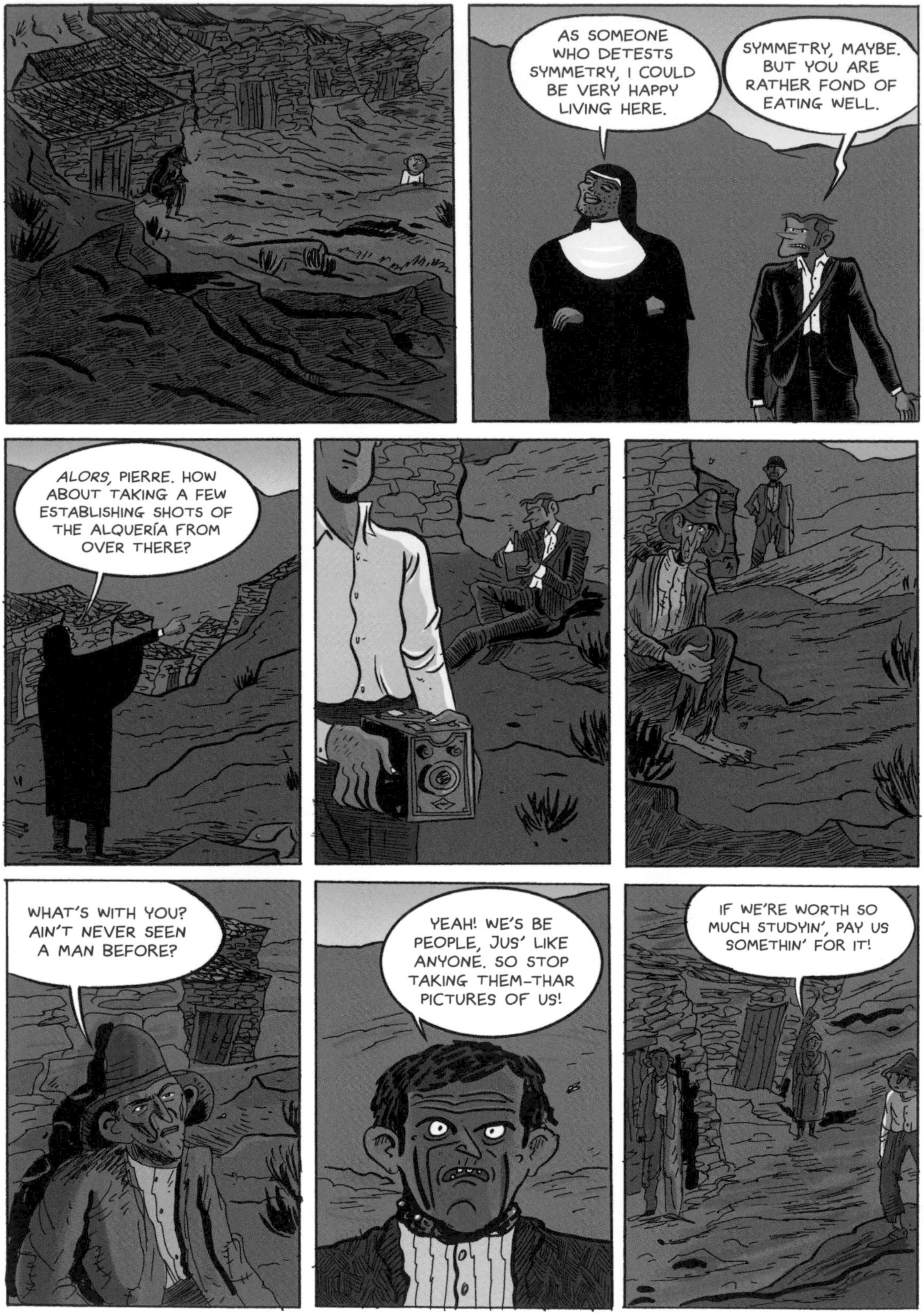
AS SOMEONE WHO DETESTS SYMMETRY, I COULD BE VERY HAPPY LIVING HERE.
SYMMETRY, MAYBE. BUT YOU ARE RATHER FOND OF EATING WELL.
ALORS, PIERRE. HOW ABOUT TAKING A FEW ESTABLISHING SHOTS OF THE ALQUERÍA FROM OVER THERE?
WHAT'S WITH YOU? AIN'T NEVER SEEN A MAN BEFORE?
YEAH! WE'S BE PEOPLE, JUS' LIKE ANYONE. SO STOP TAKING THEM-THAR PICTURES OF US!
IF WE'RE WORTH SO MUCH STUDYIN', PAY US SOMETHIN' FOR IT!

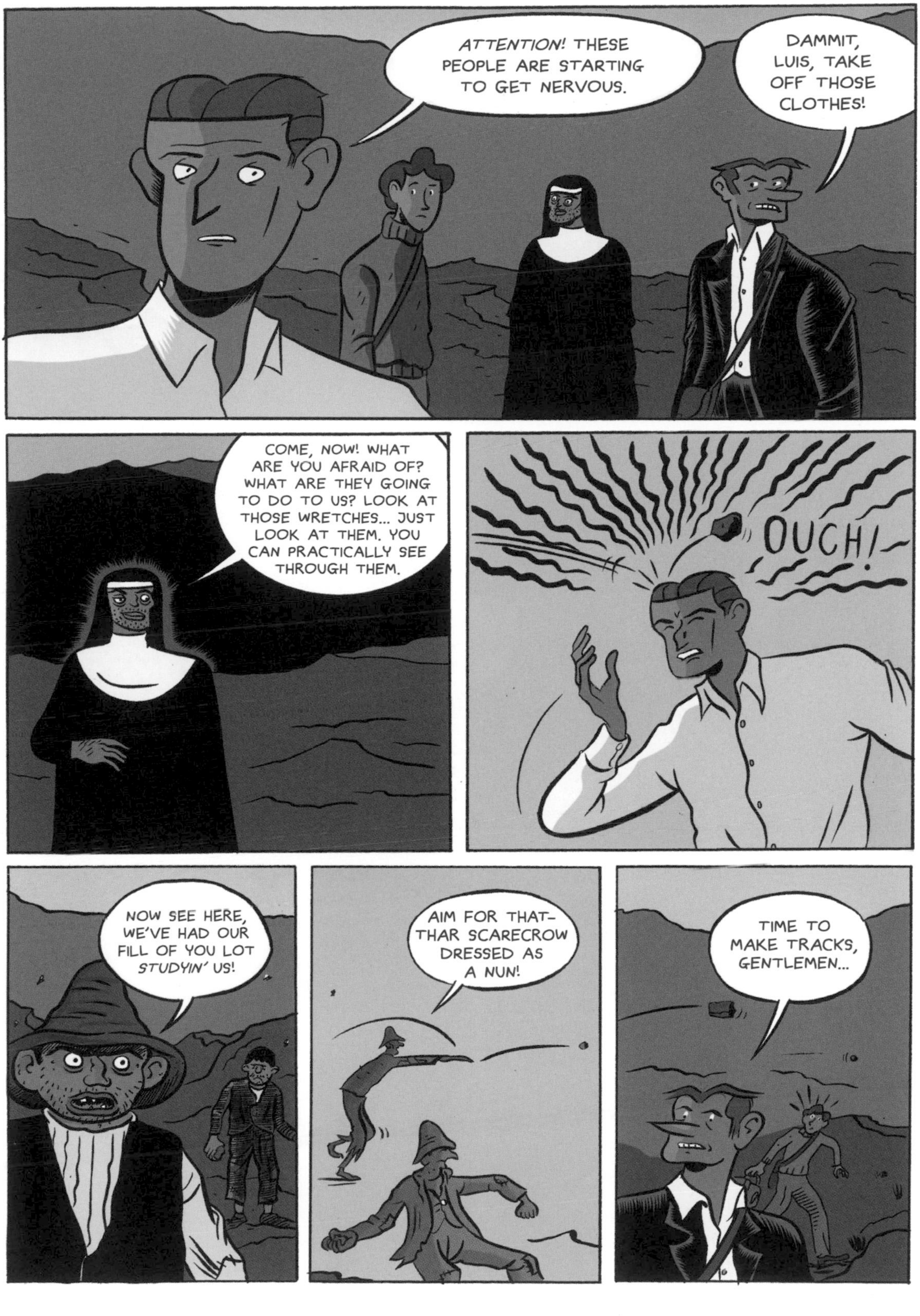

ATTENTION! THESE PEOPLE ARE STARTING TO GET NERVOUS.
DAMMIT, LUIS, TAKE OFF THOSE CLOTHES!
COME, NOW! WHAT ARE YOU AFRAID OF? WHAT ARE THEY GOING TO DO TO US? LOOK AT THOSE WRETCHES... JUST LOOK AT THEM. YOU CAN PRACTICALLY SEE THROUGH THEM.
OUCH!
NOW SEE HERE, WE'VE HAD OUR FILL OF YOU LOT *STUDYIN'* US!
AIM FOR THAT-THAR SCARECROW DRESSED AS A NUN!
TIME TO MAKE TRACKS, GENTLEMEN...

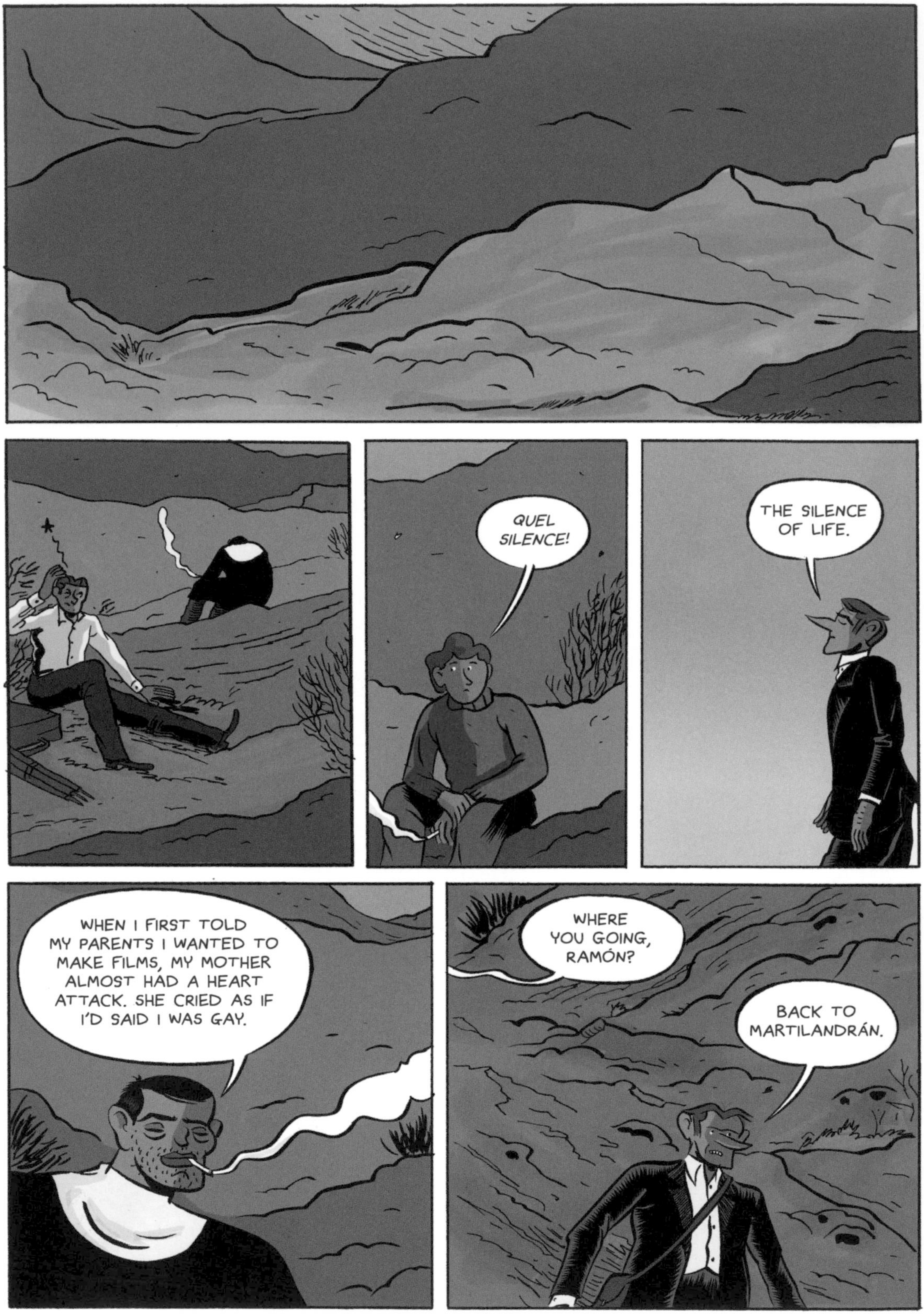
QUEL SILENCE!
THE SILENCE OF LIFE.
WHEN I FIRST TOLD MY PARENTS I WANTED TO MAKE FILMS, MY MOTHER ALMOST HAD A HEART ATTACK. SHE CRIED AS IF I'D SAID I WAS GAY.
WHERE YOU GOING, RAMÓN?
BACK TO MARTILANDRÁN.

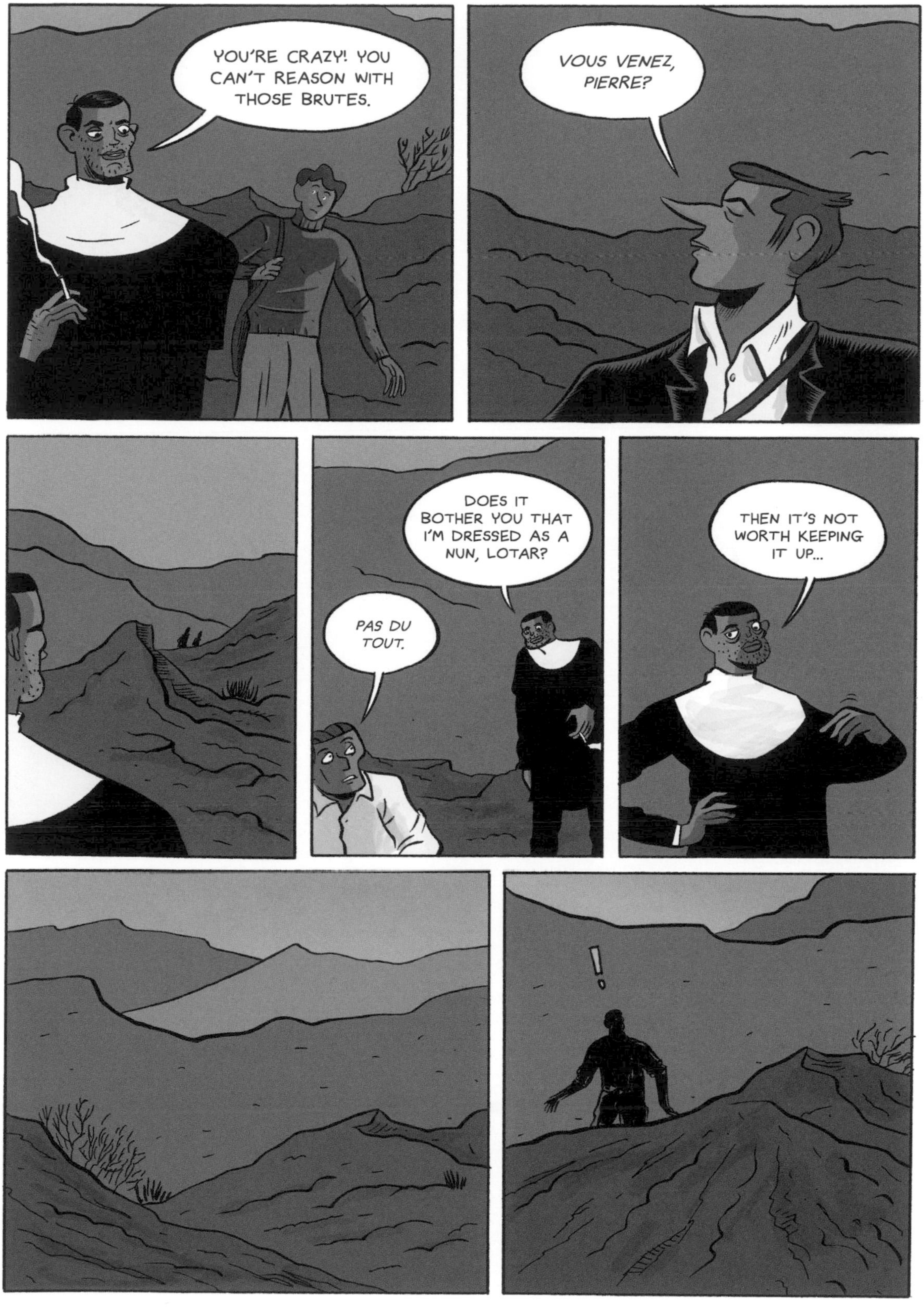
YOU'RE CRAZY! YOU CAN'T REASON WITH THOSE BRUTES.
VOUS VENEZ, PIERRE?
DOES IT BOTHER YOU THAT I'M DRESSED AS A NUN, LOTAR?
PAS DU TOUT.
THEN IT'S NOT WORTH KEEPING IT UP...
!

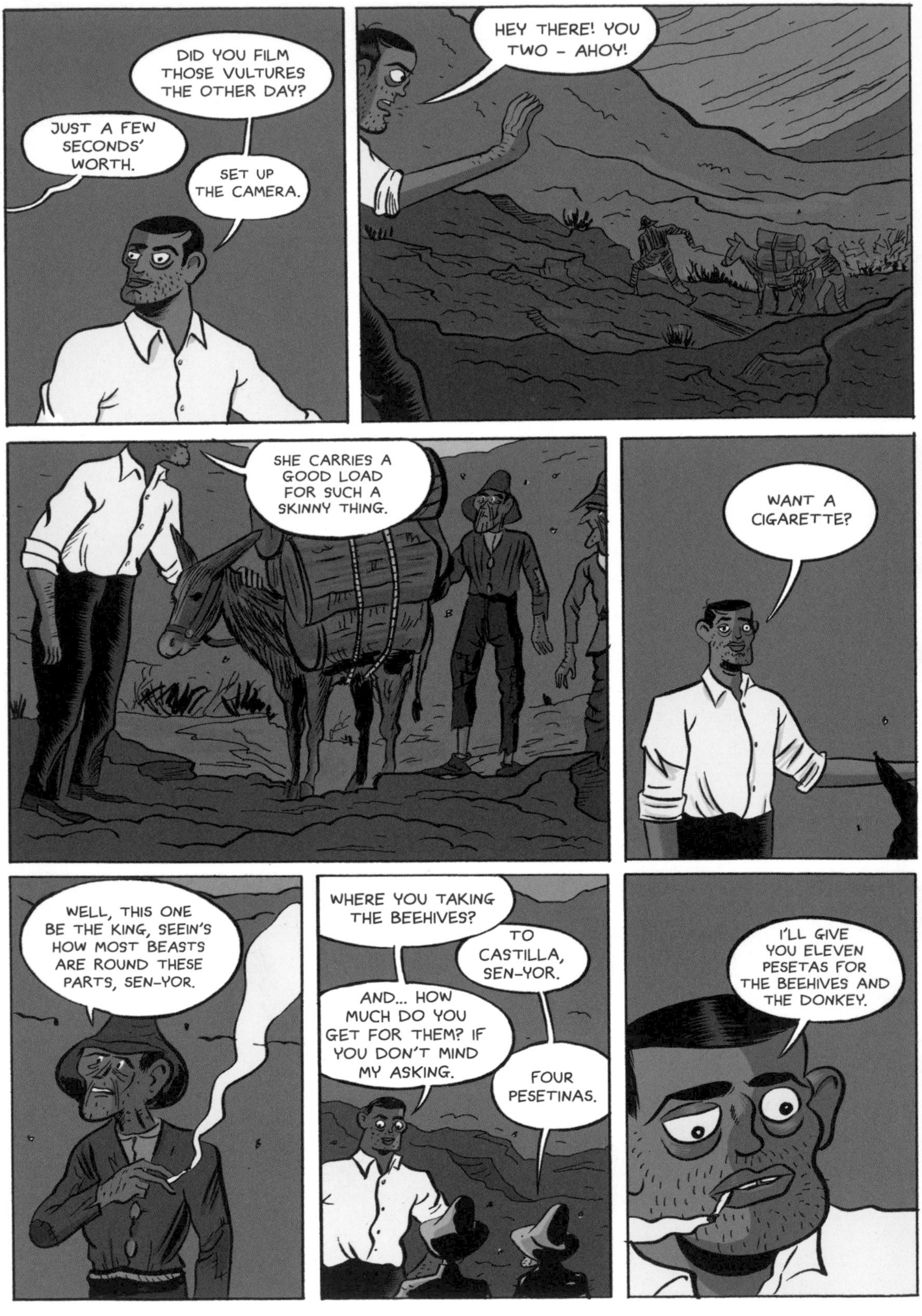
DID YOU FILM THOSE VULTURES THE OTHER DAY?
JUST A FEW SECONDS' WORTH.
SET UP THE CAMERA.
HEY THERE! YOU TWO - AHOY!
SHE CARRIES A GOOD LOAD FOR SUCH A SKINNY THING.
WANT A CIGARETTE?
WELL, THIS ONE BE THE KING, SEEIN'S HOW MOST BEASTS ARE ROUND THESE PARTS, SEN-YOR.
WHERE YOU TAKING THE BEEHIVES?
TO CASTILLA, SEN-YOR.
AND... HOW MUCH DO YOU GET FOR THEM? IF YOU DON'T MIND MY ASKING.
FOUR PESETINAS.
I'LL GIVE YOU ELEVEN PESETAS FOR THE BEEHIVES AND THE DONKEY.

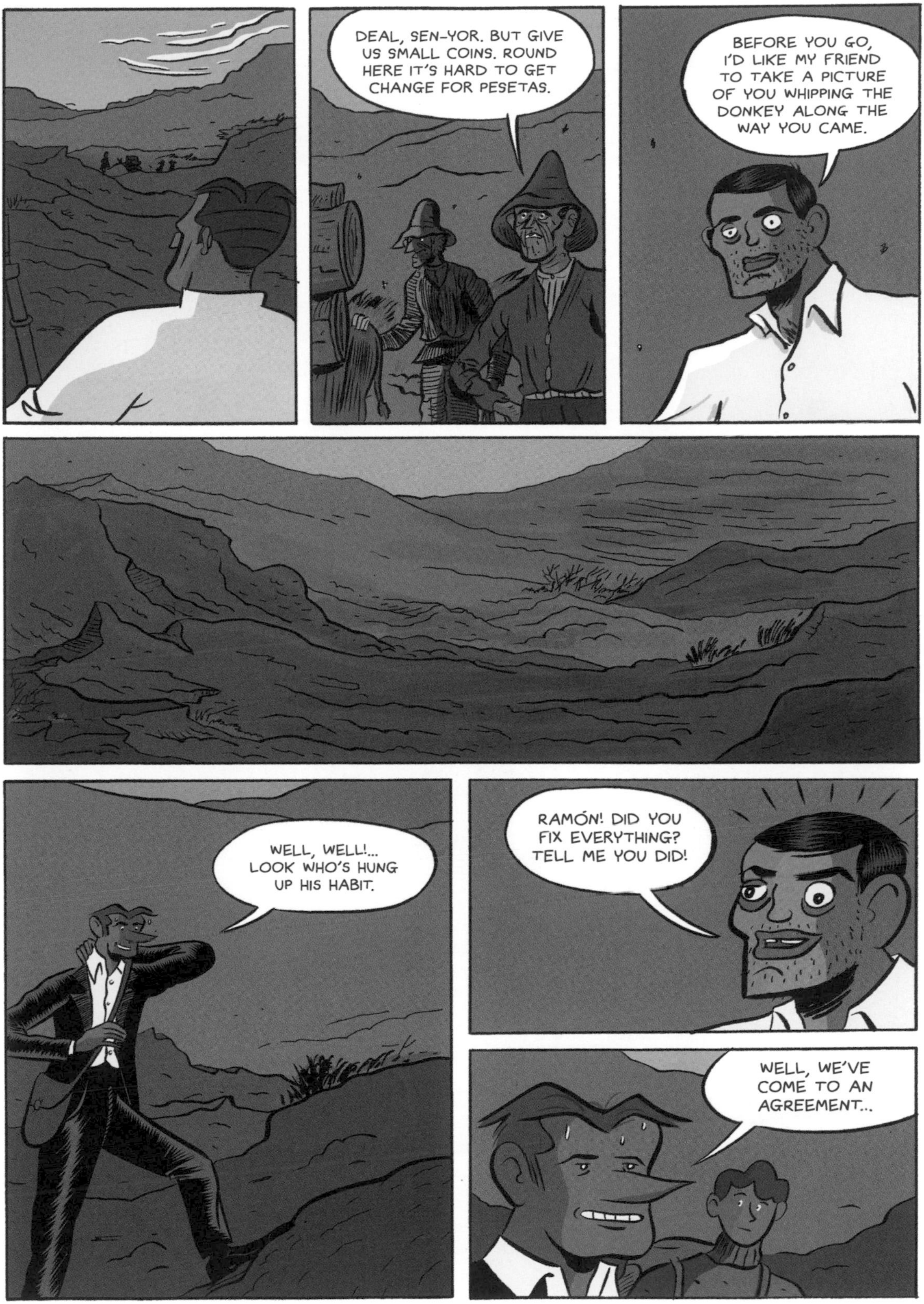
DEAL, SEN-YOR. BUT GIVE US SMALL COINS. ROUND HERE IT'S HARD TO GET CHANGE FOR PESETAS.
BEFORE YOU GO, I'D LIKE MY FRIEND TO TAKE A PICTURE OF YOU WHIPPING THE DONKEY ALONG THE WAY YOU CAME.
WELL, WELL!... LOOK WHO'S HUNG UP HIS HABIT.
RAMÓN! DID YOU FIX EVERYTHING? TELL ME YOU DID!
WELL, WE'VE COME TO AN AGREEMENT...

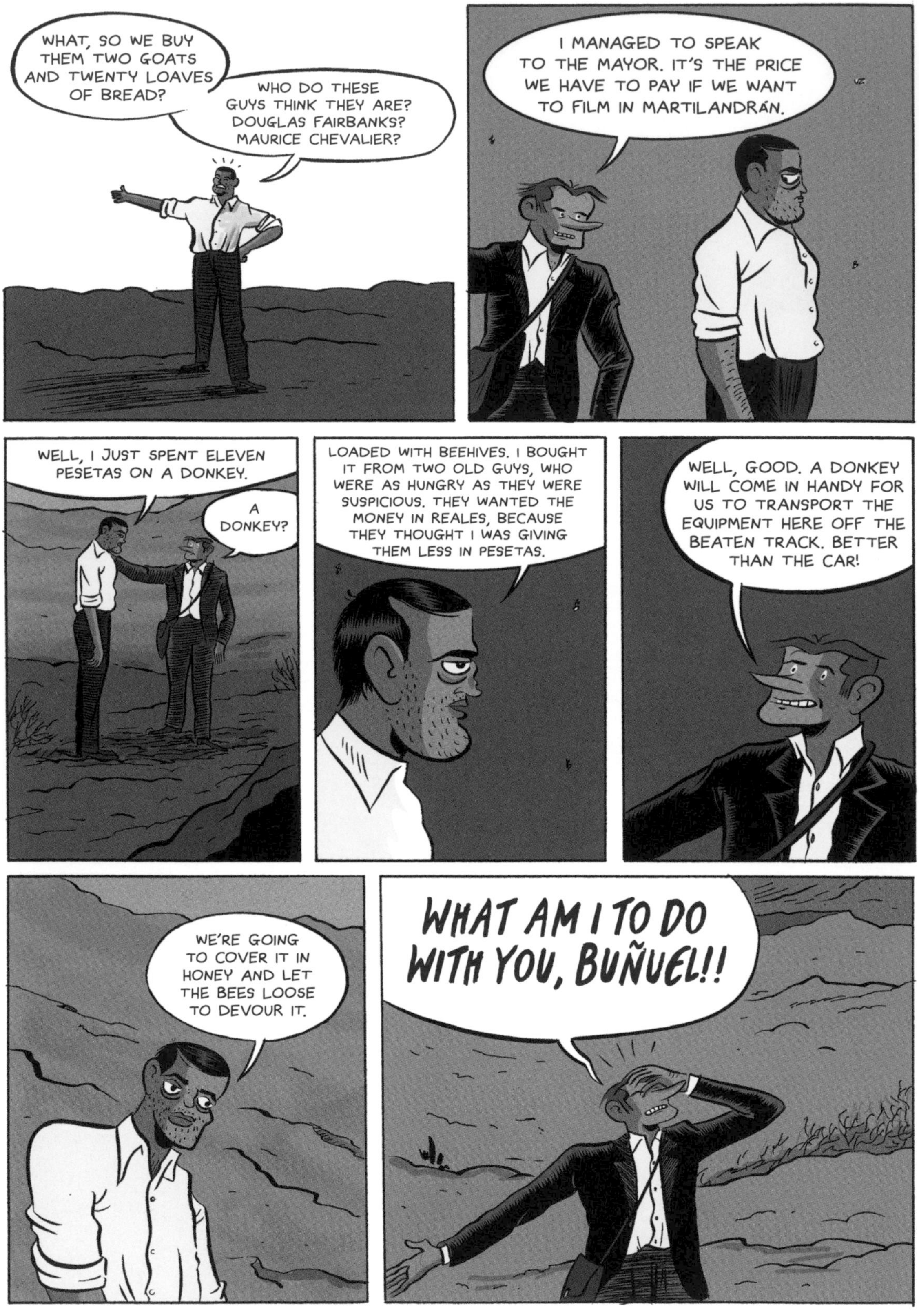
WHAT, SO WE BUY THEM TWO GOATS AND TWENTY LOAVES OF BREAD?
WHO DO THESE GUYS THINK THEY ARE? DOUGLAS FAIRBANKS? MAURICE CHEVALIER?
I MANAGED TO SPEAK TO THE MAYOR. IT'S THE PRICE WE HAVE TO PAY IF WE WANT TO FILM IN MARTILANDRÁN.
WELL, I JUST SPENT ELEVEN PESETAS ON A DONKEY.
A DONKEY?
LOADED WITH BEEHIVES. I BOUGHT IT FROM TWO OLD GUYS, WHO WERE AS HUNGRY AS THEY WERE SUSPICIOUS. THEY WANTED THE MONEY IN REALES, BECAUSE THEY THOUGHT I WAS GIVING THEM LESS IN PESETAS.
WELL, GOOD. A DONKEY WILL COME IN HANDY FOR US TO TRANSPORT THE EQUIPMENT HERE OFF THE BEATEN TRACK. BETTER THAN THE CAR!
WE'RE GOING TO COVER IT IN HONEY AND LET THE BEES LOOSE TO DEVOUR IT.
WHAT AM I TO DO WITH YOU, BUÑUEL!!

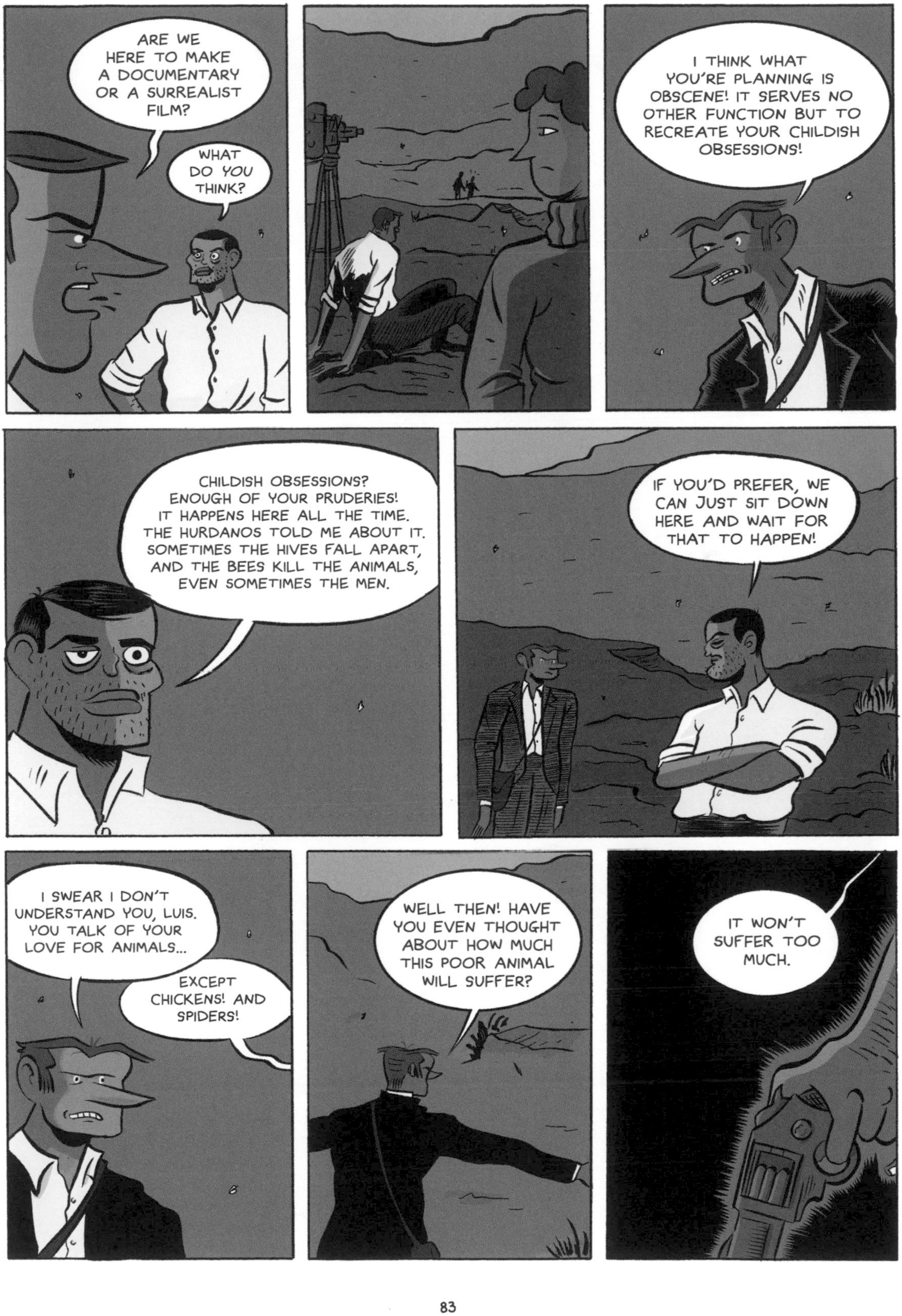
ARE WE HERE TO MAKE A DOCUMENTARY OR A SURREALIST FILM?
WHAT DO YOU THINK?
I THINK WHAT YOU'RE PLANNING IS OBSCENE! IT SERVES NO OTHER FUNCTION BUT TO RECREATE YOUR CHILDISH OBSESSIONS!
CHILDISH OBSESSIONS? ENOUGH OF YOUR PRUDERIES! IT HAPPENS HERE ALL THE TIME. THE HURDANOS TOLD ME ABOUT IT. SOMETIMES THE HIVES FALL APART, AND THE BEES KILL THE ANIMALS, EVEN SOMETIMES THE MEN.
IF YOU'D PREFER, WE CAN JUST SIT DOWN HERE AND WAIT FOR THAT TO HAPPEN!
I SWEAR I DON'T UNDERSTAND YOU, LUIS. YOU TALK OF YOUR LOVE FOR ANIMALS...
EXCEPT CHICKENS! AND SPIDERS!
WELL THEN! HAVE YOU EVEN THOUGHT ABOUT HOW MUCH THIS POOR ANIMAL WILL SUFFER?
IT WON'T SUFFER TOO MUCH.

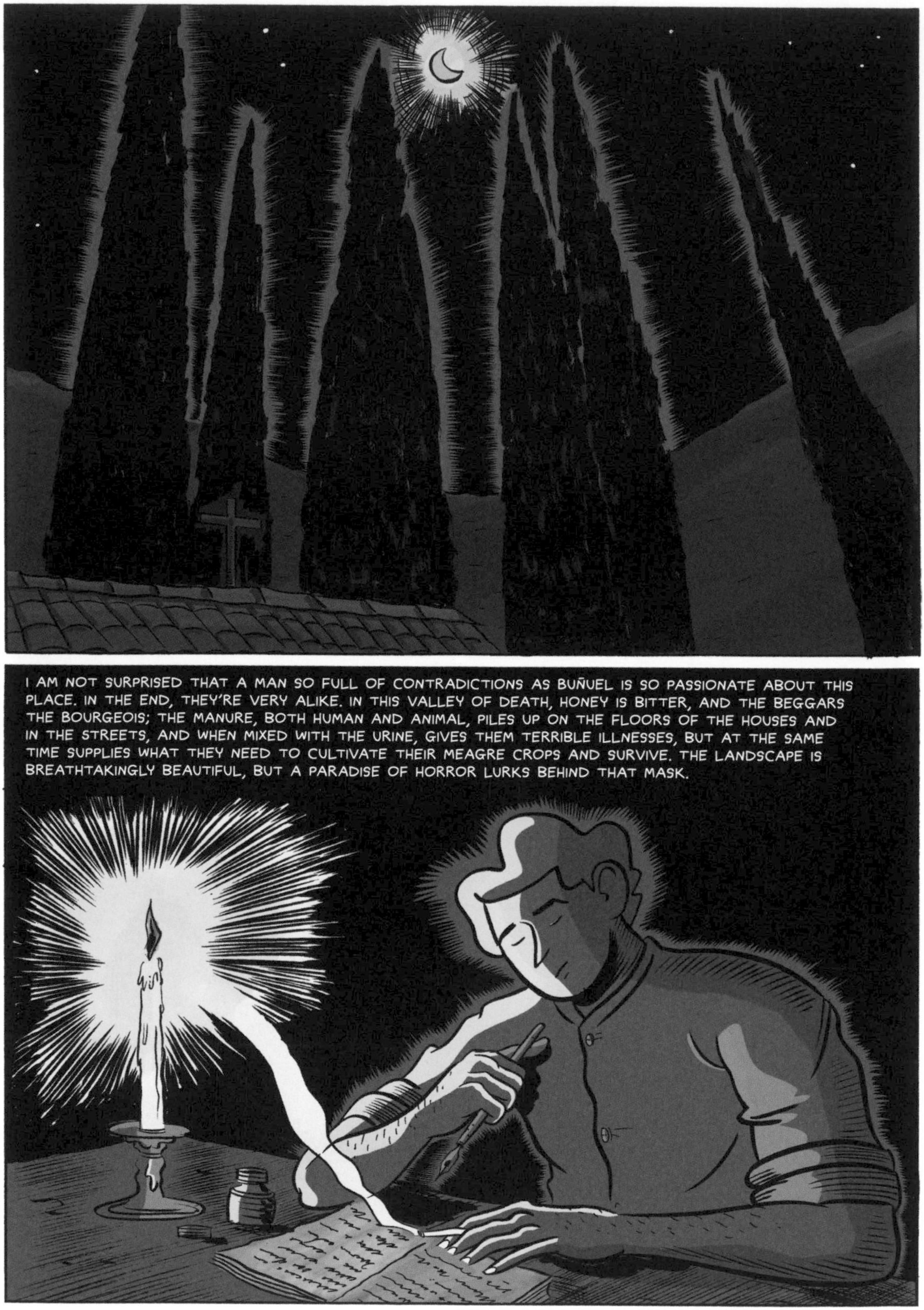
I AM NOT SURPRISED THAT A MAN SO FULL OF CONTRADICTIONS AS BUÑUEL IS SO PASSIONATE ABOUT THIS PLACE. IN THE END, THEY'RE VERY ALIKE. IN THIS VALLEY OF DEATH, HONEY IS BITTER, AND THE BEGGARS THE BOURGEOIS; THE MANURE, BOTH HUMAN AND ANIMAL, PILES UP ON THE FLOORS OF THE HOUSES AND IN THE STREETS, AND WHEN MIXED WITH THE URINE, GIVES THEM TERRIBLE ILLNESSES, BUT AT THE SAME TIME SUPPLIES WHAT THEY NEED TO CULTIVATE THEIR MEAGRE CROPS AND SURVIVE. THE LANDSCAPE IS BREATHTAKINGLY BEAUTIFUL, BUT A PARADISE OF HORROR LURKS BEHIND THAT MASK.

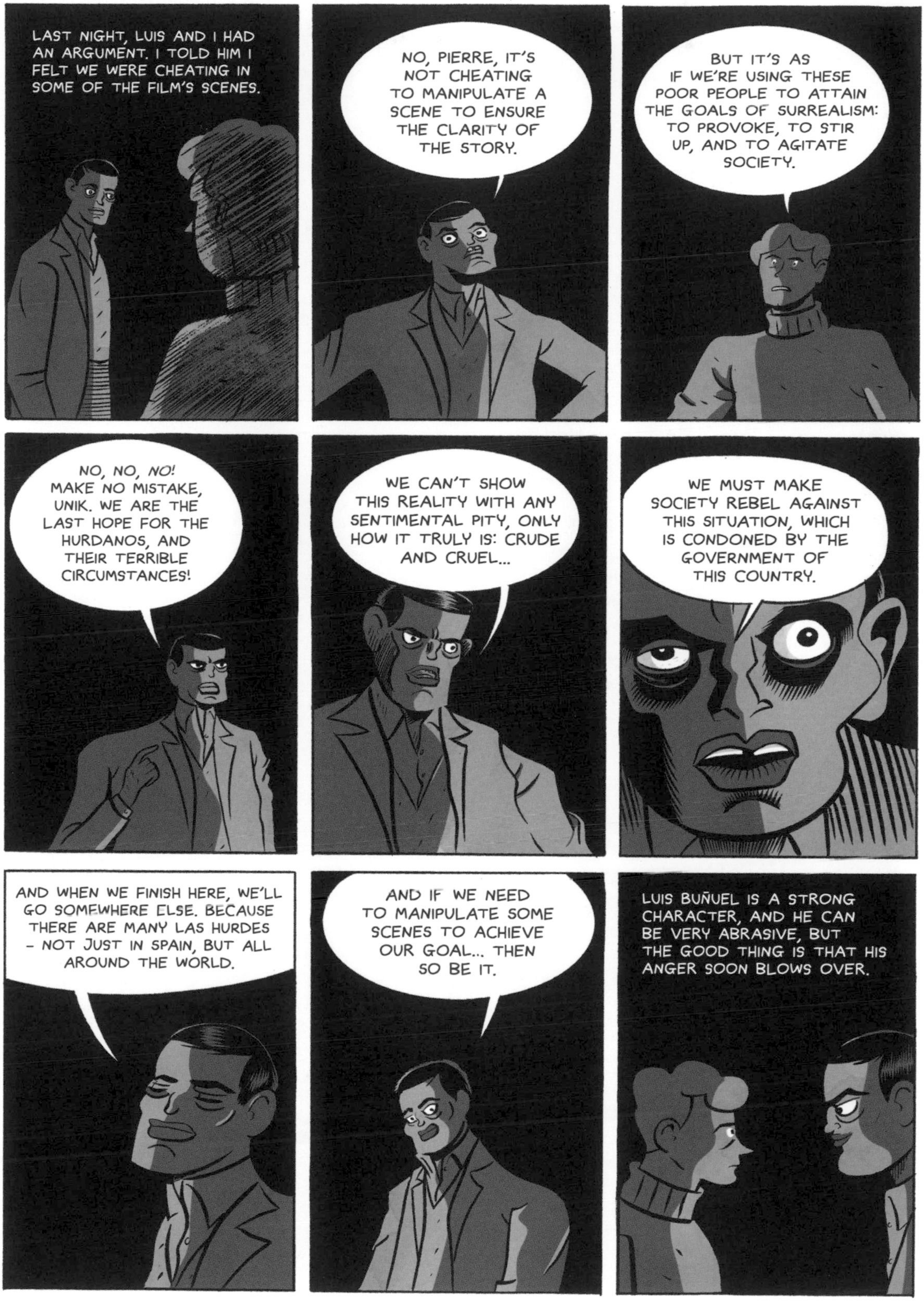
LAST NIGHT, LUIS AND I HAD AN ARGUMENT. I TOLD HIM I FELT WE WERE CHEATING IN SOME OF THE FILM'S SCENES.
NO, PIERRE, IT'S NOT CHEATING TO MANIPULATE A SCENE TO ENSURE THE CLARITY OF THE STORY.
BUT IT'S AS IF WE'RE USING THESE POOR PEOPLE TO ATTAIN THE GOALS OF SURREALISM: TO PROVOKE, TO STIR UP, AND TO AGITATE SOCIETY.
NO, NO, *NO!* MAKE NO MISTAKE, UNIK. WE ARE THE LAST HOPE FOR THE HURDANOS, AND THEIR TERRIBLE CIRCUMSTANCES!
WE CAN'T SHOW THIS REALITY WITH ANY SENTIMENTAL PITY, ONLY HOW IT TRULY IS: CRUDE AND CRUEL...
WE MUST MAKE SOCIETY REBEL AGAINST THIS SITUATION, WHICH IS CONDONED BY THE GOVERNMENT OF THIS COUNTRY.
AND WHEN WE FINISH HERE, WE'LL GO SOMEWHERE ELSE. BECAUSE THERE ARE MANY LAS HURDES - NOT JUST IN SPAIN, BUT ALL AROUND THE WORLD.
AND IF WE NEED TO MANIPULATE SOME SCENES TO ACHIEVE OUR GOAL... THEN SO BE IT.
LUIS BUÑUEL IS A STRONG CHARACTER, AND HE CAN BE VERY ABRASIVE, BUT THE GOOD THING IS THAT HIS ANGER SOON BLOWS OVER.

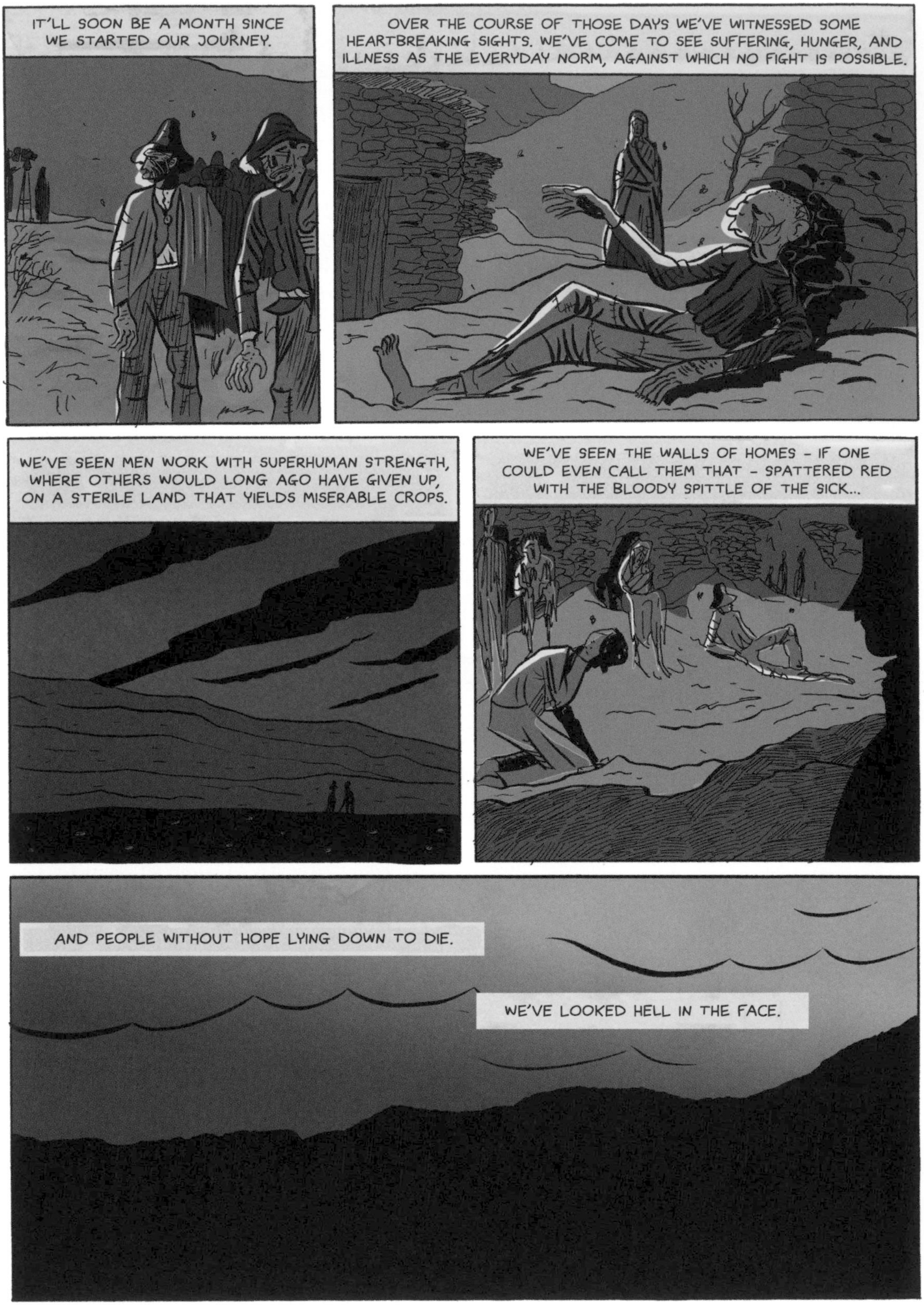
IT'LL SOON BE A MONTH SINCE WE STARTED OUR JOURNEY.
OVER THE COURSE OF THOSE DAYS WE'VE WITNESSED SOME HEARTBREAKING SIGHTS. WE'VE COME TO SEE SUFFERING, HUNGER, AND ILLNESS AS THE EVERYDAY NORM, AGAINST WHICH NO FIGHT IS POSSIBLE.
WE'VE SEEN MEN WORK WITH SUPERHUMAN STRENGTH, WHERE OTHERS WOULD LONG AGO HAVE GIVEN UP, ON A STERILE LAND THAT YIELDS MISERABLE CROPS.
WE'VE SEEN THE WALLS OF HOMES - IF ONE COULD EVEN CALL THEM THAT - SPATTERED RED WITH THE BLOODY SPITTLE OF THE SICK...
AND PEOPLE WITHOUT HOPE LYING DOWN TO DIE.
WE'VE LOOKED HELL IN THE FACE.

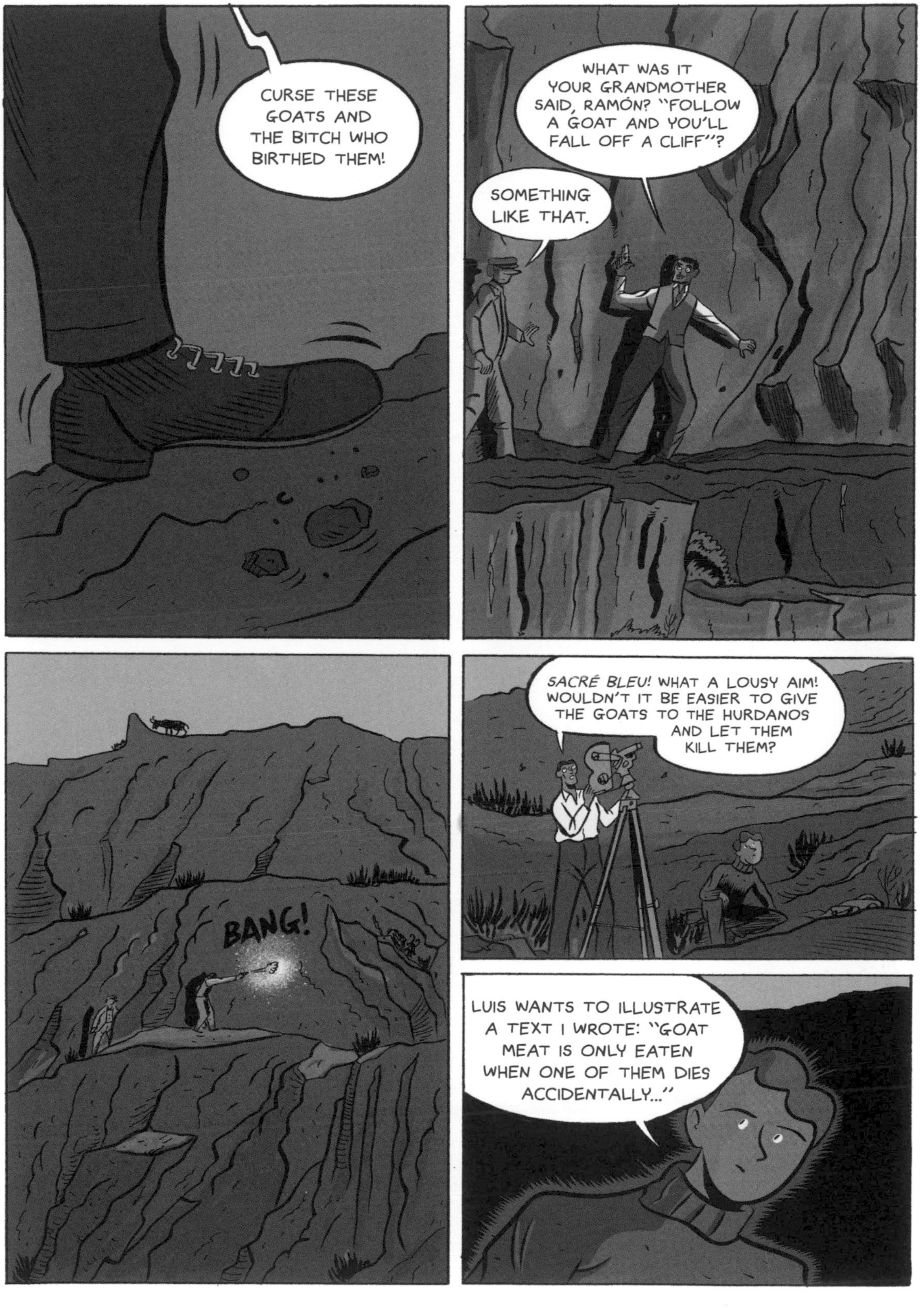
CURSE THESE GOATS AND THE BITCH WHO BIRTHED THEM!
WHAT WAS IT YOUR GRANDMOTHER SAID, RAMÓN? "FOLLOW A GOAT AND YOU'LL FALL OFF A CLIFF"?
SOMETHING LIKE THAT.
BANG!
SACRÉ BLEU! WHAT A LOUSY AIM! WOULDN'T IT BE EASIER TO GIVE THE GOATS TO THE HURDANOS AND LET THEM KILL THEM?
LUIS WANTS TO ILLUSTRATE A TEXT I WROTE: "GOAT MEAT IS ONLY EATEN WHEN ONE OF THEM DIES ACCIDENTALLY..."

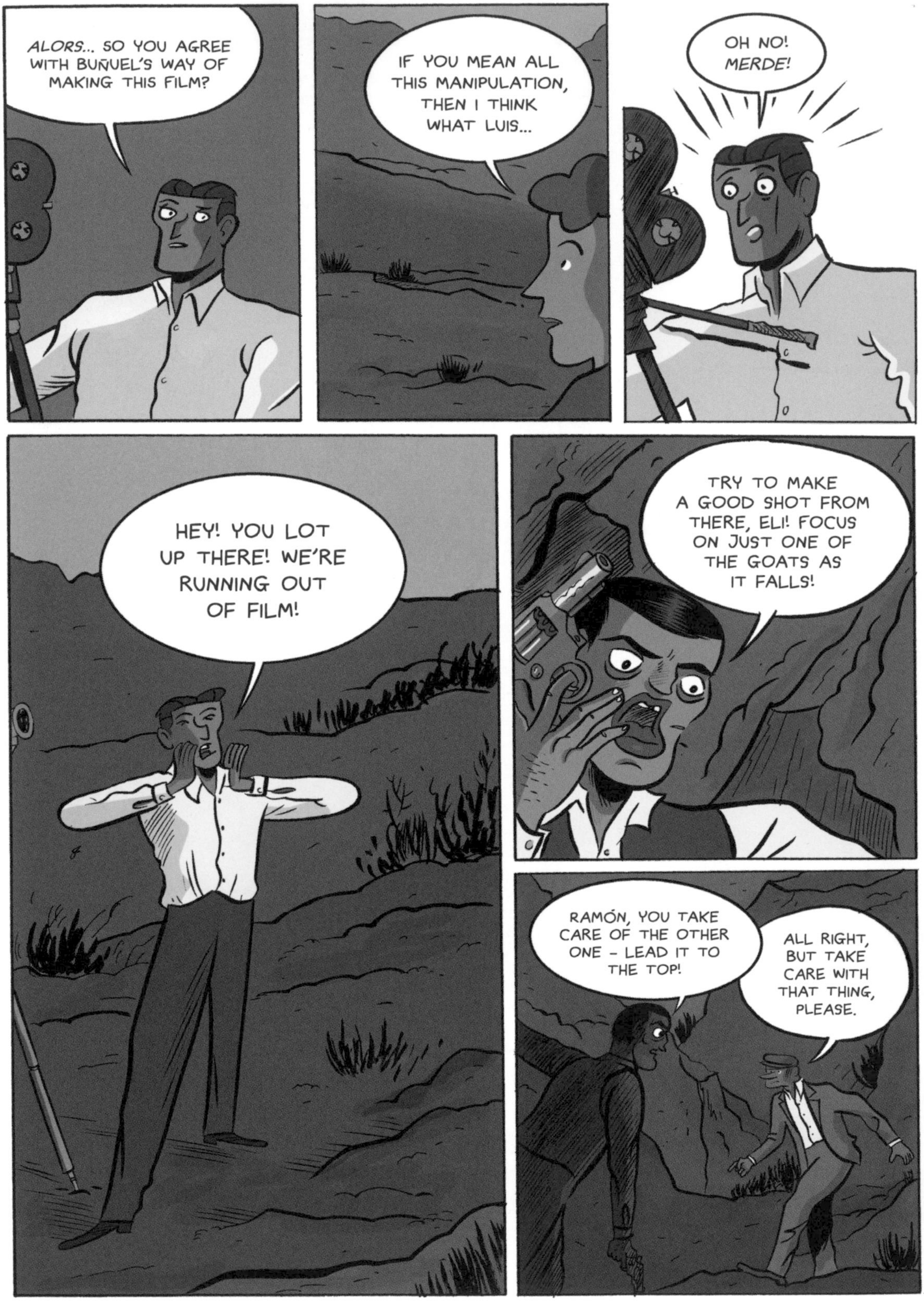
ALORS... SO YOU AGREE WITH BUÑUEL'S WAY OF MAKING THIS FILM?
IF YOU MEAN ALL THIS MANIPULATION, THEN I THINK WHAT LUIS...
OH NO! MERDE!
HEY! YOU LOT UP THERE! WE'RE RUNNING OUT OF FILM!
TRY TO MAKE A GOOD SHOT FROM THERE, ELI! FOCUS ON JUST ONE OF THE GOATS AS IT FALLS!
RAMÓN, YOU TAKE CARE OF THE OTHER ONE - LEAD IT TO THE TOP!
ALL RIGHT, BUT TAKE CARE WITH THAT THING, PLEASE.

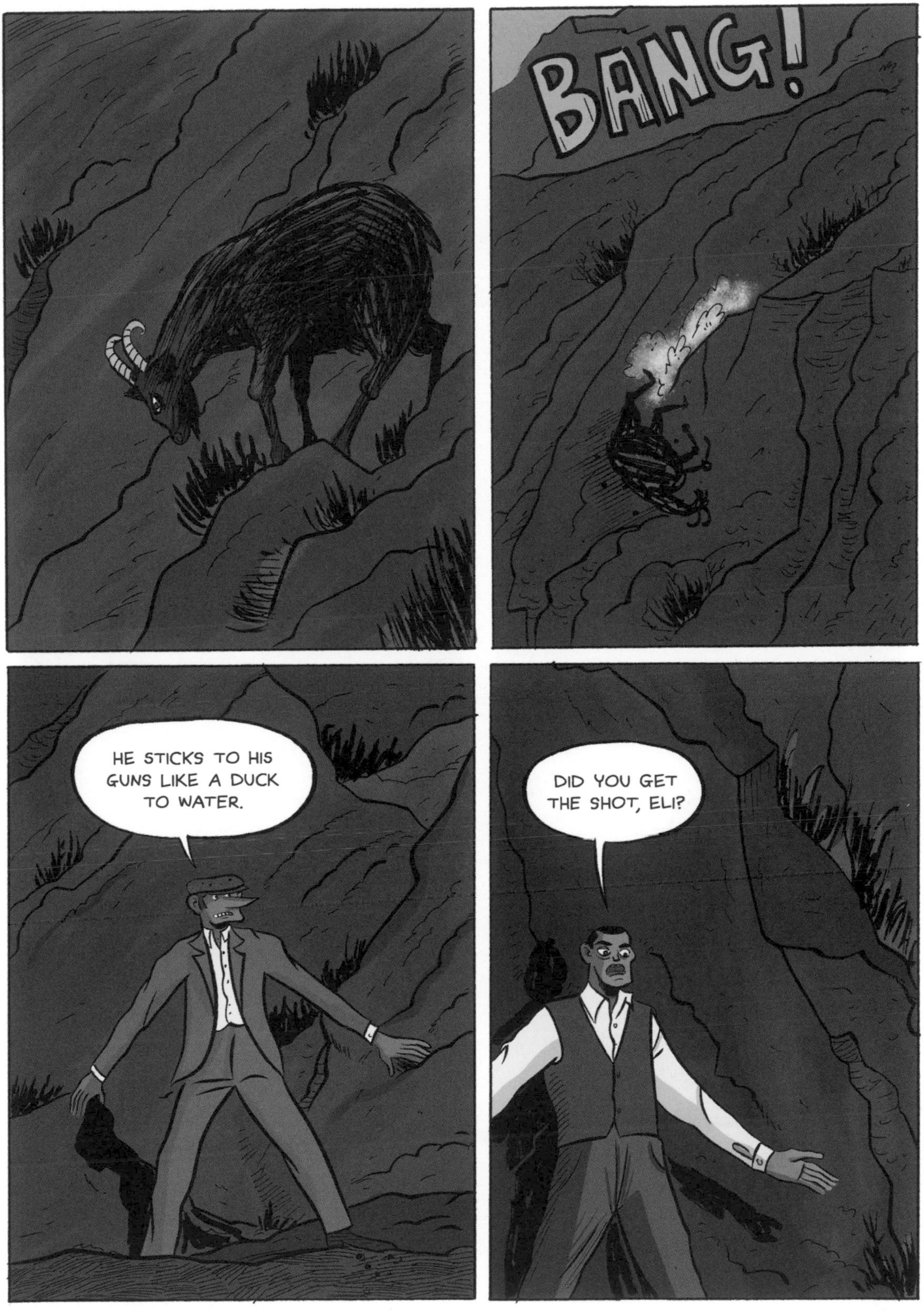
BANG!
HE STICKS TO HIS GUNS LIKE A DUCK TO WATER.
DID YOU GET THE SHOT, ELI?

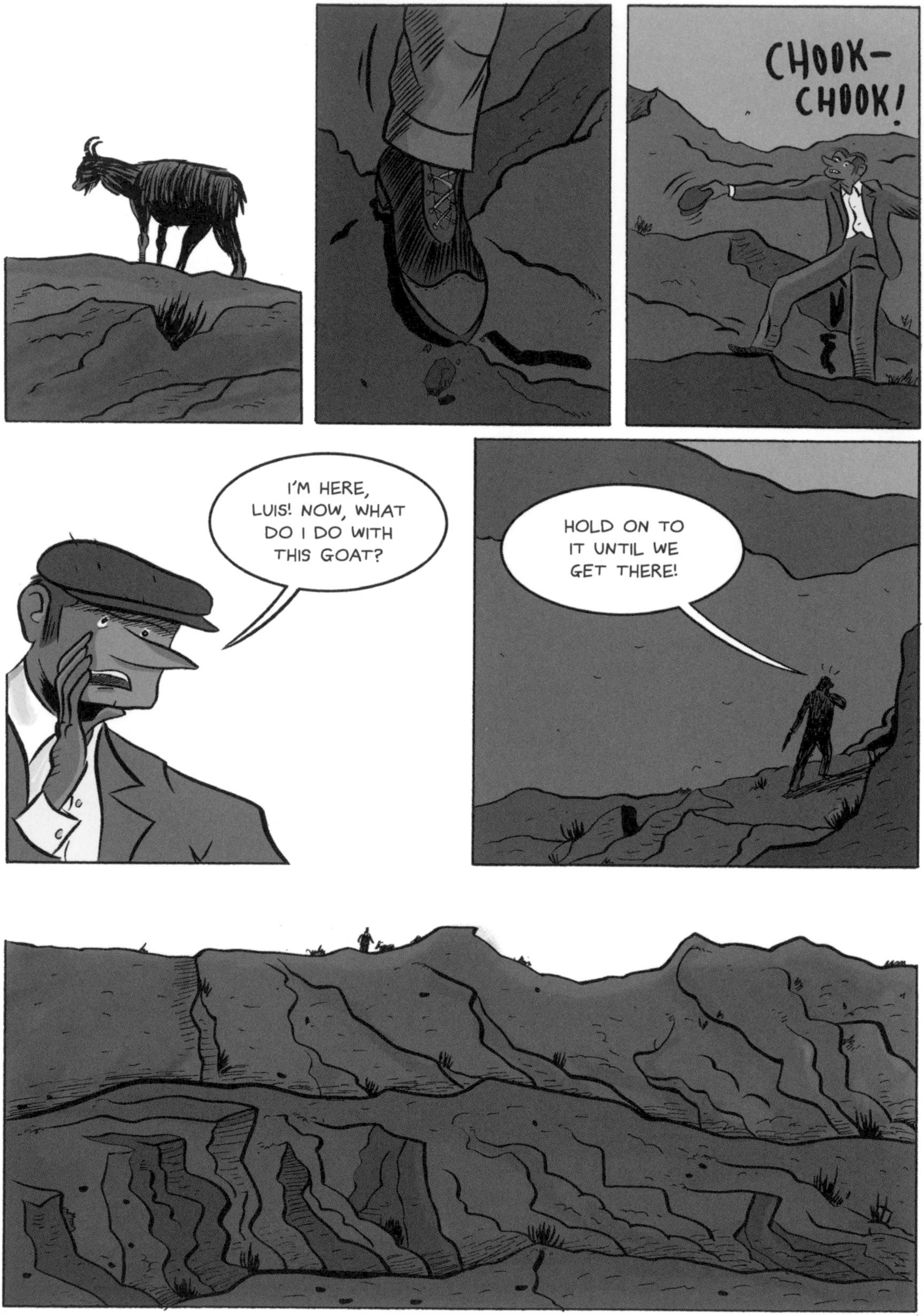
CHOOK-
CHOOK!
I'M HERE, LUIS! NOW, WHAT DO I DO WITH THIS GOAT?
HOLD ON TO IT UNTIL WE GET THERE!

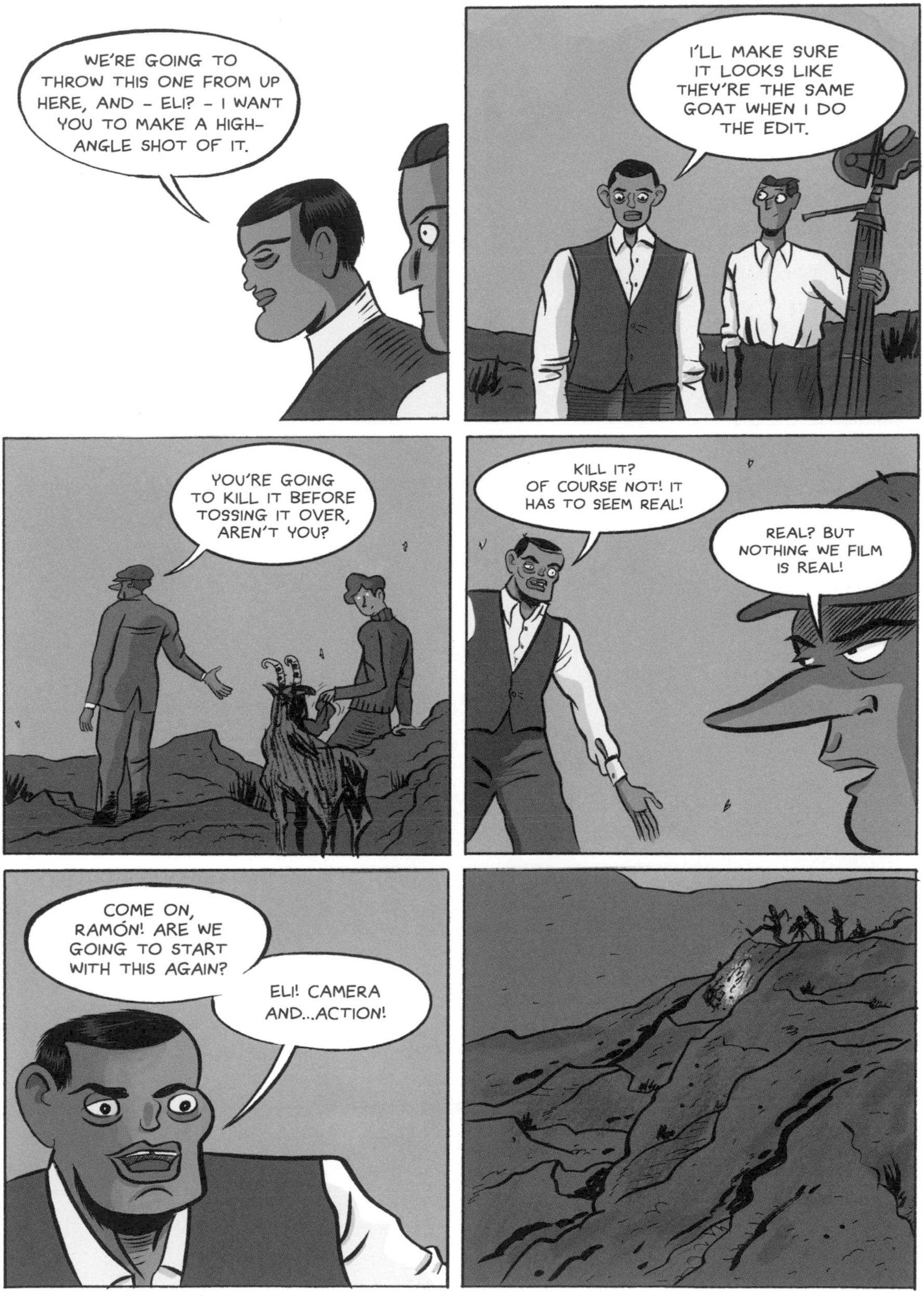
WE'RE GOING TO THROW THIS ONE FROM UP HERE, AND - ELI? - I WANT YOU TO MAKE A HIGH-ANGLE SHOT OF IT.
I'LL MAKE SURE IT LOOKS LIKE THEY'RE THE SAME GOAT WHEN I DO THE EDIT.
YOU'RE GOING TO KILL IT BEFORE TOSSING IT OVER, AREN'T YOU?
KILL IT? OF COURSE NOT! IT HAS TO SEEM REAL!
REAL? BUT NOTHING WE FILM IS REAL!
COME ON, RAMÓN! ARE WE GOING TO START WITH THIS AGAIN?
ELI! CAMERA AND...ACTION!

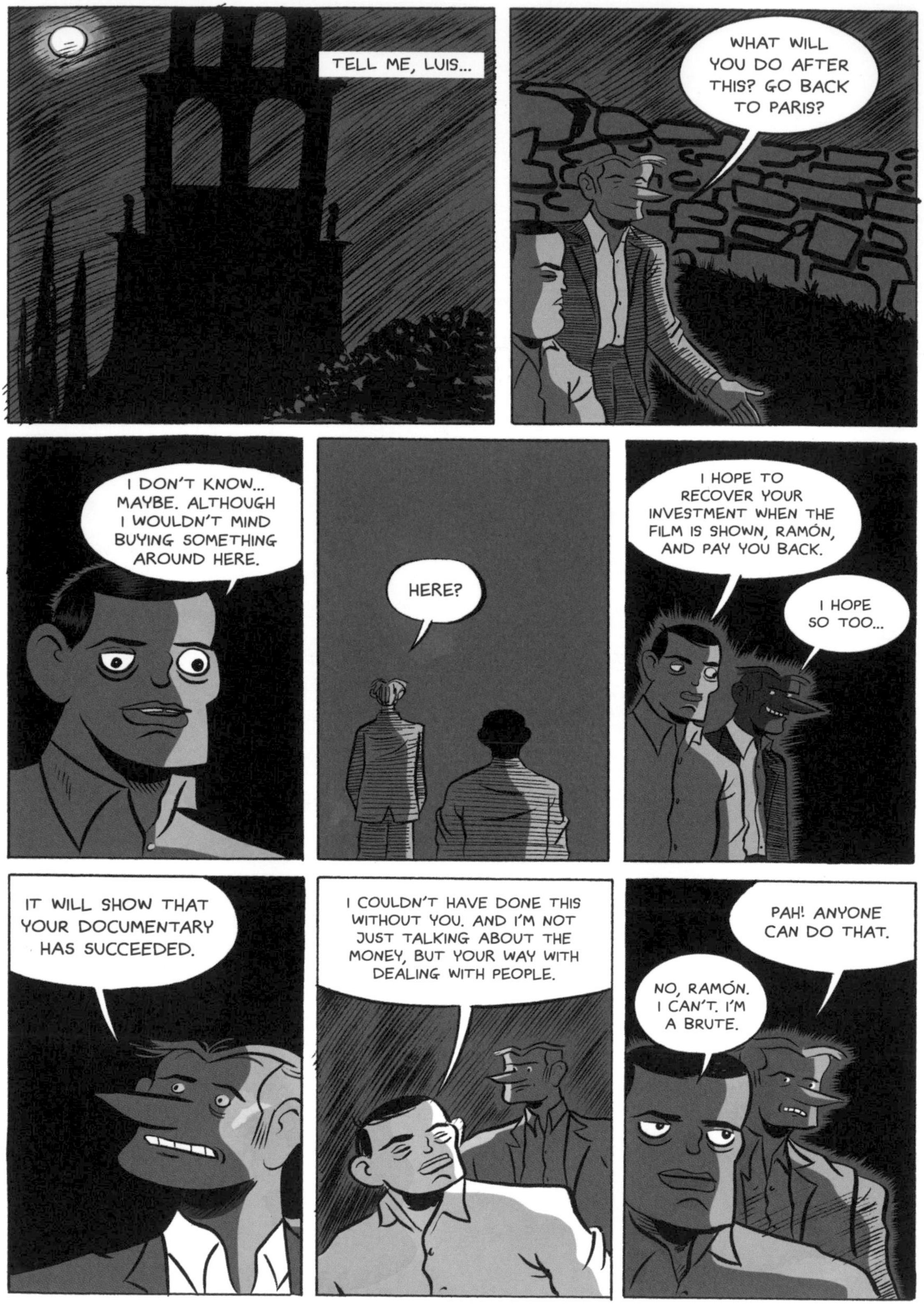
TELL ME, LUIS...
WHAT WILL YOU DO AFTER THIS? GO BACK TO PARIS?
I DON'T KNOW... MAYBE. ALTHOUGH I WOULDN'T MIND BUYING SOMETHING AROUND HERE.
HERE?
I HOPE TO RECOVER YOUR INVESTMENT WHEN THE FILM IS SHOWN, RAMÓN, AND PAY YOU BACK.
I HOPE SO TOO...
IT WILL SHOW THAT YOUR DOCUMENTARY HAS SUCCEEDED.
I COULDN'T HAVE DONE THIS WITHOUT YOU. AND I'M NOT JUST TALKING ABOUT THE MONEY, BUT YOUR WAY WITH DEALING WITH PEOPLE.
PAH! ANYONE CAN DO THAT.
NO, RAMÓN. I CAN'T. I'M A BRUTE.

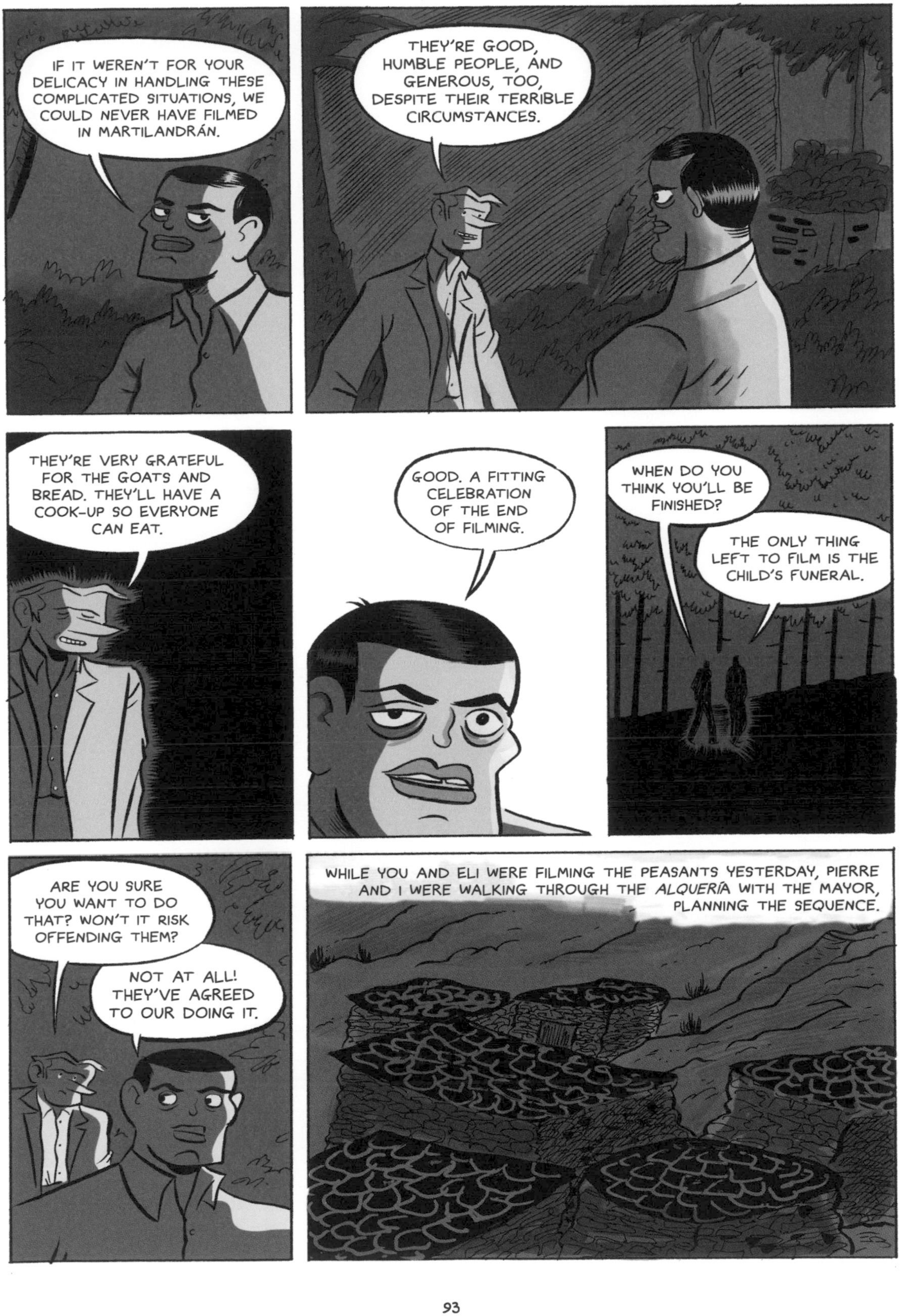
IF IT WEREN'T FOR YOUR DELICACY IN HANDLING THESE COMPLICATED SITUATIONS, WE COULD NEVER HAVE FILMED IN MARTILANDRÁN.
THEY'RE GOOD, HUMBLE PEOPLE, AND GENEROUS, TOO, DESPITE THEIR TERRIBLE CIRCUMSTANCES.
THEY'RE VERY GRATEFUL FOR THE GOATS AND BREAD. THEY'LL HAVE A COOK-UP SO EVERYONE CAN EAT.
GOOD. A FITTING CELEBRATION OF THE END OF FILMING.
WHEN DO YOU THINK YOU'LL BE FINISHED?
THE ONLY THING LEFT TO FILM IS THE CHILD'S FUNERAL.
ARE YOU SURE YOU WANT TO DO THAT? WON'T IT RISK OFFENDING THEM?
NOT AT ALL! THEY'VE AGREED TO OUR DOING IT.
WHILE YOU AND ELI WERE FILMING THE PEASANTS YESTERDAY, PIERRE AND I WERE WALKING THROUGH THE *ALQUERÍA* WITH THE MAYOR, PLANNING THE SEQUENCE.

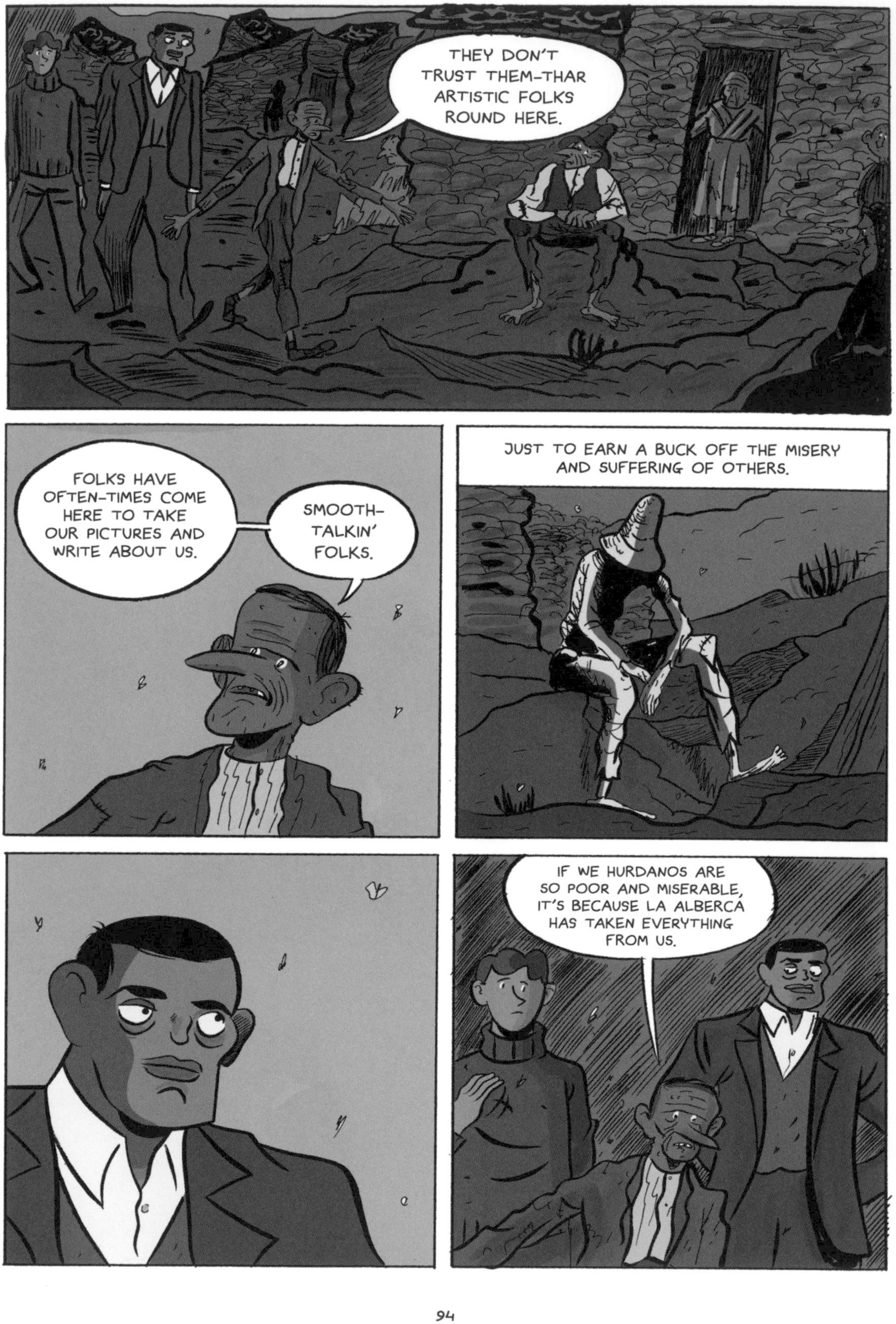
THEY DON'T TRUST THEM–THAR ARTISTIC FOLKS ROUND HERE.
FOLKS HAVE OFTEN–TIMES COME HERE TO TAKE OUR PICTURES AND WRITE ABOUT US.
SMOOTH–TALKIN' FOLKS.
JUST TO EARN A BUCK OFF THE MISERY AND SUFFERING OF OTHERS.
IF WE HURDANOS ARE SO POOR AND MISERABLE, IT'S BECAUSE LA ALBERCA HAS TAKEN EVERYTHING FROM US.

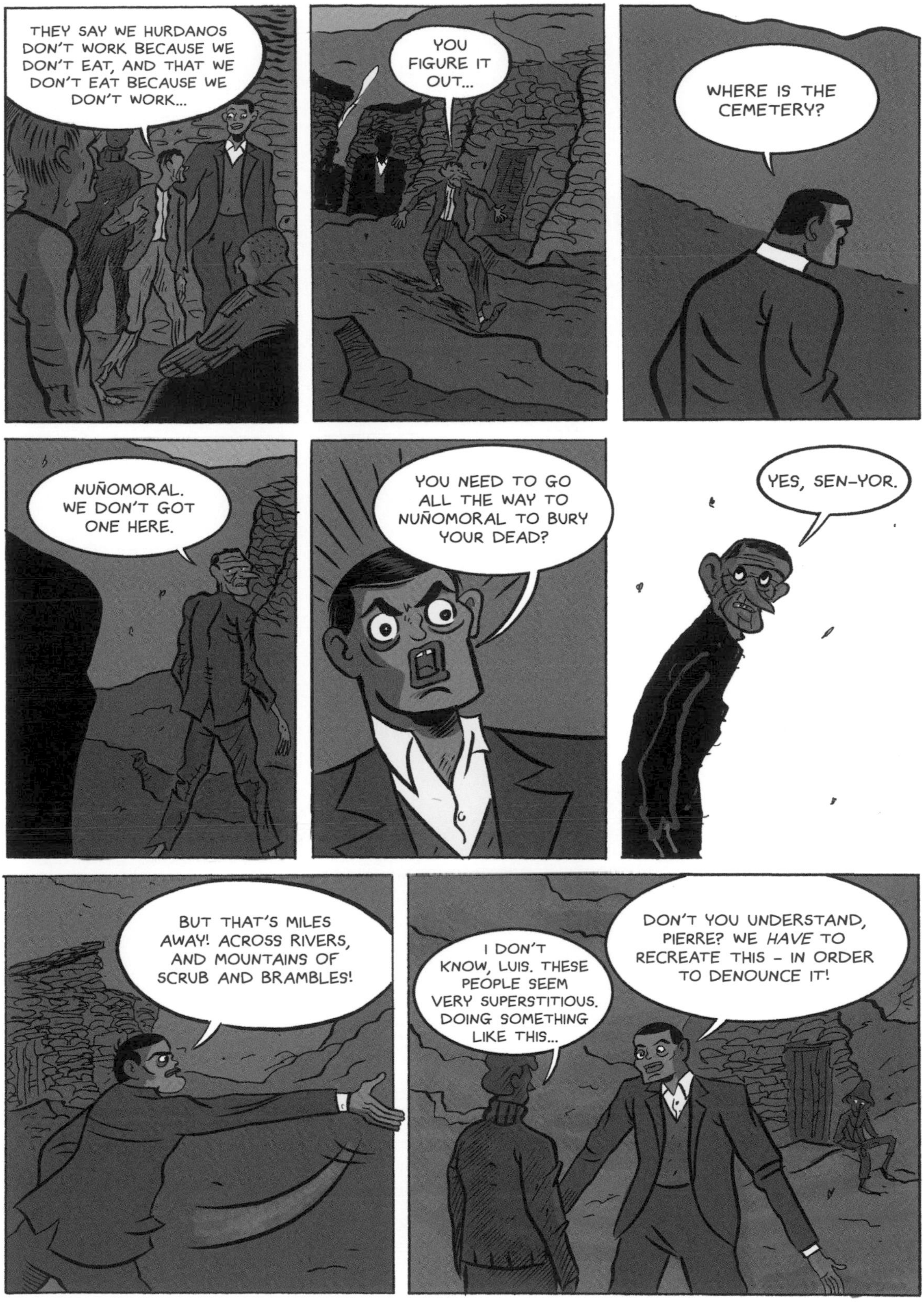
THEY SAY WE HURDANOS DON'T WORK BECAUSE WE DON'T EAT, AND THAT WE DON'T EAT BECAUSE WE DON'T WORK...
YOU FIGURE IT OUT...
WHERE IS THE CEMETERY?
NUÑOMORAL. WE DON'T GOT ONE HERE.
YOU NEED TO GO ALL THE WAY TO NUÑOMORAL TO BURY YOUR DEAD?
YES, SEN-YOR.
BUT THAT'S MILES AWAY! ACROSS RIVERS, AND MOUNTAINS OF SCRUB AND BRAMBLES!
I DON'T KNOW, LUIS. THESE PEOPLE SEEM VERY SUPERSTITIOUS. DOING SOMETHING LIKE THIS...
DON'T YOU UNDERSTAND, PIERRE? WE *HAVE* TO RECREATE THIS - IN ORDER TO DENOUNCE IT!

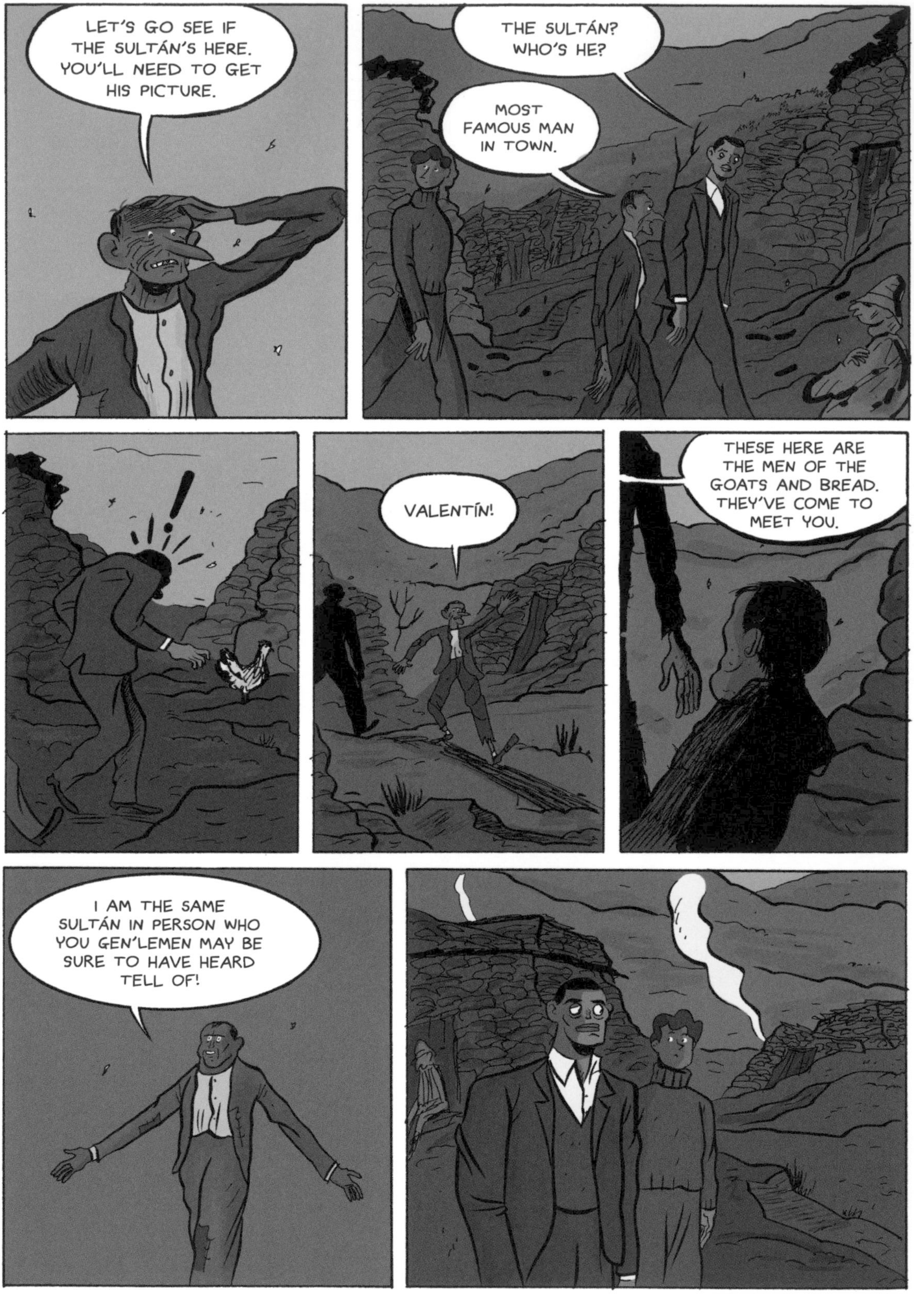
LET'S GO SEE IF THE SULTÁN'S HERE. YOU'LL NEED TO GET HIS PICTURE.
THE SULTÁN? WHO'S HE?
MOST FAMOUS MAN IN TOWN.
!
VALENTÍN!
THESE HERE ARE THE MEN OF THE GOATS AND BREAD. THEY'VE COME TO MEET YOU.
I AM THE SAME SULTÁN IN PERSON WHO YOU GEN'LEMEN MAY BE SURE TO HAVE HEARD TELL OF!

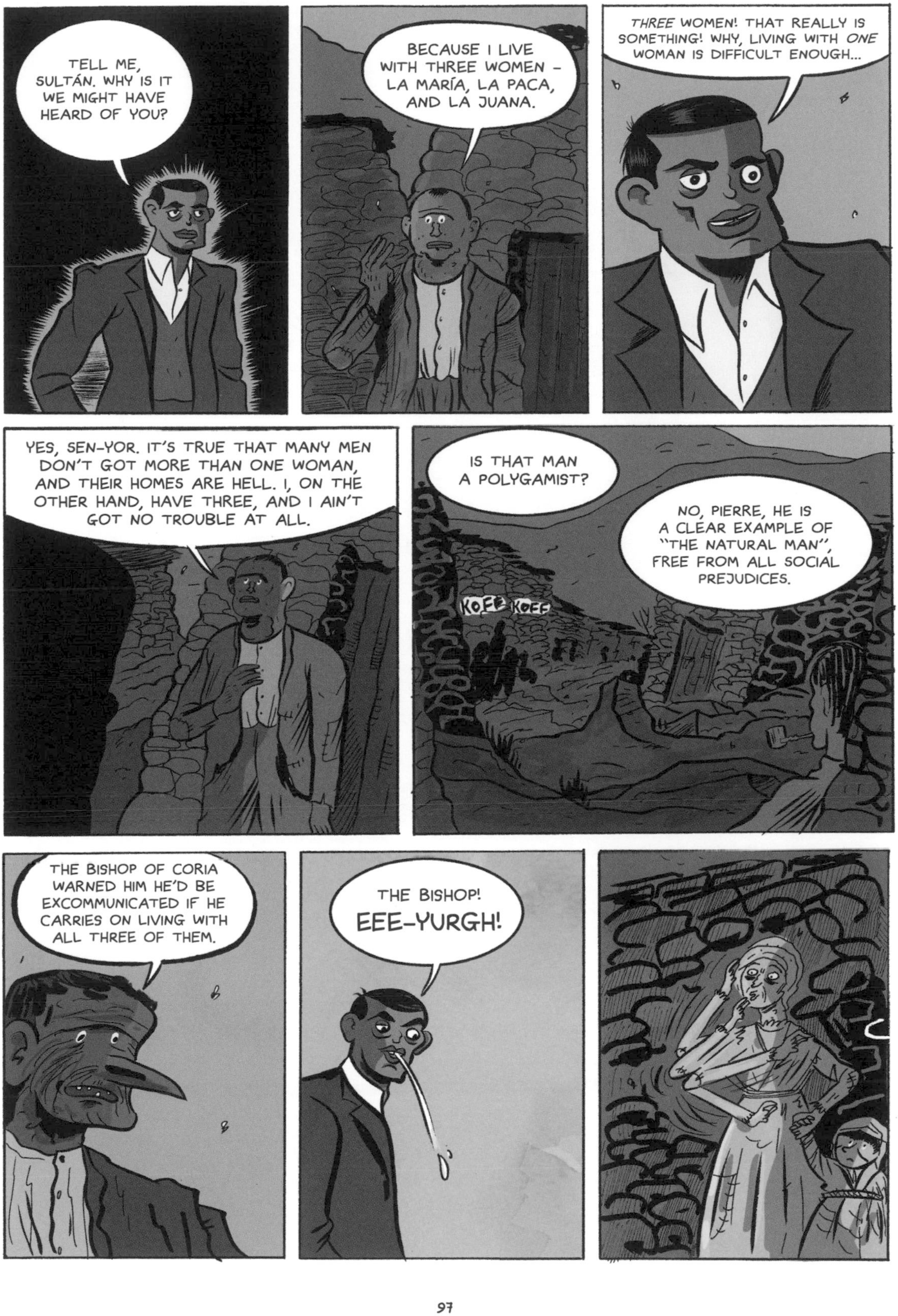
TELL ME, SULTÁN. WHY IS IT WE MIGHT HAVE HEARD OF YOU?
BECAUSE I LIVE WITH THREE WOMEN – LA MARÍA, LA PACA, AND LA JUANA.
THREE WOMEN! THAT REALLY IS SOMETHING! WHY, LIVING WITH *ONE* WOMAN IS DIFFICULT ENOUGH...
YES, SEN-YOR. IT'S TRUE THAT MANY MEN DON'T GOT MORE THAN ONE WOMAN, AND THEIR HOMES ARE HELL. I, ON THE OTHER HAND, HAVE THREE, AND I AIN'T GOT NO TROUBLE AT ALL.
IS THAT MAN A POLYGAMIST?
NO, PIERRE, HE IS A CLEAR EXAMPLE OF "THE NATURAL MAN", FREE FROM ALL SOCIAL PREJUDICES.
KOFF KOFF
THE BISHOP OF CORIA WARNED HIM HE'D BE EXCOMMUNICATED IF HE CARRIES ON LIVING WITH ALL THREE OF THEM.
THE BISHOP! EEE-YURGH!

AY, AY, AY!

CETTE FILLE – WHAT IS WRONG WITH 'ER?

DON'T KNOW, SEN-YOR. SICK FOR DAYS, SHE JUST DONE LAY DOWN THERE TO DIE.

WHERE DOES IT HURT, LITTLE ONE?

BELLY AND BELOW.

APPENDICITIS, MAYBE?

THAT WOULD BE TERRIBLE.

S'IL VOUS PLAÎT... ALLOW ME... OPEN YOUR MOUTH, MA PETITE.

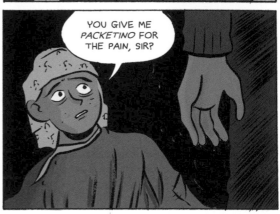

YOU GIVE ME PACKETINO FOR THE PAIN, SIR?

WHAT IS SHE SAYING?

PACKETINOS ARE PACKETS OF MEDICINE. YOU BE A DOCTOR?

PROBABLY NOTHING BUT PERIOD PAINS.

ROUND HERE WE DON'T GOT NO DOCTORS NOR MEDICINES. BUT WE KNOW MANY REMEDIES TO CURE FOLK AND BEASTS.

HERNIA CURED BY RUBBING WITH LIZARDS... RHEUMATISM WITH SHEEP FAT...

FEVER BY EATING SEVEN LUPINS ON AN EMPTY STOMACH.

AND FOR STOMACH ACHE, BEST THING IS COFFEE WITH ANISE.

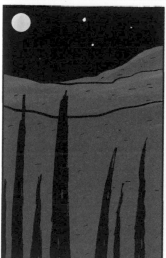

OH, RAMÓN! AND IF YOU FIND A LIZARD WITH A SPLIT TAIL, YOU'LL BE LUCKY FOR LIFE!

THESE ARE ALL JUST THE SUPERSTITIONS OF A PRIMITIVE PEOPLE.

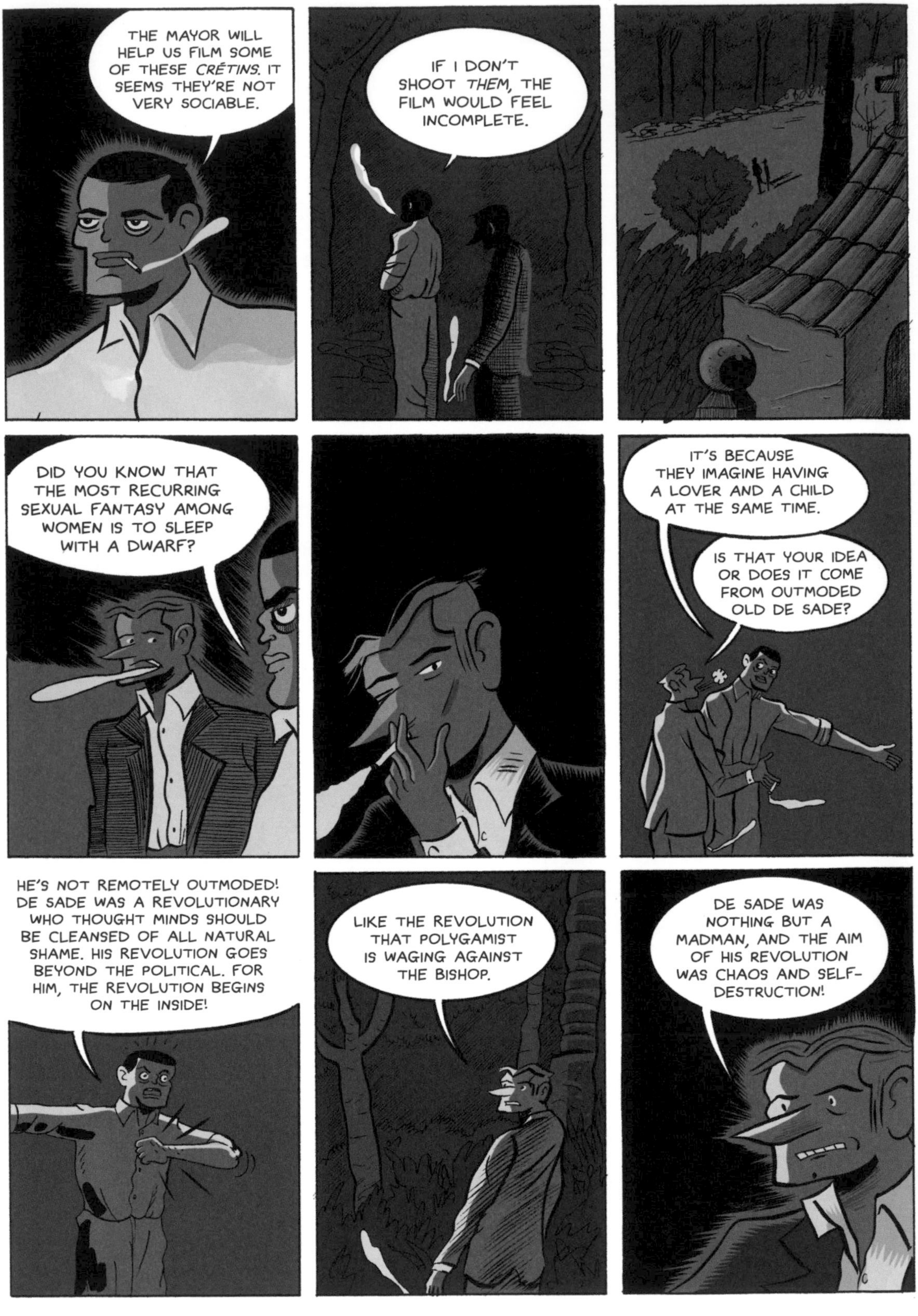
THE MAYOR WILL HELP US FILM SOME OF THESE *CRÉTINS*. IT SEEMS THEY'RE NOT VERY SOCIABLE.
IF I DON'T SHOOT *THEM*, THE FILM WOULD FEEL INCOMPLETE.
DID YOU KNOW THAT THE MOST RECURRING SEXUAL FANTASY AMONG WOMEN IS TO SLEEP WITH A DWARF?
IT'S BECAUSE THEY IMAGINE HAVING A LOVER AND A CHILD AT THE SAME TIME.
IS THAT YOUR IDEA OR DOES IT COME FROM OUTMODED OLD DE SADE?
HE'S NOT REMOTELY OUTMODED! DE SADE WAS A REVOLUTIONARY WHO THOUGHT MINDS SHOULD BE CLEANSED OF ALL NATURAL SHAME. HIS REVOLUTION GOES BEYOND THE POLITICAL. FOR HIM, THE REVOLUTION BEGINS ON THE INSIDE!
LIKE THE REVOLUTION THAT POLYGAMIST IS WAGING AGAINST THE BISHOP.
DE SADE WAS NOTHING BUT A MADMAN, AND THE AIM OF HIS REVOLUTION WAS CHAOS AND SELF-DESTRUCTION!

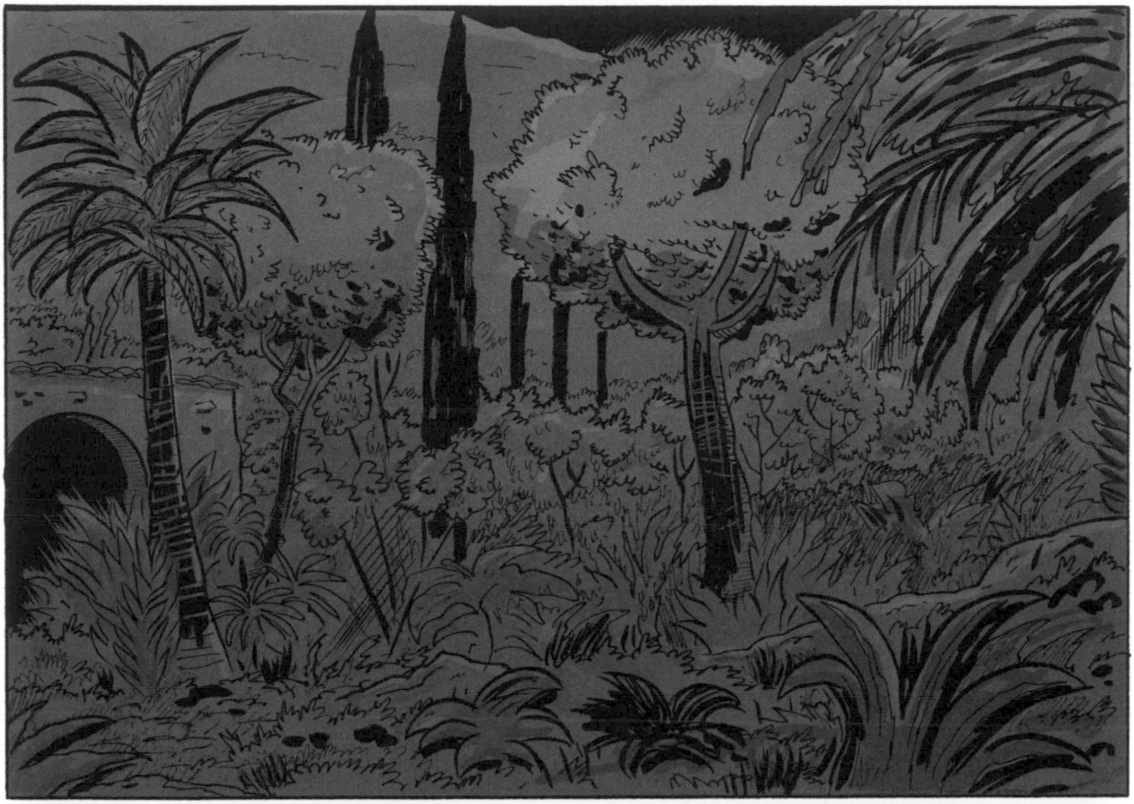

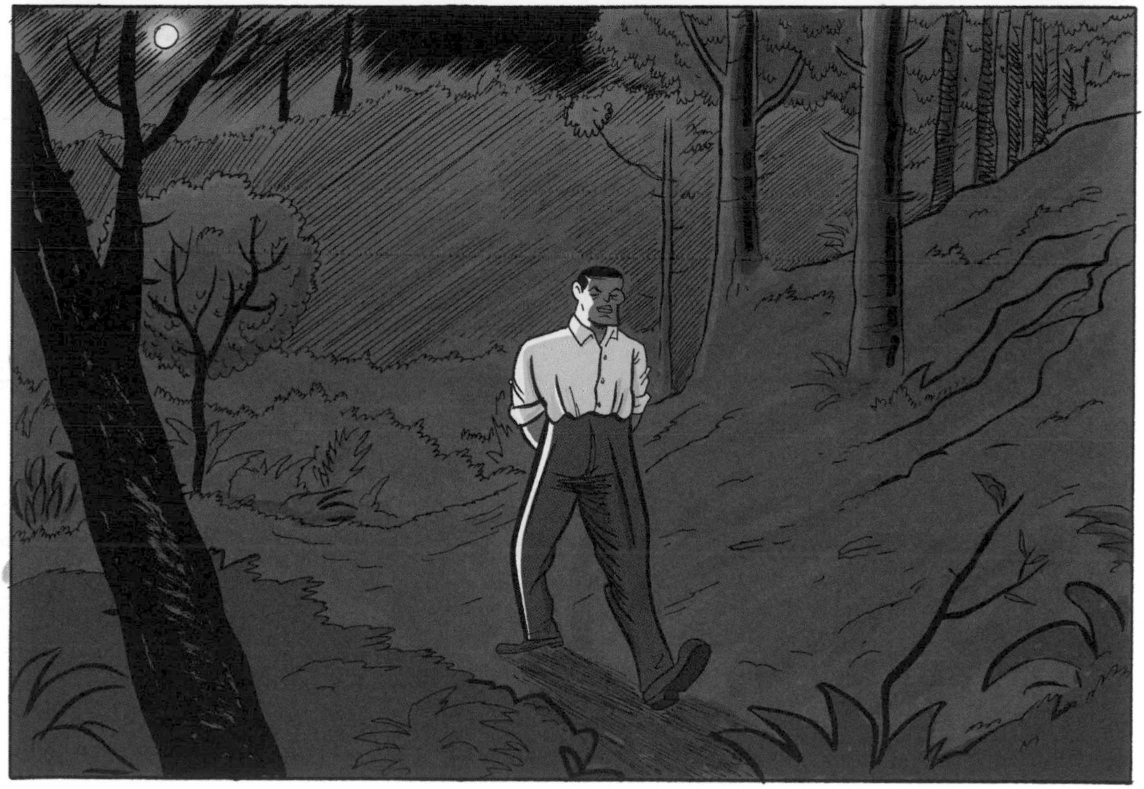

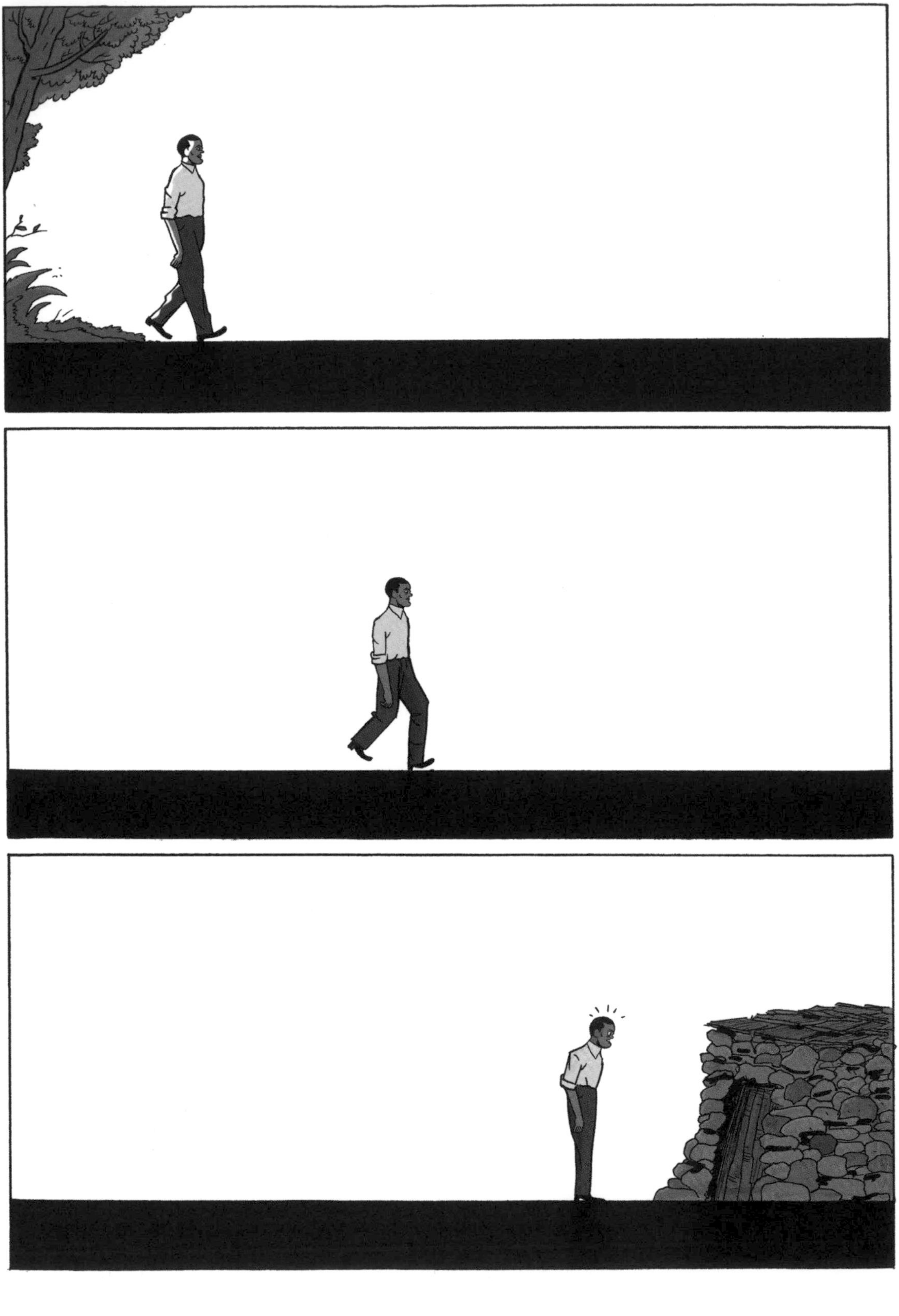

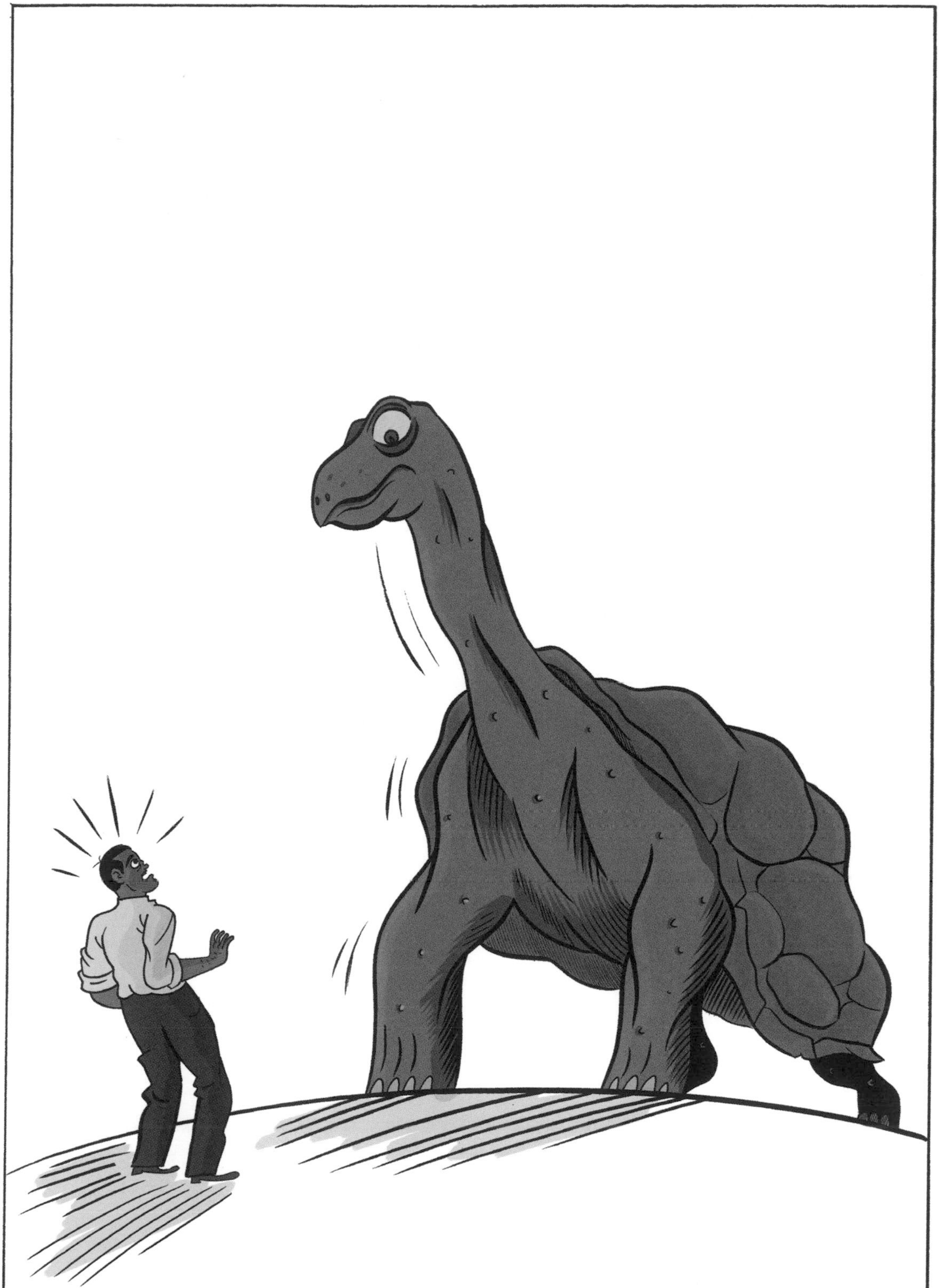

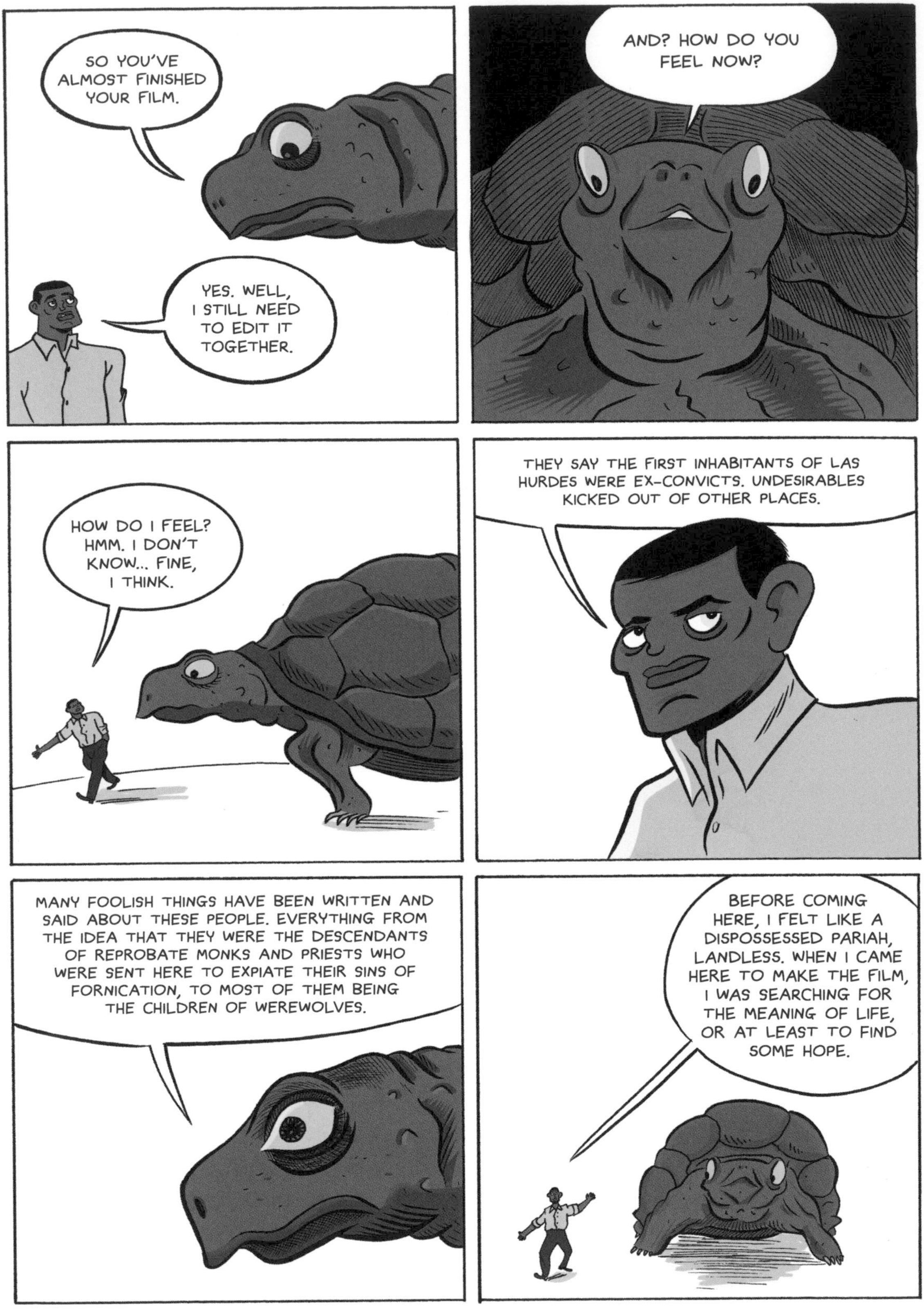
SO YOU'VE ALMOST FINISHED YOUR FILM.
YES. WELL, I STILL NEED TO EDIT IT TOGETHER.
AND? HOW DO YOU FEEL NOW?
HOW DO I FEEL? HMM. I DON'T KNOW... FINE, I THINK.
THEY SAY THE FIRST INHABITANTS OF LAS HURDES WERE EX-CONVICTS. UNDESIRABLES KICKED OUT OF OTHER PLACES.
MANY FOOLISH THINGS HAVE BEEN WRITTEN AND SAID ABOUT THESE PEOPLE. EVERYTHING FROM THE IDEA THAT THEY WERE THE DESCENDANTS OF REPROBATE MONKS AND PRIESTS WHO WERE SENT HERE TO EXPIATE THEIR SINS OF FORNICATION, TO MOST OF THEM BEING THE CHILDREN OF WEREWOLVES.
BEFORE COMING HERE, I FELT LIKE A DISPOSSESSED PARIAH, LANDLESS. WHEN I CAME HERE TO MAKE THE FILM, I WAS SEARCHING FOR THE MEANING OF LIFE, OR AT LEAST TO FIND SOME HOPE.

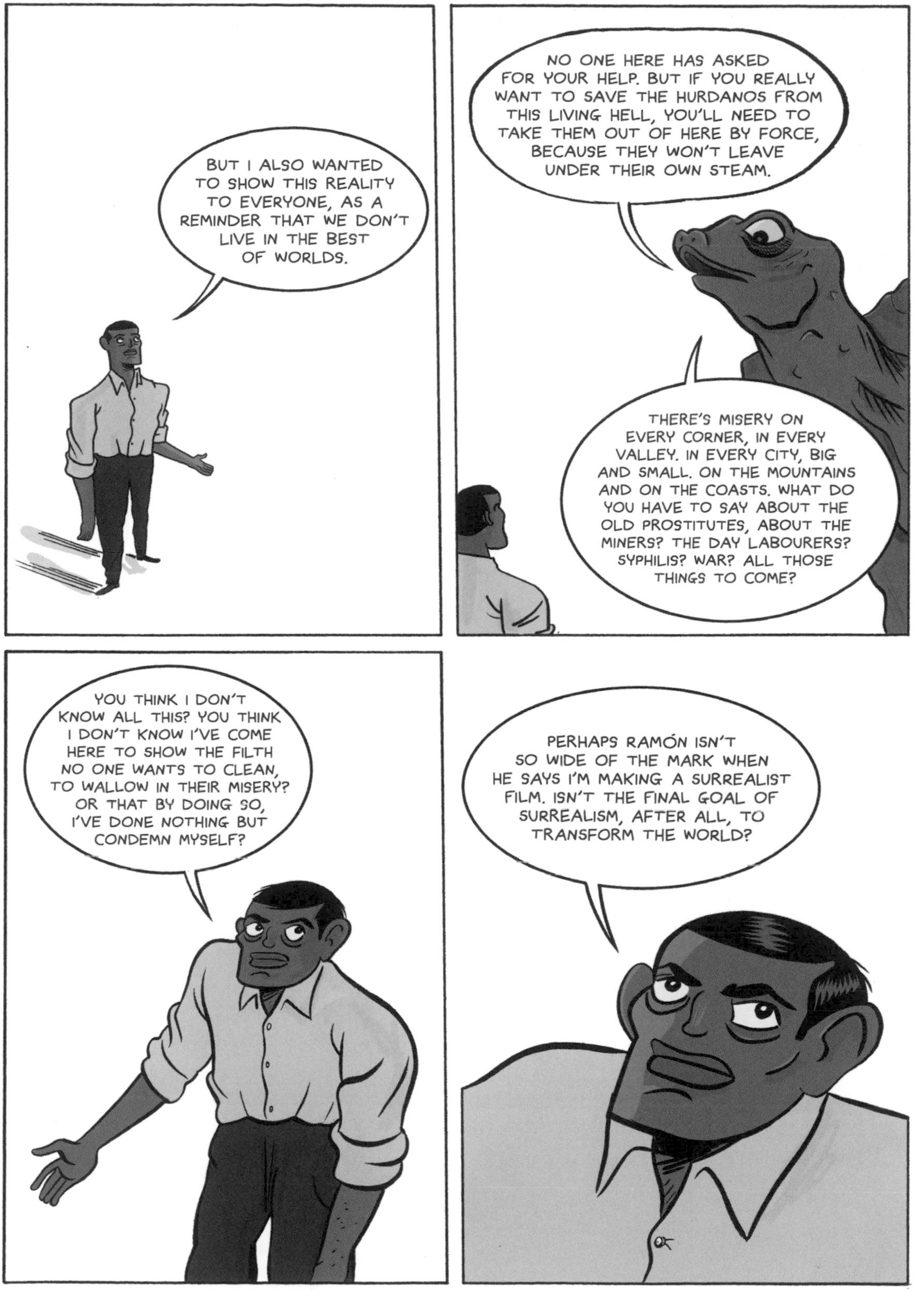
BUT I ALSO WANTED TO SHOW THIS REALITY TO EVERYONE, AS A REMINDER THAT WE DON'T LIVE IN THE BEST OF WORLDS.
NO ONE HERE HAS ASKED FOR YOUR HELP. BUT IF YOU REALLY WANT TO SAVE THE HURDANOS FROM THIS LIVING HELL, YOU'LL NEED TO TAKE THEM OUT OF HERE BY FORCE, BECAUSE THEY WON'T LEAVE UNDER THEIR OWN STEAM.
THERE'S MISERY ON EVERY CORNER, IN EVERY VALLEY. IN EVERY CITY, BIG AND SMALL. ON THE MOUNTAINS AND ON THE COASTS. WHAT DO YOU HAVE TO SAY ABOUT THE OLD PROSTITUTES, ABOUT THE MINERS? THE DAY LABOURERS? SYPHILIS? WAR? ALL THOSE THINGS TO COME?
YOU THINK I DON'T KNOW ALL THIS? YOU THINK I DON'T KNOW I'VE COME HERE TO SHOW THE FILTH NO ONE WANTS TO CLEAN, TO WALLOW IN THEIR MISERY? OR THAT BY DOING SO, I'VE DONE NOTHING BUT CONDEMN MYSELF?
PERHAPS RAMÓN ISN'T SO WIDE OF THE MARK WHEN HE SAYS I'M MAKING A SURREALIST FILM. ISN'T THE FINAL GOAL OF SURREALISM, AFTER ALL, TO TRANSFORM THE WORLD?

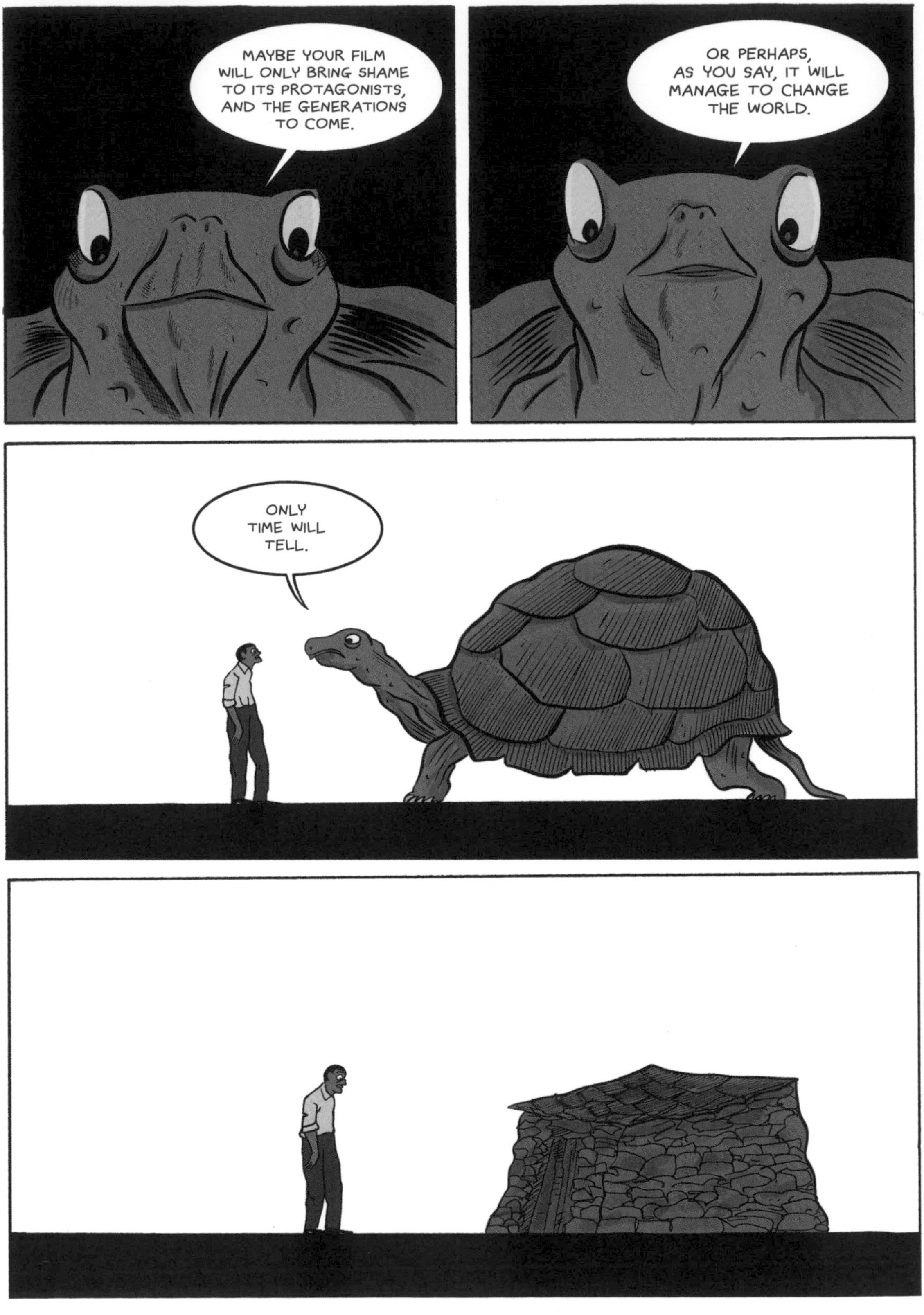
MAYBE YOUR FILM WILL ONLY BRING SHAME TO ITS PROTAGONISTS, AND THE GENERATIONS TO COME.
OR PERHAPS, AS YOU SAY, IT WILL MANAGE TO CHANGE THE WORLD.
ONLY TIME WILL TELL.

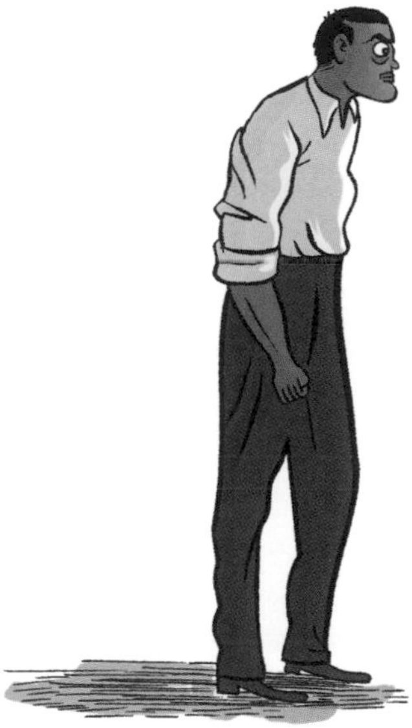

FERMÍN
SOLÍS

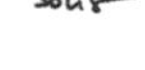

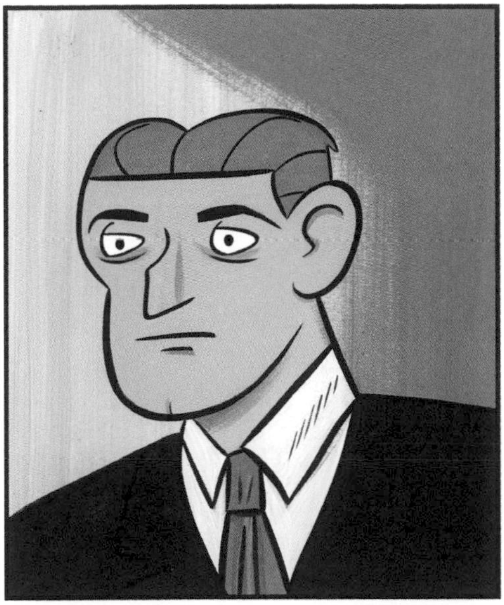

ELI LOTAR CONTINUED TO DEPICT SUCH ISSUES AS HUNGER, THE WORLD OF WORK, AND SOCIAL ISOLATION. IN 1946, HE DIRECTED THE DOCUMENTARY *AUBERVILLIERS*. HE DIED IN PARIS IN 1969.

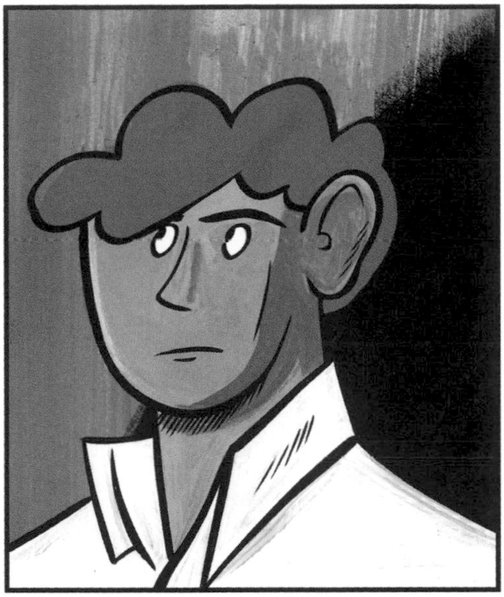

PIERRE UNIK WAS ARRESTED BY THE NAZIS AND SENT TO A CONCENTRATION CAMP, FROM WHICH HE MANAGED TO ESCAPE. HE DIED IN 1945, CRUSHED BY AN AVALANCHE.

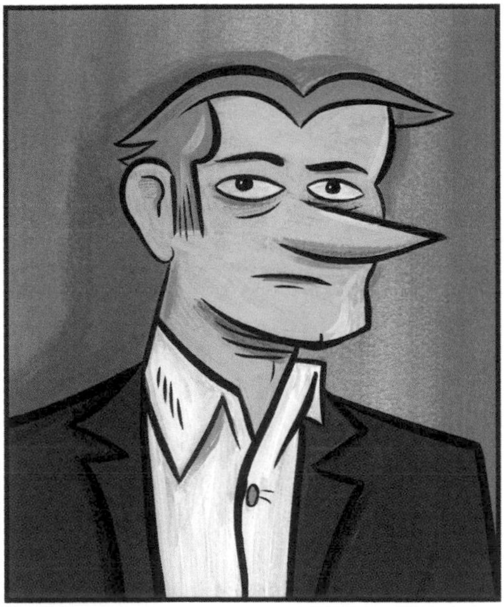

WHEN THE SPANISH CIVIL WAR BROKE OUT IN 1936, A GROUP OF MEN FROM THE EXTREME RIGHT SOUGHT OUT **RAMÓN ACÍN** AT HIS HOME IN HUESCA. HE MANAGED TO ESCAPE, BUT THEY ARRESTED HIS WIFE, SAYING THEY WOULD EXECUTE HER IF ACÍN DIDN'T TURN HIMSELF IN. RAMÓN PRESENTED HIMSELF THE NEXT DAY, AND THEY WERE BOTH SHOT.

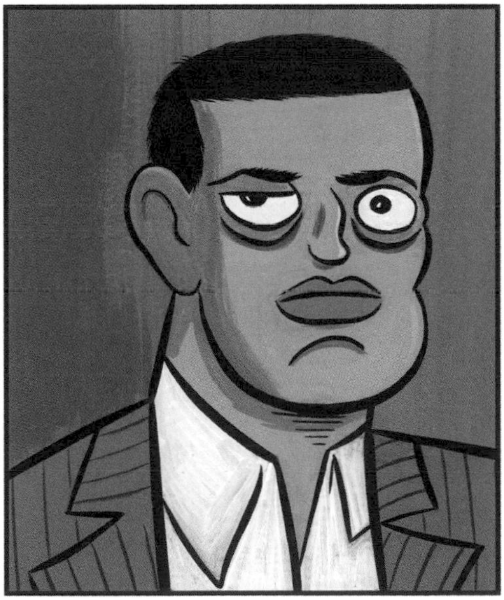

LUIS BUÑUEL DIDN'T DIRECT ANOTHER FILM UNTIL HE MADE *LOS OLVIDADOS (THE YOUNG AND THE DAMNED)*, SEVENTEEN YEARS AFTER *LAS HURDES: LAND WITHOUT BREAD*.

FERMÍN SOLÍS (BORN IN MADROÑERA IN 1972) IS A COMICS
ARTIST AND ILLUSTRATOR. HIS FIRST CARTOONS WERE
PUBLISHED IN THE FANZINES *SUBTERFUGE* AND *CABEZABAJO*,
FOLLOWED BY WORKS OF BROADER SCOPE, INCLUDING
THE SERIES STARRING HIS ALTER EGO MARTÍN MOSTAZA:
LOS DÍAS MÁS LARGOS (2003, WINNER OF THE PRIZE FOR
DEBUT AUTHOR AT THE 2004 SALÓN DEL CÓMIC OF
BARCELONA), *EL AÑO QUE VIMOS NEVAR* (2006), AND *MI
ORGANISMO EN OBRAS* (2011). FERMÍN SOLÍS ESTABLISHED
HIS INTERNATIONAL PROFILE AS A SPANISH ARTIST WITH
THE PUBLICATION OF HIS GRAPHIC NOVEL *BUÑUEL: EN
EL LABERINTO DE LAS TORTUGAS* (2008), ORIGINALLY
PUBLISHED IN BLACK AND WHITE, WHICH WAS A FINALIST FOR
THE SPANISH NATIONAL AWARD FOR COMICS. ASIDE FROM
HIS COMICS WORK, HE HAS ALSO WRITTEN AND ILLUSTRATED
A NUMBER OF CHILDREN'S BOOKS. HIS BOOKS HAVE BEEN
TRANSLATED AND PUBLISHED IN THE UNITED STATES,
CANADA, GERMANY, FRANCE – AND NOW IN THE U.K.

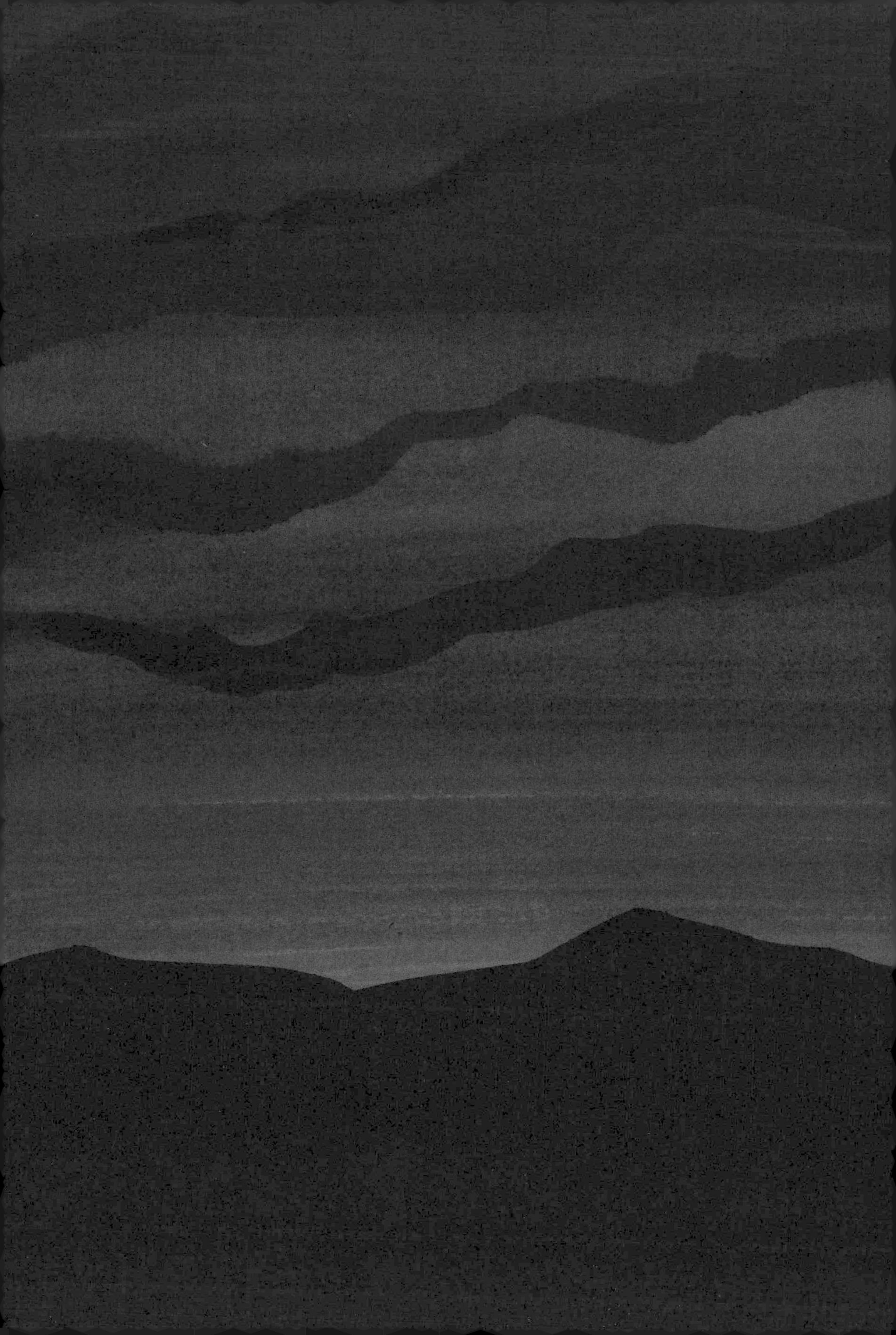